Routledge Advances in Communication and Linguistic Theory

Roy Harris, *University of Oxford*

1. Words—An Integrational Approach
Hayley G. Davis

2. The Language Myth in Western Culture
Edited by Roy Harris

3. Rethinking Linguistics
Edited by Hayley G. Davis & Talbot J. Taylor

4. The Written Language Bias in Linguistics
Its Nature, Origins and Transformations
Per Linell

5. Language and History: Integrationist Perspectives
Edited by Nigel Love

6. Language Teaching
Integrational Linguistic Approaches
Edited by Michael Toolan

Language Teaching

Language Teaching

Integrational Linguistic Approaches

Edited by Michael Toolan

First published 2009
by Routledge
270 Madison Ave, New York, NY 10016

Simultaneously published in the UK
by Routledge
2 Park Square, Milton Park, Abingdon, Oxon OX14 4RN

Routledge is an imprint of the Taylor & Francis Group, an informa business

© 2009 Taylor & Francis

Typeset in Sabon by IBT Global.
Printed and bound in the United States of America on acid-free paper by IBT Global.

All rights reserved. No part of this book may be reprinted or reproduced or utilised in any form or by any electronic, mechanical, or other means, now known or hereafter invented, including photocopying and recording, or in any information storage or retrieval system, without permission in writing from the publishers.

Trademark Notice: Product or corporate names may be trademarks or registered trademarks, and are used only for identification and explanation without intent to infringe.

Library of Congress Cataloging in Publication Data
Language teaching: Integrational linguistic approaches / edited by Michael Toolan.
    p. cm. — (Routledge advances in communication and linguistic theory ; 6)
  Includes bibliographical references and index.
1. Languages, Modern—Study and teaching.   I. Toolan, Michael J.
  PB35.I478 2008
  418.0071—dc22
                    2008034970

ISBN10: 0-415-95753-2 (hbk)
ISBN10: 0-203-88226-1 (ebk)

ISBN13: 978-0-415-95753-3 (hbk)
ISBN13: 978-0-203-88226-9 (ebk)

Contents

List of Figures   vii

Introduction: Language Teaching and Integrational Linguistics   1
MICHAEL TOOLAN

1   Implicit and Explicit Language Teaching   24
ROY HARRIS

2   Learning to Write: Integrational Linguistics and the Indian Subcontinent   47
RUKMINI BHAYA NAIR

3   Language Learning, Grammar, and Integrationism   73
DANIEL R. DAVIS

4   Grammaticality and the English Teacher in Hong Kong: An Integrationist Analysis   88
CHRISTOPHER HUTTON

5   Integrationism, New Media Art and Learning to Read Arabic   104
SALLY PRYOR

6   Teaching a Foreign Language: A Tentative Enterprise   120
EDDA WEIGAND

7   Assessing Students' Writing: Just More Grubby Verbal Hygiene?   140
MICHAEL TOOLAN

8   Integrational Linguistics and Language Teaching   156
CHARLES OWEN

Notes on Contributors   177
Index   179

Figures

2.1	Velars.	53
2.2	Palatals.	53
2.3	Retroflexes.	54
2.4	Dentals.	54
2.5	Labials.	54
2.6	Semivowels.	54
2.7	Fricatives.	55
2.8	Vowels.	55
2.9	Consonant-vowel combinations.	56
2.10	Miscellaneous consonants (part of an extended character set used mostly to capture the sounds of sounds of 'foreign' words).	56
2.11	Recto of ten-rupee banknote.	60
2.12	Verso of ten-rupee banknote.	60
2.13	Illustration of the Indian national flag containing the Ashokan wheel.	65
5.1	Still from *Postcard From Tunis*; the white asterisk indicates the location of Tunis.	104
5.2	The moving screen cursor in *Postcard From Tunis*.	111
5.3	An example of graphic forms in *Postcard From Tunis* that trigger the same sound through rollover interaction.	112

viii *Figures*

5.4	Still from *Postcard From Tunis* showing a screen containing dynamically reflexive written signs.	113
5.5	Still from *Postcard From Tunis*.	116
5.6	Still from *Postcards From Writing* where rollover activity differentiates a written sign from a written form.	118
6.1	Speaking as acting	124
6.2	Basic dialogic speech act types.	124
6.3	Speaking, teaching and learning.	125
6.4	Teaching as tentative action.	125
6.5	Principles of Rhetoric.	128
6.6	The speech act as an open set of utterances.	130

Introduction
Language Teaching and Integrational Linguistics

Michael Toolan

What might be the consequences, for how language teaching would be understood and conducted, of adopting an integrational linguistic perspective? That is the question which the papers gathered here attempt to address. The integrational linguistic perspective is so radically different from most contemporary theories of language that it may be useful to sketch here some of its basic assumptions, before reviewing a selection of the questions that it raises for language teaching.

COMMUNICATION IS NOT ACHIEVED VIA PREEXISTING SIGNS

A first and fundamental assumption of integrationism is that people use signs in order to communicate, but signs do not come ready-made and predetermined, any more than communicational situations do. New communicational situations require us to adapt as best we can (within the biomechanical, macrosocial, and circumstantial conditions or constraints that obtain), and central to that situated communicative adaptation is the creation of new signs. All signs in use are, strictly, *new* signs. We are continually engaged in using speech, and writing, and other signifying resources, in 'forms' and to induce the apprehension of 'meanings' that vary from one specific occasion to the next. Often enough we are intent on suppressing the intrinsic indeterminacy of forms and meanings, keen to treat—and have our interlocutors treat—particular signs as if they were essentially repetitions of prior instances; but integrationism is adamant that such standardizing and codifying have their source in our social and political practices and not at all in language viewed as an object of theoretical scrutiny. Rather, it has to be the case that language itself is fluid and indeterminate as to form and meaning; only such a foundational semiological indeterminacy can lead to a coherent explanation of what are normally referred to as language variation and language change, whose ultimate source is the inescapable temporal dimension of all human signifying.

As a consequence, for integrational linguists human beings are sign makers and not merely implementers of instructions linked to repertoires of fixed signs with which, if they were merely robots, they might have been programmed. From this perspective it could even be misleading to call humans 'language makers', unless it is emphasized that by language here ('what is made') is meant nothing like the notionally stable, determinate objects (typically called 'the English language', 'the French language', and so on) assumed to have a standard form and, in recent Western sociopolitical history, often powerfully associated with nationhood and national identity.

Thus, integrational linguistics is radically at odds with much mainstream linguistic theory, which assumes that languages are essentially stable systems comprising units and rules for their combination, amenable to scientific enquiry. Insofar as the language teaching profession has accepted and adopted the mainstream view, we believe its practices and methods are sometimes grounded in quicksand.

LANGUAGE USE AS SIGN-CREATION, NOT FIXED-CODE TELEMENTATION

Creating signs always involves the contextualized integration of activity, constrained by (and only by) broad biomechanical, macrosocial and circumstantial factors:

> Biomechanical factors pertain to the organic and neuro-physiological mechanisms which underlie communicative behaviour and their exercise in particular physical circumstances. Macrosocial factors pertain to culture-specific patterns of organisation within which communication situations occur. Integrational [= circumstantial] factors pertain to the fitting together of all these within a particular set of circumstances in ways which make sense to the participants involved. (Harris 1993: 321–2; quoted in Wolf and Love 311–2)

In any communicational situation, one interactant may well attempt to understand what the other interactant intends and means (although no physical or metaphorical 'giving' or 'getting' or 'sending' or 'transferring' is involved). Integrational proficiency arises from a mutual orientation (an orientedness to the other person, and to the situation in which both people—in a two-party interaction—find themselves) which does not amount to 'thinking as one' or total shared knowledge. Communicational understanding is a matter of sign-creating, not of sign-decoding, and the two axioms of integrational semiology mean that "the only facts an integrationist recognizes are those recognized in the communication situation by the participants themselves" (Harris 1998: 144). Although this may at first seem disconcerting, it only reflects how lay participants have always proceeded, asking each other to "repeat, clarify, explain, amplify, to agree or disagree, and so on" (145), constantly monitoring the 'what was said' and the 'what was meant', the 'facts' of the situation, and never justified in proceeding in cast-iron (automatic) confidence in mutual understanding.

'EXTREME' REJECTION OF THE MODEL OF LANGUAGE AS FIXED-CODE THOUGHT-TRANSFER

From these premises, as numerous integrationist publications have described, a thoroughgoing revision of thinking about language and linguistics follows. To begin with, the theoretical basis of much recent Western thinking about language is rejected as a myth—in fact, the language myth. The myth, most eloquently articulated by Saussure but traceable through many versions back to Aristotle, is that a language is a fixed system of signs fusing determinate forms to determinate meanings, deployed by interactants so that the thoughts of one interlocutor can be reliably conveyed to another: at its core, a language is a closed system for thought-transfer. It has to be closed; otherwise one speaker's signs might not match with another speaker's and, in terms of the logic of the model, communication would break down since the particular thought would not transfer reliably. The integrationist phrase to sum up this language story is 'fixed-code telementation'.

Fixed-code telementation is unforgettably encapsulated, integrationists contend, in the passage in Saussure's *Cours de linguistique générale* that accompanies and explicates a diagram depicting two schematic human heads facing each other and talking to each other (*Cours*, pp. 27–32; Harris trans., 1983, 11–15). But it is present tacitly and often explicitly in nearly every introductory textbook on linguistics, where unquestioned allusions are made to the addressee 'getting' or decoding what the sender has written or said, where references are made to 'matching' of forms with meanings (both assumed to be determinate), and wherever a language is assumed to be an autonomous system that can be studied *largely* freed from contexts of use. There are not many propositions that integrationists take unqualified from Saussure, but one we embrace is that the student of linguistic communication—anyone who wishes to develop a coherent theory of language—should begin by attending to the perspective of the language user themselves. And from that perspective all the evidence points to variability of signs, with changing circumstances, and to the use of those signs for a variety of purposes besides the attempted replication of thoughts. And yet the language myth of language as an autonomous objectifiable code for telementation remains an immensely powerful picture. It arguably continues to hold cognitively captive people in a variety of fields, when they review the role of language in their practices; those fields include the legal profession, the language teaching profession, schools of art criticism and theory, and traditions of scientific report and description.

Just one of the ways in which the language myth continues to hold sway is in the general reaction to integrationist critique of it, by most linguists and language academics: integrationism is 'too extreme', or goes too far, in its wholesale rejection of fixed-code telementationism and its corollary processes of abstraction and idealization. Integrationists argue, against these counsels of moderation, that only such total rejection gives any chance of rebuilding linguistic theorizing on a genuinely different footing, since half-rejections leave in place a residue of code-fixity incoherently combined with contextualism. They also contend that the moderate position often reflects a limited interest in fundamental questions of language theory, where the researcher is really more content to apply and elaborate a received account, without examining underlying premises thoroughly.

STANDARD LANGUAGES AND LINGUISTIC FACTS

The language myth of fixed-code telementationism is a powerfully generative one, integrationists argue. Among the dependent myths that it helps underwrite is the notion that standard languages themselves exist as first-order stable codes, rather than as a culturally embedded evaluation of that kind of language associated with high-status speakers and writers using the language in formal contexts. Additionally, the language myth directly supports the assumption that there are discrete first-order objects called languages, each with its own system, speakers, and history, so that linguistic analysis must begin by focussing upon one or more such languages. By contrast, integrationism refuses to adopt the notions of distinct languages and standard languages as foundational theoretical idealisations, regarding them as contingent and reductive (stereotyping) characterizations that have emerged to meet specific cultural and political purposes in particular historical contexts. It therefore equally rejects a covert hierarchy in which 'native speakers' are regarded as the most authoritative speakers of languages. The integrationist point is not that concepts like 'the English language' and 'standard language' are *merely* sociopolitical and therefore to be dismissed by linguists; rather that they *are* sociopolitical and therefore merit a different kind of consideration by linguists. Integrationists want linguists to shake off the illusion that these concepts are objectively grounded in linguistic facts, detachable from sociopolitical circumstances and contingencies, and confront the fact that the concepts are often articulated by considerations of power, interest, and exclusion. Despite the elaborate machinery of scientific linguistic categories and analyses, there are no politics-free linguistic facts.

REFLEXIVITY

The study of language behaviour is fundamentally different from scientific studies generally, on account of its intrinsic and essential reflexivity: all language study is a using of the thing to be understood in the process of understanding. We use—we must use—language in the study of language; and typically we rely heavily on a particular kind of language—writing— which appears to afford a stable and enduring spatial inspection of linguistic phenomena. By contrast, the geologist does not and could not conduct her study of rocks 'in rocks', and the same radical distinction between the object of study and the fundamental means with which that object is described and analysed obtains in all the sciences. Unless we are willing to regard, for example, a series of paintings (without a trace of accompanying verbal explanation) about a linguistic topic as a scientific treatment of it, we lack parity of conditions with the true sciences. In short, we cannot conduct a sustained study of language without using language, and integrationists see this as only an extension of the more fundamental idea that we cannot take any steps in signifying communication without some awareness of the process and reflection on the hazarded attribution of a signifying function to some elements in the stream of ongoing activity.

LINGUISTIC SCIENCE, LANGUAGE TEACHING, AND PROGRESS

A corollary of the viewpoint which conceives of languages as fixed-code systems is the conviction that they are amenable to scientific study and that linguistics is that science. It is then but a short step to deducing that the scientific explanations yielded by linguistics must inevitably or eventually enhance language teaching. Many linguists are eager for the conferral of scientific status on their discipline. But what does it mean to call a field of enquiry 'a science'? A broad characterization would be one that declares science to be any part of a community's "knowledge of, and power to control Nature" (Porter 1987: 8). That nature-controlling knowledge and power are reflected in a community's technology and in its systematic, replicable, falsifiable-prediction-carrying accounts of phenomena. Science, in these broad terms, is a large part (always to be taken in conjunction with culture) of what makes human development other than and more than blind Darwinian natural selective adaptation on the basis of unplanned fitness for new circumstances.

A characterization that is a good deal more focussed and robust, however, is claimed by and conceded to the natural sciences, with an insistence on the relevance of insider knowledge and outsider ignorance, on expertise and on conceptual and descriptive completeness, and it is usually with this more expert and predictive knowledge that linguists have sought to be associated. If there is one single characteristic which is absolutely defining of the hard sciences but whose applicability to linguistics remains still open to debate, it is the founding presumption that a genuine science must manifestly enlarge or develop with the passage of time, and such advances must bring progress in applied fields. Whatever the object of enquiry may be—illness and the body, thermodynamics, the formation of mountain ranges, climate change, etc.—the more it is scientifically understood the more it is assumed to be better understood, and this in turn is expected to enable risks, dangers, and malfunctions to be more quickly and efficiently addressed. By the same token, a field of human activity that did not over time manifestly furnish a fuller or more revealing account of the phenomena under consideration—e.g. art criticism—should be in no danger of being conceived of as a science. Where science and scientific method are applied to any area of human interest they should enable that area to be engaged with better, faster, more efficiently, and more effectively. It is hard to deny that in a host of natural and material sciences, and their applications, from civil engineering to medicine, there is abundant evidence of progress, improved results and outcomes, over recorded history. The motif of progress not only applies to the sciences; it underpins their rationale, the fundamental theory of what a science is, does, and is for. By extension, any field whose practitioners might wish to promise to interested parties, stakeholders, or clients that their work promises improvements, progress, etc., may well seek to present that field as a science, or scientific. On the other hand, those who practice any of the arts, or the law, would not normally have any strong attachment to a progress metaphor, or a belief that the culture, or their own contribution to it, could in any way be regarded as an improvement on the cultural productions of earlier generations.

Within this broad and admittedly simplified framework, where does linguistics sit? Is it like biochemistry, which, applied to human physiology, can enable medicine to do an increasingly good job? Or is it more akin to literary studies or art criticism, which at their best may help us better appreciate and understand the verbal and visual arts which engender them, but which it would be unreasonable to expect directly to foster better art or literature? Integrational linguistic principles suggest that it is self-damaging mythopoeia for linguists to continue to imagine they are prosecuting a science, along with false expectations of 'progress' in linguistic matters. The reason is in part to do with the fact that integrationism takes the cotemporal integration of linguistic and nonlinguistic activity really seriously, so that extraction of 'the linguistic parts' of human interaction so as to see and reproduce them the more quickly, accurately, deeply, or purely is self-defeating. Genuine sciences, by contrast, are studies of phenomena which are not so thoroughly constrained by their necessary ontological integration with their encompassing contexts of occurrence.

The reality is that there is relatively sparse conclusive evidence of significant advances in learners' language proficiency that can be specifically attributed to today's advanced linguistic insights and applications, by comparison with learners' proficiency attainments of twenty years ago, fifty years ago, or two hundred years ago. Here we confront the elephant in the room; or, to change metaphors, we are expected to admire the language-learning emperor, dressed in the new clothes known as linguistics-informed language teaching. There is no incontrovertible evidence of progress in language teaching *as a science* (or as an application of a science). Every teacher, at some level of reflection, knows this; but the implications are often denied or ignored.

Alongside the foregoing scepticism, it must be acknowledged that some kinds of progress in matters pertaining to language teaching have been achieved and will continue to emerge, with positive consequences for those who are learning languages. An array of teaching methods have been adopted over the years, and the narrative of movement (not without forms of pendular return) from grammar/translation to audio-lingual immersion to communicative language teaching to presentation-practice-production to task-based teaching is a familiar one. Debates continue over forms of 'real' or authentic 'data' (sometimes characterized as the unteachable chaos of real-time interaction) versus the invented but strategic and relevant examples, designed to bring sense to the learner's 'zone of proximal linguistic development' in the target language; and perhaps they always will. It is difficult to see how these culture-embedded conversations over methods, syllabus, and curriculum could possibly be concluded by scientific scrutiny.

In summary, with the post-Saussurean emergence of linguistics as a science, and the bringing of linguistics to bear on language learning and language teaching, it should follow that linguistically informed language learning and teaching should themselves have become 'more scientific'. But there is strikingly little evidence that modern language teaching and learning programmes, *directly or indirectly assisted by insights afforded by linguistic science*, are significantly better, quicker, more efficient, etc., than the processes of language learning and teaching adopted in earlier times, prior to the modern era of 'linguistic science', or undertaken by those today who ignore the assistance of linguistics.

Thus, the focus here is on the damaging impact of standard linguistics on language teaching. Insofar as language teaching has improved—and there is a variety of evidence that in many respects it has—it has done so by sidestepping orthodox linguistic assumptions. Here one might mention advocacy of a corpus-based 'lexical syllabus' of the kind proposed by Sinclair and Renouf (1988) and implemented in Willis and Willis (2007), in which the commonest word forms in a language and their central patterns of usage and the combinations into which they enter would be focussed upon (e.g. by having learners study multiple instances of use, harvested from a suitable corpus). According to Tognini-Bonelli, such a change would involve students in attempting to "formulate the rule in the presence of the evidence" (2001: 43) rather than simply passively receiving them from the teacher. And the use of corpus evidence exposes students to *variation*. "To learn to cope with variation, it is argued, is a very healthy process for the student and it is similar to the process of first language acquisition" (2001: 43). Teacher and students have substantially altered roles in such a scenario, and have become more like 'co-workers'. Quoting from Johns (1991: 1) Tognini-Bonelli remarks:

> The task of the learner is to discover the foreign language, and . . . the task of the language teacher is to provide a context in which the learner can develop strategies for discovery—the strategies through which he can learn how to learn.

Task-based and lexis-oriented teaching is of course only one of many successful initiatives that have come to prominence in language teaching in recent years, and no general survey of their effectiveness can be attempted here, where the interest is in what integrationism might bring to language teaching. But even these progressive contributions have arguably been shackled by the enduring institutional (educational, governmental) inclination to measure success by reliance on mainstream linguistic idealisations such as the fluent native speaker. As a result, as Graddol has noted, standard practices in the teaching of English as a foreign language have tended to ensure failure:

> Modern foreign languages, English amongst them, have traditionally belonged to the secondary school curriculum, with learners rarely starting study before the age of 11 or 12. They have focused on the language as a timetabled subject, with stress on such things as grammatical accuracy, native speaker-like pronunciation, and literature.
>
> When measured against the standard of a native speaker, few EFL learners will be perfect. Within traditional EFL methodology there is an inbuilt ideological positioning of the student as outsider and failure—however proficient they become.
>
> Although EFL has become technologised, and has been transformed over the years by communicative methods, these have led only to a modest improvement in attainment by learners.
>
> The model, in the totality of its pedagogic practices, may even have historically evolved to produce perceived failure. Foreign languages, in many countries, were largely learned to display social position and to indicate that your family was wealthy enough to have travelled to other countries. Even if you do not accept the argument that the tradition is ideologically designed as a gatekeeping device which will help the formation of elites, it is nevertheless true that the practice of EFL can and does tolerate high levels of failure. In those countries where passing English exams has been made a condition of promotion or graduation, it has often led to considerable stress and resentment

by learners, rather than significantly enhanced levels of proficiency. (Graddol 2006: 83–84)

IMPLICATIONS OF INTEGRATIONISM FOR LANGUAGE TEACHING

The papers collected here aim to demonstrate the relevance of an integrational linguistic perspective to a practical, real-world activity, namely, the teaching of languages. They try to do this by demonstrating how an integrational linguistic stance can help disentangle the conflicting considerations and contradictory assumptions that arise in a host of language-teaching situations: first, second-, and foreign-language classrooms in a diversity of settings (including India, the UK, the United States, and Hong Kong), with different age-groups of students, whether the focus is on speech or writing, and in more informal settings also.

In view of the importance to integrationism of linguistic reflexivity, one thread in the integrational approach to language teaching is the need for greater attention to that reflexivity, on the part of teacher and learner alike. This is evident in an earlier article (Davis 1994) by one of the present volume's contributors, Daniel Davis, reporting on his teaching of a course in American English as a foreign language when he was resident in Hong Kong. Davis began by examining the students' own interests, purposes, and misconceptions. For example, they were aware of the prestige of American English but had some wayward ideas about how it tends to differ from other varieties of English. They were also aware, as he was, of the double bind that prompted them to 'embrace' American English (even though this also opened them to constant reminders of the 'inferiority' of their English relative to the fluent native speakers whom they routinely encountered) as a passport to better jobs with international prospects, while feeling a counter-pull of loyalty and affiliation to their home language (often Cantonese) or to the national language of Mandarin.

The course was initially oriented to the students' own declared interest in 'the features' of American English, using a textbook on English varieties which purported to distinguish the key features of American English which contrast with other national and regional varieties, and drew students to see the theoretical and practical limitations of such an approach. The theoretical problems arise when any attempt is made to apply a Saussure-derived structuralist concept of a language (including fixed-code telementationism) to the situation described; the practical problems emerge when the inventory of features defining of 'American English' set out in the textbook are found to be absent or only intermittently present in actual samples of American speech and writing, and equally partially present in other distinguished varieties. By these means, Davis drew students to reflect much more fully on the stereotypicality of these asserted national and regional varieties, and the cultural and political work that they perform (as distinct from the apolitical linguistic description they are often claimed to provide). As Davis notes, students can come to see more clearly the contingency of the notion of 'standard English', and the political pressures that motivate the postulating of such a category and the importance accorded to it ('international intelligibility' being a robust example of political motivation). None of this made life easier for his Hong Kong students, Davis recognizes; but it did enrich their reflections on whether, behind any pressure they encountered to replace their native Hong Kong English by American English, a form of stereotyping discrimination was at work.

In the present volume, Davis considers the consequences of integrationist sentiments for the language-immersion class which, in its contrived and ritual aspects, he calls a game, one in which the student relinquishes a large part of his or her autonomous agency while trying to role-play being a native speaker. Inevitably, artificiality and stereotypicality dominate, making it the more difficult for such activities to deliver on their promise of nurturing a proficiency that is *transferable* to real-world interactions. But Davis recognizes that there are benefits along with the drawbacks in the teaching method under scrutiny (a theme taken up in Hutton's chapter also). In the case of the immersion class, students "who can allow themselves to perceive and adopt the teacher's phonetic and phonological norms" can greatly improve their pronunciation of the target language. But against this Davis cites the recurrent difficulty that such a learner meets when moving from the classroom to the street, the shop, the office, or the café, where the target language is used as a vernacular: the classroom-immersion version of the language inevitably fails fully to reflect all the "communicationally relevant aspects of the language contexts it purports to model". Davis is similarly careful when he turns—quite autobiographically—to discussion of the studying of Welsh grammar and prepositions. At first glance a more segregationist language-system-assuming topic than 'prepositions in Welsh' is hard to imagine; but like other integrationists Davis is at pains to emphasize that integrationists are as prepared to study prepositions as the next linguist, provided that their ontological status is not assumed to be beyond scrutiny (e.g. as a foundational, first-order, unit of a language's system of syntax). Prepositions have the place they have, Davis suggests, by virtue of their role in a deeply rooted historical and political literacy tradition (in which a need for a category of prepositions arises). If Welsh were an oral language only, there is a sense in which it could be argued that it might have no prepositions at all, so that teaching them to learners of the language would be absurd. The claim might be maintained if, for example, speakers of the language demonstrated fluency and flexibility across many years of using the language, without ever mentioning or drawing attention to particular distinctly prepositional segments of the speech continuum. The same distinction is recognized in Harris's paper where he warns against a conflation of proficiency *in* a language with knowing something *about* a language.

A chief motivation of integrational linguists' interest in language teaching is our belief that language-teaching programmes in Western literate societies are themselves often powerful disseminators of the language myth and objectivist segregational ideas about language. If that belief is correct, those programmes are conveying, alongside help and benefits of a more specific or local kind, a powerfully general misrepresentation of the nature of the language, what is entailed in knowing it, and what the basis for projecting and maintaining a standard language is. The programmes are also still often designed for the convenience of teachers, as opposed to attempting to take the pupils' present preparedness and abilities as the starting point.

Can language teaching dispense with the language myth? How would language teaching look different with any, or a minimum of, concessions to fixed-code telementational segregationist objectivist assumptions? Can we have language teaching without languages—that is, without all the implicit political and social baggage that reification of languages and standards and examinations brings with it?

The idea of language teaching without a focus on languages (the English language, 'standard English', and so on) is not mere politically correct piety, but a possible solution to an enduring conundrum. The conundrum is rehearsed in Christopher Hutton's paper, where he quotes a German university teacher of English (Erling 2002), who questions whether her students' saying "I learn English since ten years" is simply a 'typical German error' or a quite normal feature of the new native Englishes of Ghana, India, and elsewhere, hence by extension acceptable in German English. Erling wonders whether, as a teacher of English, she should continue to correct such an utterance, or now accept it relative to a different standard.

The example is eloquent of the need, first, for recognition of regional differences of norm, and ultimately for recognition that kinds of language may vary and differ not only with region but on a number of other contextualizing bases also. What works linguistically between male middle-class lawyers in a business interaction in central London may not be effective between female teachers in the high-school staffroom in a Mumbai suburb. But regionalism is as good a basis on which to start recognizing distinctions as any: it may well be that *I learn English since ten years* is readily accepted and responded to, without stigma of 'illiteracy', in some parts of the world, even if in Britain (in the classroom, in public discourse, in professional interactions, etc.) people might (a) notice the absence of an aspect marker and past participle ending in the verb and (b) substitute *for* for *since* in the adverbial of time duration. But where that utterance is so accepted without objection, it would be a misrepresentation to describe the situation as indicative of *spread* (of some different norm), or of enlargement, or of widening, or of 'relaxation of norms' or, pace Erling, of "a broader interpretation of the standard" (2002: 12). It is simply that language is customarily used (again, with all necessary conditions noted: in prestige situations, between educated people, etc.) in one way in one region and in a different way in another region. There is no good news here for proponents of the idea of a 'widening circle' of English speakers, soon to encompass the whole world. On the contrary, a question like 'Is German English a New English in Kachru's second or Outer Circle, developing its own norms; or is it (still) in the third or Expanding Circle, dependent on Inner Circle norms, like Japan, Brazil, etc.?' cannot be given a single answer. At the very least, two answers are needed, and perhaps many: the English of German students in Berlin is very much within the Outer Circle; that of ordinary people in many other parts of Germany, who may not have been educated beyond high school, remains entirely in the third or Expanding Circle. The widening-circle metaphor fails to dislodge 'language myth' thinking, because it assumes that 'the English language' can change to align with global and New English reality (here, presumably by abandoning aspectual distinctions, and accepting indiscriminately any preposition of time with following time phrase) and still, at its postulated 'core', within the Inner Circle, stay the same. But for speakers like me who would never say *I learn English since ten years*, the language would have powerfully, and confusingly, not stayed the same.

The emergence of different norms in different contexts of situation is a phenomenon well-known to language teachers. They naturally ask what Erling asks: what forms or grammar should we teach ("where should I use my red pen?") faced with this diversity of 'standards'? Hutton's integrationist response to some of these difficulties is to urge much greater use of corpus-based reference tools, and of the World Wide Web itself, as an enormous multilingual corpus. Using a commercial search engine (or one of the more sophisticated search facilities now available to language teachers and learners such as Webcorp (http://www.webcorp.org.uk) may do much to limit the authority of the native speaker in matters of appropriate grammar and usage. And unlike traditional dictionaries and grammars it is hugely to its and the user's advantage that the Web is overwhelmingly an aggregation of real instances of language usage, albeit, to date, predominantly written usage. But still cause for concern must be the fact that the Internet is in its vast chaotic extent largely oblivious to or silent about matters of context of situation, whether varying by region or on some other basis.

COTEMPORAL INTEGRATION OF LEARNERS AND TEACHERS

The focus of these chapters is language teaching not language learning, and we assume that there are many respects in which the activities and processes involved in teaching are entirely separate from those involved in learning. First- and second-language acquisition can proceed without anything approximating language teaching being involved, while it is only too evident that language teaching can take place without much or any learning occurring as a result. Nevertheless, it would be disingenuous, and counter to integrationist assumptions, to pretend that language teaching did not typically take place because, cotemporally, someone was intent on language learning taking place. As a result, it is not possible or appropriate to discuss language teaching without having some regard for the learner and the processes of learning, even though these are not the direct concern of this collection.

Mention has just been made of the cotemporal, and it should at once be acknowledged that cotemporality, a cornerstone of integrationism, should have important consequences for the integrational conception of language teaching. This is because, in the most general terms, 'understanding' itself is "subject to the principle of cotemporality, i.e. is limited by what, at any given time, participants are aware of and how they contextualize this in relation to past and (projected) future experience" (Harris 1998: 105). As a result, an integrationally reconceived language teaching should involve a thoroughgoing focus on the two (unshared) perspectives of the teacher and the learner (in the canonical dyadic teacher-pupil interaction), a focus on their assumptions and particular goals during any specific encounter or lesson. In addition, the implication must be that teacher and learner should attend very fully to the contextualization that each of them is necessarily and continuously projecting, as enablement of their interaction with the other party.

MEDIATION

One way of maintaining a constructive distance between linguists and language teachers is to argue that they have radically different methods and goals, and to propose that an intermediary cadre and profession is needed. Such a subdiscipline has indeed emerged over the last half-century, and is known as applied linguistics. The name would suggest that this subdiscipline might in principle address all kinds of applications of linguistics; in practice, other 'applications' have hit upon their own compound denomination (sociolinguistics, psycholinguistics, literary linguistics, forensic linguistics), and applied linguistics has stabilized as predominantly the theory and practice of applying linguistics in language teaching and learning.

One of its most influential champions, Henry Widdowson, has often insisted on its distinct and important role and viewpoint, which is neither that of the idealizing and abstracting linguistic scientist (*langue*-tied) nor of the classroom teacher, but is that of an interpreter, making sense of linguistics for teachers:

> The essential issue for applied linguistics is whether, how, and how far the ideas and findings that have been refined out of actual data by idealisation and analysis can be referred back reflexively to the domains

of folk experience whence they came and be made relevant in practice.
. . . Mediating between disciplinary expertise and folk experience is, of course, a tricky thing to do, and given the authority accorded to experts and the low esteem in which folk ideas are held, it is not something everybody would think worth doing. (Widdowson 2005: 20)

Mediating, however, is precisely what Widdowson sees applied linguists doing. They mediate between the linguistic experts as one party, and, somewhat ambiguously, either the 'folk experience' of ordinary people such as language learners (as in the aforementioned quotation) or the practices of language teachers (as an earlier article implies: Widdowson 2000). But is the claimed mediation bidirectionally transitive? There seems rather more mediating of linguistics to the folk, rather than the other way about, despite the insistence, at the close of Widdowson's 2005 article (echoing a similar sentiment in Widdowson 1980), that applied linguistics must start with folk experiences of real-world language, and reformulate these in different terms. It does this rather than assuming that the perspective of the linguist and his or her model of 'the language' (and of language acquisition, language change, language pathology, etc.) should come first, and then be used to make sense of folk experience:

Rather, [applied linguistics] takes an approach that is the reverse of this in that it explores how the problems that folk experience with language in real-world domains might be clarified, reformulated, made more amenable to solution by reference to the abstract representations of language that linguistics (hyphenated and otherwise) has to offer. (2005: 25)

But this does not make clear just what sort of help, for what sort of problems, the 'abstract representations of language' offered by linguistics can or might provide. If starting with folk experience were seriously and strictly observed, there would be no danger of assimilating the procedure to that of the visiting anthropologist, who typically has been prepared for fieldwork in such an objectivizing way that full adoption of the insider's perspective is impossible. By contrast, the integrationist is committed, as a theoretical principle, to the proposition that the linguist's abstract representations can be no more intrinsically especially useful in the course of a person's language learning than other metalinguistic strategies, articulated vaguely or in detail, by the learner and any teachers or co-interactants involved.

Integrationism is sceptical about the value of either 'spatial' or temporal externality to the actual communicational exchange as experienced by those who are parties to it, calibrating intentions and effects, assaying purposes, agreement, compliance, and so on, without benefit of any kind of fixed chart by means of consultation of which they could 'confirm' that the other party had understood them and vice versa. The 'spatial' externality is reflected in accounts of language learning that privilege outsiders, experts, abstraction, idealization, system, and code. The temporal externality to the current exchange that is commonly privileged is the past, and more particularly the past linguistic experience of the interactants, or the past linguistic behaviour of larger groups of users of the language (however these may be sifted and refracted in grammars, dictionaries, corpora, thesauri, usage guides, precepts, and so on). What Harris says in the course of discussing his own first encounter with the word *moshpit* (in the course of reading a newspaper article about the music scene in Sicily) is relevant here. Harris's situated bafflement with *moshpit* is a typical language learner dilemma, only different in degree from my difficulties with the stream of sound on my *Beginning Danish* audiotape, which, the accompanying book assures me, can be rendered in writing as *Jeg hedder George Wilson*. Harris's encounter with *moshpit* chiefly raised difficulties of meaning, while my engagement with the audiotape and accompanying text raised difficulties of form, spelling, and pronunciation. Both types of difficulties derive from the nature—the indeterminacies—of signs.

> A further . . . mistake [is] supposing that coming across a word for the first time is a 'special case' and therefore unreliable as a guide to 'the nature of meaning'. The integrationist, on the contrary, maintains that what happens in this 'special case' is what happens in *every* case, except that the similarity is disguised by our hubristic readiness to assume that our past linguistic experience provides all the information we need in order to assign semantic values in present and future cases. (Harris 1998: 70)

Because language proficiency is something developed and renewed on a moment–to–moment (or exchange-to-exchange) basis (rather like physical fitness), and because no package (neither the linguist's nor the language teacher's nor that 'package' comprising all our past linguistic experience in the target language) of fixed signs and rules for their combination will reliably provide all the guidance we need to make sense of and in present and future exchanges, the abstract representations of the linguist or the ordinary learner can only at best try to set limits on the indeterminacies. But, it logically follows, these attempted delimitations, constrainings and codifyings carry their own health warning, that they cannot be assumed to apply to the new case. An exactly parallel vacuous rule of thumb applies in legal determinations of the meanings of terms: it is appropriate to rely on dictionary definitions, except where they 'clearly' are inappropriate.

IMPLICIT LANGUAGE TEACHING

Roy Harris begins his keynote chapter in dry ironic mode, quoting two original thinkers (Tagore and Nowakowski) who cannot be suspected of carrying 'the heresy of integrationism'; what attracts Harris is the exceptional originality or creativity of these artists' contributions. The 'creative initiative' of the human individual, intent on devising signs to further interactional goals, is primary in all human communication, Harris asserts. Such creative initiative is what he finds damagingly neglected in both the explicit content of much conventional classroom language teaching, and in the implicit messages that language teaching often imparts.

Harris is particularly critical of how we neglected language teaching's implicit instruction, the 'something other, and more' that any teacher sponsors, ratifies, or communicates as reasonable and proper, in the course of teaching. To take an example from my own schoolboy experience, it was unremarkable for a male secondary school teacher in Britain forty years ago to smoke a pipe in the classroom; this taught the lesson that smoking was a right and proper thing to do in the classroom or office (my impression is that cigarettes, by contrast, were frowned upon, which taught its own little lesson about class in the other sense). The class could easily be 'on' the human respiratory system and the vulnerability of the lungs to diseases and damage; hence, the teacher's implicit instruction can be seen as at odds with, if not negating, their explicit instruction. Does the impressionable schoolboy, embarking on his first forays into smoking and drinking at the local pub, emulate his admired teacher who smokes or this same teacher who has taught him the aetiology of lung cancer? The boy, it might be replied, should do as the teacher says, not as he does—it shouldn't be so hard to separate the 'science' conveyed in the classroom from the form, culture, and other 'white noise'. But are they in actuality so separable? The teacher, pausing to puff on his meerschaum, takes the tobacco smoke into his lungs, expels that air, now phonated, in order to explain infections of the lungs. Pulmonic egression is here undetachably integral to the explaining of potential impairments to pulmonic egression. Nor need or should the sense of the fundamental integration, in every teaching situation, of the message and the medium, the explicit science and the implicit culture, stop here with a focus on the teacher. Consider what can happen to the schoolboys when our pipe-puffing teacher, outlining the sources of lung diseases, turns to an explanation of 'secondary smoking': consider how at this cotemporal point the boys may become more reflexively aware of their own breathing, and the present risk to their own lungs. Even if this example is atypically vivid, ironic, and physicalist, it may stand as a warning of the consequences of teaching (including language teaching) as an inescapably integrational activity, with overlooked 'secondary' effects and consequences—more often intellectual and cultural than directly physical—that may even override the declared primary goals.

Turning to his own experience as schoolchild, subject to being taught French, Latin, and English, Harris suggests that a 'projective' strategy was adopted by teachers of the first two of these languages, while a 'reductive' mode applied to English. Taught about French 'from scratch', everything absorbed in the French classes was an expansion or enlarging of the reach: eventually young Harris might be able to use his French beyond the classroom, even in France. English classes were tout autre chose. Harris was already quite proficient in written and spoken English as used beyond the classroom: now it was time to learn to reconceive it by focusing in on it as a decontextualized object removed from human activities, a matter of clauses with subjects, gerunds, tenses, and inflections.

Harris rails against the use of grammar books and other teaching methods and materials, composed on the evident basis of the student having at least some proficiency in the language, in the very different situation where students have almost no knowledge of the target language. He also comments on the nationalistic imperative: the pressure to declare (i.e. invent) a standard language as the cultural home of the constructed nation. Standard English as proclaimed in countless language teaching textbooks and government documents is, Harris bluntly declares, a systematization and simplification of linguistic reality, and reflects the elite's attempt—consonant with numerous parallel attempts through history—to dictate behaviour (here, linguistic behaviour) to the restless lower classes. We might add that the pedagogic and policy treatments of Standard English are much inconvenienced by the fact that the entity they invoke seems to defy comprehensive ostension or description. Standard languages are—at least in part—works of the imagination, or of imagined glottic communities (on a par with Anderson's characterization of nation-states as imagined communities: Anderson 1983). This is reflected in textbook descriptions of it, such as they are, which are largely couched in negative terms: in Standard English one does not write *ain't* or use multiple negation, one does not say *they was* or *he were*, and so on. By contrast, the aggregations called regional dialects—which have at least a flickering real existence—have a positive characterization: in Black Country dialect you say *Yam going dowun the towun. Am yow cumming with me, babs?*

Harris ends with a disturbing suggestion: today (in the UK at least), perhaps more than ever before, the language teacher's freedom to change methods and teaching assumptions are hemmed in by national codes, curricula, examinations, and performance criteria—part of the late-capitalist rewriting of the social contract that is replacing interpersonal trust by tickbox cliché-governed accountability. This elaboration of exams and accounting, far from bringing scope for reform and innovation, has rather tended to entrench the old segregationist language myth.

LANGUAGE IN INDIA: THE INTEGRATION OF SCRIPTS

In her essay, Rukmini Bhaya Nair uses integrational criticisms of prevalent linguistic thinking (with respect to telementation and scriptism) in a revaluation of what has developed—and what has perhaps been suppressed or denied—in the cultures of writing (with all that writing and access to writing enables, in the way of education, development, democracy) in India. Bhaya Nair discusses the relationships between various Indic scripts and such desiderata as learnability, emotional engagement, and self-perception (are some scripts significantly easier to learn, significantly more facilitative of self and emotions?); she comments on the performing of nationality and nationhood, and the cultural implications (*e pluribus scripsi, unum populum?*); and, broaching the transnational or global issues, she considers "the vexed relationship" between syllabic Indian scripts and the alphabetic Roman or Western one (the 'foreign' hand in which much of India's state business is expressed and enshrined). She ends with fascinating speculations about the possible futures of scripts in India, which may soon come to be almost fantastically more available or accessible to readers of other scripts, via instantaneous translation techniques enabled by digital technology. A form of open-source shareware script manipulation is in prospect, which may end by rendering computer-mediated writing (now far more important than handwriting in middle-class India, as in many countries) readable by all others proficient in any one Indic script, whatever the source Indic script may have been. Locally invented technologies that can convert Hindi to Tamil or translate Malayalam into Bengali not merely promise but perform a profound form of conversion, in which diversity persists alongside (indeed, becomes the precondition of) inclusion by conversion. Indic script diversity, it seems, might gradually reduce to a matter of computer-enabled formatting and reformatting; but it is important to see that this is a rebuff to scriptist segregational theory rather than an endorsement of it.

Among other things, Bhaya Nair discusses the role of indigenous mother tongues and the 'father script' of English in India: it is as if Indians can *say* what they think and feel in their 'local' languages but when things get serious enough to be written down (science, government, law, property) they should 'put it down in English'. The implications of Bhaya Nair's topic range widely, as the role and status of English around the world continues to shift rapidly, with India as a crucial test case. Soon there may be more native speakers of English in India than in the UK, a cohort speaking a new New English second in size only to the old New English spoken in America. Globally, they could come to wield considerable influence (Indian English as the 'flagship' New English), even if nationally, being just another minority language, the impact might be slight (cf. American English, generally 'owned' as much by African, Asian and European Americans as by those with a specifically English ancestry).

OWNERSHIP BY BIRTH

Christopher Hutton's essay begins with a series of telling anecdotes about influential figures in Hong Kong lamenting the standard of English in that region (what he calls a 'prevalent discourse of decline'). Part of what is interesting about such laments (from a judge, a businessman, a wealthy public figure, etc.) is that from time to time we hear variants of such laments, concerning one prestige language or another, in almost every country of the world. There are global tendencies here. In Britain from time to time schoolchildren's performance on ability tests at age 11 are reported and laments go up about the persistent 'low standards' of achievement in literacy and numeracy. As for British pupils' collective performance in the learning of foreign languages, this is now deemed so dire as to be almost beyond rescue. We've stopped making jokes about speaking "schoolboy/girl French" throughout our adult lives since, frankly, even that level of proficiency in the dominant language of our closest continental neighbours seems generally to be dwindling. And at the time of writing (February 2008), it is being proposed that the brief oral test of proficiency should no longer figure in the lower public examination in a foreign language (for 16-year-olds), on the grounds that it is "too stressful".

Hutton shows how complex is the linguistic and educational situation of Hong Kong. Although attempts (sometimes successful) were made in the colonial period to teach through the mother tongue (i.e. Cantonese), when the Hong Kong government pushed for mother tongue as medium of instruction in secondary schools there was a mass revolt by parents, who knew the importance of English for the professions and better-paid jobs and rejected the 'win-win' promise of both better Cantonese-medium school education and better English-as-a-second-language proficiency. Hutton emphasizes the local political effects, not least in the staff room, caused by the abrupt introduction of Native English Teachers (NETs) in schools, intended to serve as advisers and a 'resource'. And yet, he also notes, there is some irony in the exceptionalism that makes English the only language where it is now widely questioned (at least by applied linguists) whether being a native speaker is a desirable prerequisite of its teachers. More ironies emerge when the automated grammar checker that comes as part of Microsoft Word is let loose on example writing errors cited in the HK government report on the Language Proficiency Assessment for Teachers. The ironies extend to an examination system which is either blind or brazenly un-self-critical about dictating to and constraining students while using ludic, rule-flouting poems as 'set texts'. Like others before him, Hutton concludes that the fundamental issue is one of authority or ownership, and in his view modern linguistics, which still reverences the native speaker, has too uncritically embraced a Romantic-organicist concept of the native speaker. Most thought-provoking is his suggestion that the contemporary inclination to make a linguistic exception of globalized English has only proven or strengthened the Herder-Humboldt Romanticist rule; that rule is that native speakers on their native ground know their language best (better than the Other, speaking

English Elsewhere). Hutton's conclusion is significantly muted: integrationism may be incapable of radically reforming language teaching, but its scope for understanding new language technologies should not be neglected, at the same time as it can help us to historicize and relativize the still-powerful and powerfully damaging model of language ownership which confers a special status on the 'native speaker'.

WHAT SHOULD BE TAUGHT, WHAT DOES GET TAUGHT?

The next three chapters look again at foreign and native-language teaching. In a sense, all three authors are concerned with the social position of the student embedded in a context of language teaching, and are concerned with how the teacher and learner can best deflect or negotiate the powerful segregationist expectations that each may tend to attribute to the other (especially, the segregating of language from context).

Edda Weigand's chapter includes an outline of her views on dialogic interaction—action games—and proposes that this is the essential background that must be taken into consideration in designing materials aimed at fostering effective 'competence-in-performance' in a foreign language. Her chapter takes up the challenge presented to language teachers by the integrationist premise of the strict inseparability of language from context. She argues the need to teach "the communicative ability of effective language use", and proposes that is best achieved by modelling interaction as the negotiating of interests and purposes in what she calls "dialogic action games". Foreign-language instruction becomes chiefly a matter not at all of informing (or 'conduit' metaphor telementation) but of teacher-student mutual *adaptation*, mirroring as fully as possible the adaptation that applies, to a greater or lesser degree and unilaterally or bilaterally, whenever a less proficient and more proficient language user interact. Weigand includes in her chapter reflections on some of the practical consequences, in foreign-language teaching, of taking her dialogic action game approach, and analyses some authentic examples of foreign-language teaching.

Sally Pryor's discussion of language teaching by way of digital, Web-based 'postcards' is as focused on practice as Daniel Davis's essay. Spending time among Arabic-speakers in Tunis, Pryor acquired some spoken and written Arabic, but without benefit of any formal teaching or lessons. A new media artist, Pryor has made that experience the basis of two inventive CD-based artworks, *Postcard from Tunis* and *Postcards from Writing*; these constitute artistic interpretations of integrationist ideas about communication, and like all art they avoid asserting or implying that the conveying of information—ideas-transfer—is their primary goal. Rather, they aim to please, entertain, beguile, engage us in reflection, and by those means persuade us of the value of integrational principles. But why the postcard, as emblem, in this digital world of ours, where brief graphic contact can be made by e-mail, SMS, blog and vblog, facebook, and myspace? Only to close friends do we nowadays much bother with the frail, traveling conjunction that is a postcard, one of the last traces of handwritten interpersonal communication.

Pryor points to the familiar rough parity of writing and pictures in the ordinary postcard, the impersonality of the image wedded to the subjectivity of the written message; but she is attracted too to the way a postcard travels (often traveling 'back' from the sender's site of temporary removal, to somewhere close to home) while the sender's particular meanings may or may not. But Pryor's digital creations require more interaction from the receiver than the scanning of recto and verso demanded by the conventional postcard. They have accompanying sounds (demonstrating Arabic pronunciation of words naming things, for example), animated graphics, showing the right-to-left continuous sequence involved in writing Arabic words, and 'rollovers' activated by the viewer's mouse, uncovering further signs or optional links. So Pryor's two postcards are attempts at artistic implementation of integrational language-teaching principles.

My own chapter focuses on language performance and, especially, performance assessment, which has such a prominent role in institutionalized language teaching. Unlike other contributors to this volume, my discussion is chiefly of proficiency assessment in the context of first- or native-language education, particularly the assessment of written-language proficiency. But with due allowances for differences of knowledge base, and adjustments to the specific normative targets that will obtain in assessing writing in a native language by contrast with writing in a second or foreign language, I believe that essentially the same tensions and constraints operate.

The chapter reviews the complex layerings or framings that are involved, and that necessarily make the judgements involved partial and contingent, when formal assessment of writing attainment is undertaken (the codes, curricula, examinations, and performance criteria alluded to at the end of the Harris chapter). The situation I report is one in which there are written comments (by an external examiner) on written comments (by lecturers) on written comments (by students) on the written work of primary-school children: rampant reflexivity, or the triumph of the meta over matter. All parties are interested ones, but those interests vary and to some degree must clash. How those interests are reasonably peacefully reconciled, which I take to be a typical language-teaching scene, has everything to do with practicalities, interpersonal politics, and social pressures and little to do with the logic of science and context-free correctness. The multiplicity of interlocking frames of reference means that at no point is the work of assessment truly autonomous or independent. Furthermore, even after all these years of sociolinguistic and critical discourse enlightenment, the rationale behind some of this assessment work is, I believe, still open to the objection that it is arbitrary, or obscure, or—worst of all—class-driven.

The entire collection is responded to by my colleague Charles Owen in a healthily sceptical afterword. I alone have seen his essay: none of the contributors has had the opportunity to reply to his criticisms. This does not trouble me: integrationists welcome robust and bracing critique, and I am sure that our dialogue with attentive sceptics such as Owen will continue in other fora. Here, someone had to have the last word and I was happy to give it to a nonintegrationist. Owen speaks from long experience as a language teacher, applied linguist, and teacher of teachers, and I am sure that many in the language-teaching profession will feel his questioning of the more extreme ideas in this volume is a welcome dose of articulate reasonableness. Using the sickness metaphor rather than the more familiar religion one (and using 'self-certification'), Owen reports how the foregoing chapters threatened to infect him with the integrationist bug, but his rational and commonsensical immune system has successfully resisted this. Therefore, he says, although the 'infection' did not take hold, the exposure was good for him (and by implication could be similarly useful for others who might be equally unpersuaded, finally). Perhaps his pink and healthy tongue is in his cheek here; nevertheless, I am extremely grateful for his witty and challenging contribution.

REFERENCES

Anderson, Benedict. 1983. *Imagined Communities:* Reflections on the Rise and Spread of Nationalism. London: Verso.

Davis, Daniel. 1994. Teaching American English as a foreign language: an integrationist approach. In M. Hayhoe and S. Parker, eds., *Who Owns English?* Buckingham, UK: Open University Press.

Erling, Elizabeth J. 2002. 'I learn English since ten years': The global English debate and the German university classroom. *English Today* 70, vol. 18, no. 2, 8–13.

Graddol, David 2006. *English Next.* London: British Council.

Harris, Roy. 1993. Integrational Linguistics. *Actes du XVeme congres international des linguists*, ed. A. Crochetiere, J.-C. Boulanger, and C. Ouellon, Sainte Foy: Presses de l'Universite Laval, 321–3.

Harris, Roy. 1998. *Introduction to Integrational Linguistics.* Oxford: Pergamon.

Johns, Tim, and Philip King, eds., 1991. *Classroom Concordancing.* Birmingham University: English Language Research Journal 4.

Porter, R. ed. 1987. *Man Masters Nature.* London: BBC.

Saussure, Ferdinand de. 1983 [1916]. *Course in General Linguistics*, trans. and annotated R. Harris. London: Duckworth.

Sinclair, John, and Antoinette Renouf. 1988. A lexical syllabus for language learning. In R. Carter and M. McCarthy, eds., *Vocabulary and Language Teaching.* Harlow, UK: Longman, pp.140–60.

Tognini-Bonelli, Elena. 2001. *Corpus Linguistics at Work.* Amsterdam: John Benjamins.

Widdowson, H. G. 1980. Models and fictions. *Applied Linguistics*, 1: 165–70.

Widdowson, H. G. 2000. Object language and the language subject: On the mediating role of applied linguistics. *Annual Review of Applied Linguistics*, 20, 21–33.

Widdowson, H. G. 2005. Applied linguistics, interdisciplinarity, and disparate realities. In P. Bruthiaux, D. Atkinson, W. G. Eggington, W. Grabe, and V. Ramanathan, eds., *Directions in Applied Linguistics*. Clevedon, UK: Multilingual Matters, pp. 12–25.

Willis, D., and Willis, J. 2007. *Doing Task-Based Teaching*. Oxford: OUP.

Wolf, George, and Nigel Love, eds. 1997. Epilogue. *Linguistics Inside Out: Roy Harris and His Critics*. Amsterdam: John Benjamins.

1 Implicit and Explicit Language Teaching

Roy Harris

The minds of children of to-day are almost deliberately made incapable of understanding other people with different languages and customs. (Tagore 1961: 65)

Talking is not a language. It's not a nonsense. It's a yessence. (Nowakowski 2003)

This paper has two epigraphs. The first, in chronological order, is taken from the writings of one of the few truly radical pioneers of twentieth-century education: Rabindranath Tagore. The second is taken from an essay by one of the most innovative pioneers of book design of the last half-century: Radoslaw Nowakowski.

One reason why I choose these two quotations is that neither author can be suspected of the heresy of integrationism. But their own ways of tackling the problem of communication is, in various respects, very much in line with integrationist thinking: and what they say is of some relevance to the concerns of the language teacher.

I am particularly attracted to Nowakowski's concept of 'yessence', as opposed to 'nonsense'. Nowakowski sees, I think, that the opposition between 'sense' and 'nonsense', at least as enshrined in traditional language teaching, misses a whole dimension of linguistic activity. Underlying the notion of 'sense' is that of conformity to rules. Nowakowski, as his work bears witness, is an innovator for whom there are no rules of production, and certainly no rules of comprehension. Or if there are, it is Nowakowski who proposes them. The title of his essay from which my quotation comes is 'Why Do I Make My Books the Way I Do?' I find it interesting that his realization that talking is 'yessence' played such an important role in his radical reconceptualization of the book. In integrationist terms, what I think he is saying is that in human communication the creative initiative is always primary, never derivative. Such initiatives can perhaps be *provoked*, but never *taught*, least of all by imitation. That, indeed, is what distinguishes talking from mere speaking.

Tagore, for his part, might in some respects be considered as a forerunner of integrationist thinking. He saw that the great weakness in traditional teaching was its compartmentalization—the endeavour to treat each academic subject as a speciality in its own right, a self-contained province of knowledge, to be studied for its own sake. He also saw that the endeavour was self-defeating, because teachers, however specialized in their own eyes, always teach more than they think they are teaching. Thirdly, he saw that teachers, however well-intentioned, often adopt methods that bring about the exact opposite of what they set out to achieve.

The integrational approach to language teaching that I would like to propose is based on very similar notions to those of Tagore and Nowakowski. It might be stated as follows. Whatever language or languages you are teaching, or think you are teaching, you are always teaching something more. For one thing, whether you realize it or not, you are teaching not just English or French or Japanese, but a certain view of what *that* language is, and also a certain view of what *a* language is: because that is built into the techniques you decide to adopt in your teaching programme.

If this idea is taken seriously, it follows that language teaching is at least a two-level enterprise: it has an *explicit* level and an *implicit* level. At the explicit level, students of language X are being introduced to various practical skills in speaking and comprehending speech, or in reading and writing, or in all of these. But at the implicit level they are being encouraged to think in a certain way about how languages in general function, how language X in particular functions, how it is set up to carry out those functions, and how it consequently unites or divides individuals and communities.

If I may draw on the analogy that Nowakowski's work suggests, the way a book is made cannot but reflect, *and also project,* certain ideas about how the book relates to its reader, and how it is organized to carry out those reader-oriented functions. There is no way those implications can be neutralized, except by removing altogether the notion *that it is a book.* That is equally so *mutatis mutandis* in the linguistic case.

I want to argue, then, that the implicit and explicit levels of language teaching are intrinsically connected. This—to take a different analogy—is for roughly the same kind of reason that you cannot teach someone to ride a bicycle without persuading the learner to think of the bicycle in a certain way. You could, in theory, treat the bicycle as just a piece of machinery, with wheels and cogs and chain interconnected in a particular sequence. But if you want to teach someone to ride it, that is not sufficient. The rider needs to know such things as which way up it goes, that the pedals are worked by the feet as opposed to the hands, what the saddle is for, and so on. The 'machinery' perspective is not enough. Another perspective is required, which starts not only from the needs and purposes of the individual rider, but from the rider as one among many. Riding a bicycle is essentially a matter of *integrating* various biomechanical activities of the rider in order to produce a certain result.

In the case of bicycles, there is not too much doubt about what the apprentice rider needs to master. But in the case of languages, that is exactly where the problems about the relationship between explicit and implicit teaching begin.

The language myth of the Western tradition presents each language as a separate, independent verbal code, designed to facilitate the transfer of specific thoughts from the mind of one person to the mind of another person. For integrationists, this involves a gross misrepresentation of what actually goes on in the processes of human communication. The linguistic sign is not a determinate unit within a fixed code of any kind, either verbal or nonverbal. Signs are the contextualized products of integrated human activities. The moment we start thinking of each linguistic sign as having a separate existence of its own, independently of any communication situation, we are straightaway knee-deep in decontextualization. Our thinking is already in thrall to the language myth.

Talking to language teachers, I find that for some of them there is a major puzzle about the integrationist position. They see that if the linguistic sign is not a determinate unit, it follows that there is no such thing as a language. If a language does not exist, how can one teach it? If I am a teacher of English, surely there must be an English language that is the language I teach. If not, what am I doing? These are the kinds of questions language teachers ask about integrationism. This paper will make some attempt to answer them.

* * *

Before trying to clarify the integrationist position, I think it worth pointing out that integrationists are not the only theorists who are sceptical about the existence of such languages as teachers find themselves called upon to teach: languages called 'English', 'French', 'Japanese', and so on. Five years after I published my book *The Language Myth*, which discussed a number of difficulties with the traditional Western conception of languages, Noam Chomsky mounted a similar attack on what he called the 'commonsense notion of language'. In the same year as Chomsky's book appeared, an eminent philosopher of language, Donald Davidson, independently announced 'there is no such thing as a language. He adds: 'not if a language is anything like what many philosophers and linguists have supposed' (Davidson 1986: 174). So integrationists are not alone in regarding languages as linguistic illusions. However, the reasons adduced for the illusion itself are different.

In his book *Knowledge of Language* (1986), Chomsky wrote as follows:

> The commonsense notion of language has a crucial sociopolitical dimension. We speak of Chinese as "a language," although the various "Chinese dialects" are as diverse as the several Romance languages. We speak of Dutch and German as two separate languages, although

some dialects of German are very close to dialects that we call "Dutch" and are not mutually intelligible with others that we call "German." A standard remark in introductory linguistics courses is that a language is a dialect with an army and a navy (attributed to Max Weinreich). (Chomsky 1986: 15)

From all this Chomsky drew the conclusion that the 'commonsense' notion of language had no place in what he called 'scientific' linguistics. Tagore would have shared Chomsky's suspicions about the criteria for recognition as 'a language', particularly as applied in such a polyglot community as India. It is interesting to note that although Chomsky describes the concept of a language that he attacks as a 'commonsense' notion, while Davidson rejects the view under attack as that held by 'many linguists and philosophers', the two are remarkably similar.

However, the integrationist goes much further than either Chomsky or Davidson, in addition to doubting the credentials of anything that could be called 'scientific' linguistics. In the end, what Chomsky is complaining about in the passage just quoted is the lack of consistency in the current *de facto* use of language names. This does not constitute an argument for saying that no satisfactory criteria for assigning language names are possible: which is the integrationist position.

That integrationist claim highlights a problem that cannot be solved by appeal to politicians who are touting for votes at the next election, any more than to the existence of native speakers. For what it is to be a 'native speaker' is itself contentious, and in any case the speakers themselves are not in agreement. Nor can the problem be finessed in the long run by identifying particular items piecemeal as belonging to this language or that (as when it is said, for instance, that *butterfly* is an English word, or that *au revoir* is a French expression). For that does not illuminate the grounds on which the uncontested examples themselves escape contestation. Thus, the whole enterprise of describing something called 'language X' is undermined as soon as the constitution of the *describiendum* itself is seriously called in question.

* * *

Let us for the moment, however, assume that, contrary to what integrationists maintain, languages *do* exist. The question then arises: can languages be taught? That can easily be dismissed as a silly question: but if it *is* a silly question, it is not for the reason often adduced, namely, that the teaching of languages has been carried on successfully for hundreds and thousands of years. That response merely confuses the issue. 'Are there specialists who call themselves "language teachers"?' is a quite different question. No one in their right mind would suppose that because there are specialists who claim to be able to foretell the future by consulting the stars, we must conclude that the future can indeed be foretold by consulting the stars. The existence of astrologers is one thing: what astrology claims is another. The same applies to language teachers and the teaching of languages.

Part of the confusion is doubtless due to what in orthodox linguistics would be called the semantics of the verb *to teach*. It is important to remove this confusion at the outset, if it can be done. Let us suppose you tell me 'John taught me to swim'. Unless there is contextual evidence to the contrary, I would be inclined to take this as implying that you can now swim, or at least could swim when John finished teaching you: whereas this is not the case if you say 'John gave me swimming lessons' or 'John was my swimming instructor'. In other words, having been 'taught', in the sense of having received lessons or instruction, does not automatically entail success in the enterprise in question. Some people, regardless of how many swimming lessons they have, and however expert the instructor, will never be able to swim.

The case is rather different if you tell me 'John taught me French'. I am inclined to suppose—unless, again, there is contextual evidence to the contrary—that you are telling me no more than that John gave you French lessons, or that John was your French teacher. So saying 'John taught me French' is not quite parallel to saying 'John taught me to swim'.

Now why is this? The answer is not immediately obvious. One candidate explanation is the following. It locates the problem—to put it in very traditional terms—as residing in the object of the verb *teach*. Perhaps 'John taught me French' is more like 'John taught me physics' than like 'John taught me to swim'. In other words, the explanation would be that there is no particular achievement (like being able to swim) that is the goal of being taught physics: nothing specific that you have to be able to *do* in physics. Or, to put it another way, there is no verb *to physic* which corresponds to the verb *to swim*. You might say 'John taught me physics' but hardly 'John taught me to physic'. And if you did, I would have to ask you what you meant.

Either you can swim or you can't. *How good* a swimmer you are is another question. And if there is any doubt about whether you can swim or not, then you probably can't. But there is nothing like that when you are being taught physics.

This is one possible explanation, and I think there is something in it. That is to say, I suspect there are many language teachers who do regard, say, 'French' as being no more than another subject on the curriculum, like 'physics' or 'geography'. It is identified by having its own syllabus, its own typical exercises, tests, set books and so on. So far, so good. Unfortunately, that explanation does not get to the heart of the problem. It gets us only as far as equating 'John taught me French' with 'John was my French teacher'. I say 'unfortunately' because, in that narrowly pedagogic use of the verb *teach*, having been taught French is no guarantee of having any practical command of French at all.

* * *

There is no doubt if we look at the history of what has gone on in European classrooms for centuries past that language teachers themselves are primarily responsible for maintaining the myth that languages exist. It is in the teachers' own professional interests to do so. This was brought home to me on one occasion when I gave a lecture pointing out that no one had ever proposed an objective set of criteria that could be employed to distinguish between so-called 'standard' and 'nonstandard' forms of English. The next morning I received an irate letter from a senior lecturer in the university's language-teaching department which did not mince words. The letter was not concerned with whether my arguments were valid or not. It said bluntly: 'You are threatening our jobs.' So I know from experience that it is very difficult even to raise these issues without immediately being accused of being unhelpfully negative, or even deliberately disruptive.

The fact remains that, in the Western tradition, generation after generation has been brainwashed into accepting not only that languages exist but also, along with that, a certain view of what a language is. The brainwashing process has been in full swing since classical antiquity.

Originally, language teaching had no place in Greek schools. The first Greek teachers were the pedotribe, in charge of physical training, and the cither player, in charge of music. It was not until the classical period that we hear of a third kind of teacher, the *grammatistes*, who, as his title indicates, was in charge of teaching the *grammata,* the letters. It is with the appearance of this third type of teacher in Greek education that the history of language teaching in the West begins.

Exactly what the first *grammatistes* taught we do not know. Our documentary evidence begins with the grammar of Dionysius Thrax. It continues through Donatus and Priscian, the Renaissance vernacular grammarians, and Port Royal, down to the present day, where we end up with an enormous multimillion-dollar language-teaching industry. Its output ranges from tourist phrase books to television programmes, and its employees include university professors, recording engineers and church missionaries. All these people—and their customers—are in various ways committed, whether they realize it or not, to the twin propositions that what we *do* know about languages is *that they exist* and *are teachable* (by those qualified to teach them). So deep is the commitment that it is rarely questioned.

In the face of this vast infrastructure, devoted to identifying and selling particular languages, integrationists perversely deny that languages exist. Is this just a theoretical quibble rather than a sober statement of fact? Here is an interesting piece of anecdotal evidence. Nabokov tells us that, when he was a boy, for a number of years he did not grasp that French and Russian were different. Without realizing it, he was equally fluent in both. Those of us who were not brought up in a bilingual household like that of the young Nabokov may find it difficult to imagine that kind of experience. In my own case, which is probably not atypical for English children of my generation, I could not only speak, but read and write as well, long before it dawned upon me that there was any *other* language in the world than the one we used at home. And when it did dawn upon me, there was no doubt at all about the linguistic difference between English and non-English, because non-English was simply incomprehensible. But then, non-English is not a language.

This, I later realised, corresponds rather closely to the ancient Greek distinction between Greeks and barbarians. Barbarians are the people whose language you do not understand. That ethnocentric terminology, as Tagore would doubtless have agreed, has important implications. It means that Greek is tacitly defined as the language of those people you *do* understand: your family, your friends, your neighbours, and so on in an ever-widening circle. At the same time, it segregates that community from any other community whose members you do *not* understand. But applying the criterion of comprehension raises an even more intractable problem. How is the communicational phenomenon of comprehension to be defined?

The solution Dionysius Thrax adopts is not very convincing. (It was criticized even in antiquity.) Instead of discussing the question as open to rational debate, he simply defines the grammar he will be dealing with by reference to what he calls 'the general usage of poets and prose writers'. The implication, of course, is *Greek* poets and prose writers. In other words, he proposes a model for imitation and study. The model proposed, however, is extremely vague. Presumably the poets he has in mind would have to include Homer, while the prose writers would have to include Herodotus and Thucydides. And that already raises a problem, because—classical scholars tell us—the language of Homer was not the language of Herodotus or Thucydides. Nor was it the vernacular of Dionysius's own day. But, as a canny language teacher, Dionysius is not going to get further out of his depth. He settles it by the ancient pedagogic ploy of stipulative definition.

That in itself is a clear indication that Dionysius's programme is by no means ideologically neutral. It is already inscribed in an ongoing construction of 'Hellenism'. It is essential to such a programme to single out certain landmarks as showing what is authentically Hellenic and what is not. The language of Homer is just such a landmark. For this purpose, it has to be demonstrable that Homer's language, although outstanding and perhaps unsurpassable, is not just peculiar to Homer. It has to be 'reducible' to a schema comprehensible to Greeks of the current age. Only thus can the continuity of Hellenic culture be made to appear plausible. Once that pedagogic thread is broken, it cannot be mended. From an integrational perspective, that supplies a macrosocial explanation of why the first grammar of Greek emanates not from Athens but from Alexandria. Athens had no reason to establish its credentials in the mainstream of Hellenic culture.

Implicit and Explicit Language Teaching 31

But provincial Alexandria, founded in the wake of Alexander's conquests, certainly did.

* * *

Not the least of the reasons why Dionysius's grammar might be regarded as a landmark in language teaching is this. It is the first pedagogic text we have that is clearly based on the notion that, in order to teach pupils a language, you need to present them with a synoptic view of its basic elements and relations. Otherwise, they will not really be able to understand how it 'works'. This is in line with all Greek pedagogic enterprises, including the teaching of mathematics, geometry, logic, biology and politics. Dionysius's grammar of the Greek language presents just such a synoptic view. It is rather like treating the bicycle as a complicated piece of machinery, rather than a means of transport.

In favour of this approach, it might be argued that it is certainly an advance on what we might imagine to have been a more primitive 'pre-grammatical' form of language teaching, involving no more than repetition and rote learning. In modern terms, Dionysius's method is based on promoting what language teachers in the twentieth century belatedly started calling 'metalinguistic awareness'. In fact, most of Dionysius's grammar is just a metalinguistic catalogue, hierarchically arranged.

The point an integrationist would want to make here is this. If you teach a language by getting your students to learn some metalinguistic hierarchy of this kind, you cannot complain if they begin to conceive of *the language itself* as consisting essentially of just such a hierarchy. That is by far the easiest way for them to make sense of what they are being taught. It is the implicit lesson as opposed to the explicit lesson. Dionysius, in short, was not just teaching Greek. Whether he realized it or not, he was teaching a certain conception of what the Greek language was.

It is no coincidence in the case of Dionysius that it was a conception of the Greek language *as seen from Alexandria*. Roland Barthes somewhere says, unless my memory deceives me, that it is no use trying to elucidate what is said unless you realize that everything is said from *a certain position*. This was also the objection brought years earlier by the Oxford philosopher R. G. Collingwood against founding a theory of logic on the Aristotelian syllogism. One cannot pluck a proposition out of thin air and attach a 'meaning' to it. It has no meaning until it is considered as a contextualized utterance. Collingwood was right: his contention about meaning corresponds exactly to the integrationist position.

* * *

All the foregoing is by way of background to two general theses I wish to advance in this paper. Thesis 1 is that conceptions of what a language is, *from a certain position*, determine how languages are taught. Thesis 2 is that how languages are taught, *from a certain position*, determines conceptions of what a language is. These two theses are not contradictory but symbiotic. Let me take Dionysius as an illustration.

In various ways Dionysius's conception of the Greek language might strike us today as very curious. Not just curious but positively misleading. For a start, in Dionysius's grammar there is no syntax. Or at least nothing that linguists would nowadays call 'syntax'. And this is not just an accidental omission for which Dionysius is to blame. In his lifetime, there was no recognition of any syntactic component as part of a language. The first attempt at a comprehensive syntax of Greek was the work of Apollonius Dyscolus, some three centuries later.

What accounts for this primitive asyntactic conception of the Greek language that we find in Dionysius? Almost certainly the answer is simply that what we regard as syntax the early Greek language teachers were never required to teach. It was not part of their job. Why not? Because in the early period the Greeks regarded knowing how to put words together in order to express a coherent proposition as not so much a *linguistic* ability as an exercise of reason. That is why Dionysius stops short as soon as he has expounded his metalinguistic doctrine of the parts of speech. To put it another way, syntax disappeared down the pedagogic gap between the teaching of Greek and the teaching of logic.

But that, from an integrationist perspective, is not the gravest misconception associated with teaching languages by the Dionysian method. A more basic problem, not only with Dionysius but with any method based on 'metalinguistic awareness', is that it invites a conflation between personal linguistic proficiency *in* language X and knowing something *about* language X. In integrational terms, the difference is very clear. The activities that can be integrated in the two cases are quite different. You might as well suppose that learning a lot about the bicycle would automatically enable you to ride one. A conscientious student who had thoroughly mastered the contents of Dionysius's grammar would not *eo ipso* have improved his fluency in spoken or written Greek one iota. What he might have improved, doubtless, were his answers to metalinguistic questions in the language classroom.

* * *

If you are a language teacher, there comes a point at which you have to make up your mind about what your language teaching is geared to do. It seems to be assumed nowadays that the teaching of foreign languages is geared to being able to interact linguistically with a variety of foreigners, mostly anonymous. Some of these interactions are 'on the spot': some are 'delayed'. If you are English, you have to be taught how to order ('on the spot') a ham sandwich in a French cafe, or how to negotiate a commercial contract (possibly 'delayed') with a French company, or how to read the novels of Balzac ('delayed' indefinitely), or how to follow a film ('on the spot') by the latest French film director. Or some miscellaneous combination of those.

It is far from clear that any metalinguistic analysis of French, or even of particular dialects or other varieties of French, will help anyone to achieve success in these various objectives. I am nevertheless struck by the fact that precisely such a metalinguistic emphasis in language teaching has been maintained for centuries. It is a striking paradox that the metalanguage was never designed for our modern priorities; but we continue to use its terminology (or some historical derivatives thereof) in our present-day discussions. And this is undoubtedly one source of current confusions. All the more reason for an intelligent language teacher to take seriously the question of whether languages exist.

* * *

I return now to the vexed question of distinguishing one so-called 'language' from another. The situation Nabokov describes seems to be no more than an extension of a phenomenon commonly reported in research on language acquisition in bilingual children; namely, that the differentiation of words and constructions as belonging to two separate systems is a gradual process. 'Mixing' all and sundry indiscriminately is the primitive state. Nabokov, to the best of my recollection, does not say what actually triggered the realization that French and Russian were somehow different. But I suspect it may well have been his first encounter with a language teacher. (His parents were sufficiently affluent to employ such a person, and sufficiently enlightened not to question whether they were getting good value for their money.)

With that in mind, let me now put forward another proposition for discussion. The proposition is this: 'For many people, the initial differentiation of one "language" from another is a function of pedagogic experience.' In other words, some of us started distinguishing language X from language Y because we were *taught* to do so as part of some language-teaching programme.

For what percentage of the world's population that generalization holds I would not like to guess. Here I am concerned only with those for whom it does hold. And that class is not empty. I know, because I at least am a member of it. I also suspect, although I cannot prove, that it would have included generations of Greek and Roman schoolchildren.

I cannot speak for them, but I can speak for me. What I am talking about, as an integrationist, is trying to make sense of one's own linguistic experience. And I find I can easily make sense of some of my later notions about language and languages by reference to an important early stage in my education. During this stage, different 'languages' corresponded mainly to the content of different *lessons*. I never went through any initial phase of the kind Nabokov describes, where I grew up speaking what I only later realized were quite different forms of verbal communication. That was never part of my first-order linguistic experience.

In Britain, Disraeli's Act of 1876 made it 'the duty of the parent of every child to cause such child to receive elementary instruction in reading, writing and arithmetic'. That is the first time, as far as I know, that any form of language teaching was made obligatory in this country. I was a direct beneficiary, or helpless victim, depending on one's point of view. They (the 'authorities') caused me to receive language teaching from the first moment when I was swept up into the public educational system. But from my entry into what was then secondary education, French was what you did in French lessons, Latin was what you did in Latin lessons, and so on. The only exception, curiously enough, was English. This stood out like a sore thumb; because English was not only what you did in English lessons. It carried on outside the classroom as well. The other languages, at first, stopped short at the classroom door. The other feature that made English a linguistic oddity was that French lessons and Latin lessons were always conducted in English, whereas English lessons were never conducted in French or Latin. What a perplexing asymmetry!

As my education progressed I began to see that there were two quite different kinds of language teaching, moving in opposite directions, as it were. In French and Latin lessons the teachers were trying to set up a classroom subject *ab initio* and then, gradually, move it outside the classroom into the wider world. In English lessons it was the other way round. English I was already familiar with outside the classroom. When it moved inside the classroom, English took on a different shape. It shrank. It became reduced. It had to be looked at in an altogether narrower way. It had to be analysed by means of terms and procedures that I had never encountered elsewhere, at home or in the street. ('What is the subject of this sentence?' Can anyone imagine a more pointless question? As a child, I couldn't.)

Later still I came to realize that these two kinds of language teaching exemplify fundamentally different integrational modes. They apply, it need hardly be said, to many other forms of communication than language teaching. One integrational mode follows the direction inside > outside, or here > elsewhere, or now > then. Let us call this the 'projective' mode of integration. The other mode follows the opposite direction: outside > inside, or elsewhere > here, or then > now. Let us call this the 'reductive' mode.

These are, to be sure, very vague descriptions, but they capture an integrational opposition that I think is intuitively recognizable and that I think Tagore would have recognized. Some communicational enterprises are inherently reductive. Cartography would be an example. The mapmaker has to reduce the whole topography of external landscapes to a schema of lines and colours on a piece of paper. An example of the opposite mode would be the town planner's drawings for a suburb and a road network that have yet to be built. Here the objective is to set up a model for something that does not yet exist, but which might be brought into existence. Only when it is will it find a place on the cartographer's map. Each mode of integration has its own functions in a whole range of human enterprises, and there are some which combine both; but I am not going to say anything further about that general distinction on this occasion except that each mode has its own semiological profile. Even if the cartographer and the town planner use formally identical graphic signs, their meanings in the two cases will be different.

What I do want to say, however, is that it seems to me no accident that the first language-teaching text that has survived in the Western tradition, the grammar of Dionysius, is manifestly a text in the reductive mode. It presupposes that the pupil is already able to cope with Greek outside the classroom, at least up to a point. I do not think that Dionysius's grammar was ever designed to teach Greek to pupils who knew none. It looks to me much more like a synoptic handbook addressed to language teachers. And here we come to another communicational problem. Teachers have to put a pedagogic distance between themselves and their pupils. This is a requirement that arises out of the communication situation itself. It relates to what integrationists call the 'macrosocial' and 'circumstantial' parameters of communication. And the way language teachers have traditionally chosen to deal with that requirement is to adopt a backward-looking linguistic stance. Language teaching always casts its lot on the side of conservatism. It is always slightly—and sometimes a long way—behind the times.

In the case of Dionysius, as classical scholars have pointed out, he is teaching a pronunciation of Greek that was already archaic by the time his grammar was compiled. But it was a pronunciation necessary for appreciation of the works of the poets, in particular Homer. So there is an invisible warning inscribed at the beginning of Dionysius's text. It reads: 'Don't imagine that because you are a Greek you are competent in the Greek language.' In other words, Dionysius is implicitly rejecting the popular linguistic distinction between Greek and barbarian, based on comprehension. He is saying: 'Greek is not just what you find comprehensible in the speech around you.' And something like that has remained a professional article of faith with language teachers down to the present day. The language teacher must lay *some* claim to superior knowledge. The pedagogic rationale is simple enough. If the pupil already knows all that needs to be known, what is the point of teaching? The language teacher has to be cast in the role of someone who 'really' knows the language: and this makes language teaching an intrinsically prescriptive enterprise.

* * *

I may of course be wrong about Nabokov's great revelation. Perhaps it had nothing to do with language teaching. There are various other possibilities.

Perhaps the penny dropped when one day he realized that when you were talking to servants or labourers on the estate you had to speak Russian, because French they could not understand (whereas his family spoke and understood both). Or perhaps he suddenly realized that there were certain sounds that occurred in French words but never occurred in Russian words and vice versa.

Let me now, however, press Nabokov's anecdote a little further; doubtless further than the author himself would have wished; perhaps into the realms of science fiction. Suppose he had *never,* for some reason, had occasion to discover any difference between French and Russian. Suppose he had never had an unfortunate encounter with a language teacher. Suppose that the peasants on the family estate could understand everything he said. Suppose he had never been observant enough to realize that certain vowels occurred only in one set of words, but never in another set, and vice versa. You will doubtless object that on his first visit to Paris he would soon have found that many Parisians did not understand Russian. But let us suppose that he never went abroad. Let us suppose that he lived all his life on this isolated estate, somewhere in Russia, cut off from all contact with the outside world. The question I now want to pose is this. Given those conditions, do we have one language or two in Nabokov's linguistic community? Or does that distinction automatically collapse?

I can imagine that some language teachers would regard this as a rather desperate thought experiment, wheeled on to justify the integrationist position. So let me refer now to some experimental work by J. J. Asher, who is by no means an integrationist and therefore provides some measure of independent support.

According to Asher, in developing his own Total Physical Response' (TPR) method of language teaching, he found that *it made no difference* whether students were given instructions in Persian, Portuguese or Japanese. All three could be mixed at random, without affecting comprehension or recall (Asher 2000: 1–22). If we stop to think about this, we realize that the theoretical implications are profound. The human mind does not distinguish between one language and another in any preordained way. Nor does the innocent language learner. There is evidence from what is known in orthodox linguistics as 'code-switching' that speaks to this point too. (Although, it hardly needs saying, the orthodox term 'code-switching' already begs the very question we are discussing.)

All this seems to me very strong empirical confirmation that the integrationist position on languages and language teaching cannot be dismissed as just theoretical quibbling. The world of verbal communication does not divide up *naturally* into any set of separate systems called 'languages'. We are not dealing here with first-order *realia,* but with artificial constructs deliberately set up to further ideological objectives.

In my own case I can remember quite distinctly what at first I thought different languages were. They were alternative sets of words for the same set of objects, and alternative ways of expressing the same thoughts. It was not until many years later that I read Saussure and discovered that there was a name for this misguided view: it was known as 'nomenclaturism'. Saussure, as later did Wittgenstein, went to some pains to explain why the nomenclaturist position was mistaken. But he did not explain, at least to my satisfaction, why at a very early stage in my education I had already become a fully paid-up subscriber to the doctrine of languages as nomenclatures. As far as I recall, no one explicitly indoctrinated me. So how did I come to fall into that trap at such a tender age?

Looking back now, I have no doubt whatever about the answer. It was implicit in at least one of the pedagogic techniques employed systematically by my teachers of French and Latin. This was the rote learning of vocabulary lists. We were given lists of words for plants, trees, furniture and so on, consisting of foreign terms and their English equivalents. The class learnt them for homework and were tested on them at school the next morning. The *implicit* linguistic lesson was almost inescapable. Each foreign word had its paired English counterpart, and they were counterparts because, and only because, both were names of the same real-world item. If the French word *chien* meant 'dog', that was because the animal was one and the same on both sides of the Channel. No one told me this *explicitly:* they did not have to.

There were of course a few 'exceptions' to these Anglo-French lexical pairings: there were always 'exceptions' in language lessons. I remember our French teacher making a great song and dance about the fact that *chaise* did not mean 'chair', because, for some unexplained reason, the French attached great importance to whether or not a chair had arms. But this kind of case did not crop up very often. Fortunately for our French teacher. If it had, his task would have been incomparably more difficult, if not wellnigh impossible. By and large, you could take it for granted that whatever you wanted to talk about in English, the French had a word for it. I did not realize at the time that these correspondences had a historical explanation. It seemed to me that French and English were two different linguistic lenses through which one looked at the same world 'out there'. Nor did I realize that there were languages that projected a totally alien picture of the world from the one to which I was accustomed.

Latin was a bit of a problem, because Latin became a dead language before the invention of electric lights and motor cars. So you had to be careful when translating English passages containing terms for modern inventions. But usually that posed no pedagogic difficulty, because the snippets we had to translate had been carefully selected. In any case, it was not an insuperable problem. When due allowance was made for the late invention of the electric light and the motor car, plus the fact that Romans wore togas, the Roman world seemed very much like an earlier version of our own. Its existence did not seriously undermine my view of languages as alternative nomenclatures with clear interlingual equivalences. In a curious way, the historical example of Latin seemed to confirm that naive view.

In any case, the notion of interlingual equivalence was validated for me by that great pedagogic institution, the bilingual dictionary. One did not question the dictionary. That would have been a no-go area in the classroom. I did not know then that the Greeks and Romans had no dictionaries. Nor did I know that the dictionary was essentially a Renaissance invention, sponsored by one of the greatest macrosocial upheavals in the history of Europe: that is, the collapse of the feudal system and the emergence of the centralized nation-state as the dominant political unit. With that came an ideal that was to leave an indelible mark on all language teaching. The ideal was 'one country, one language'.

Here we have an even clearer example of linguistic ideology at work. The ideal 'one country, one language' was an indispensable adjunct of nationalism. No country could afford to appear to be culturally dependent on another. So 'languages' had to be defined in such a way as to allow them to become important badges of political independence. This was one of the early forms of what we now call 'political correctness'. In the long run, language teaching had to fall in line with this sociopolitical doctrine, regardless of whether language teachers approved of it or not. But they did not fall in line without some acrimonious disputes, as we discover when we read sixteenth-century grammarians. To put it in integrationist terms, their problem was, essentially, that dividing up the linguistic world of Europe into a determinate number of languages was theoretically insoluble, because it could be done in an infinite number of ways. So the language teachers of the Renaissance had to make some very arbitrary choices. In other words, a vague conception based simply on comprehension no longer sufficed to deal with the political pressures being exerted on this concept of 'our language'. It was no use having a national code if no one was very sure what it was.

So the next thing that happened was that language teachers were recruited willy-nilly to put this code in place. They became political agents for policies of linguistic cleansing. In many places today they still are. Given the nationalistic imperative that became increasingly pressing from the Renaissance onwards, what you might have predicted, had you been a sufficiently astute linguistic theorist, is that European language teachers, as a profession, would eventually go for constructing linguistic superfictions based on writing. And that is exactly what happened. In this country, it took the form of a mythical supercode called 'Standard English'. This term is actually an invention of nineteenth-century nationalist lexicographers; but it has caused generations of students unnecessary anxiety about whether their English was 'Standard' or not.

No such language as 'Standard English' has ever existed except in the textbooks of its pedagogic proponents. But the most paradoxical chapter in this particular episode of language teaching was contributed by linguists who should have known better. Finding themselves confronted with indisputable evidence of the nonstandardized character of English usage, they sought to explain this away by postulating a plurality of standards. Thus arose the submyths of 'Standard American English', 'Standard Australian English', 'Standard Welsh English' and even 'Standard English English'. These submyths in turn were complicated by distinguishing internally between different 'sociolects', allegedly used by members of different social classes, and therefore each having its own 'standard' form.

The absurdity of this hypothetical multistandard language is revealed by its own terminology. In every field of human activity, postulating a plurality of different standards makes a nonsense of the 'standard' itself. If a yard differs in length in different parts of the country, or from one shop to the next, then the yard is *not* a standard measurement, and no insistence on calling it a 'standard yard' will make it so. Exactly the same holds for languages, for currency, for spare parts, and for everything else where the notion of standardization applies.

'Standard English' we have to recognize as a language-teaching construct; a mythical construct that attempts to impose an arbitrary systematization on a linguistic state of affairs that itself resists systematization because it embraces too much diversity. The resistance comes from the open-endedness, the intrinsic instability and context-dependence of everyday human communication. In order to systematize or codify, one is forced to decontextualize and simplify. The lines along which that was done, in the British Isles, reflected a top-down attempt to put the lower classes in their place. What was taught as 'Received Pronunciation' was actually the pronunciation of the major English public schools, to which the lower classes had no access. This was recognized long ago by the doyen of twentieth-century English phonetics, Daniel Jones (Jones 1945: ix–x).

Any linguistic systematization is always arbitrary in the sense that some alternative systematization could have been chosen. Once we grasp that, we see that the end product—the codified object that gets to be called 'English' or 'French' or whatever—is actually an artifact of the classifications and ideological subterfuges deployed in order to produce it. As far as one can see, that is endemic in the language-teaching practices of the Western tradition.

Again, to go back to Dionysius Thrax, the pedagogic reliance on systematization is already in evidence. For Dionysius there are just eight parts of speech: no more and no less. Dionysius never considers possible alternative systems, or explains on what basis this particular systematization has been selected, or why. As far as he is concerned, the existence of eight parts of speech is just a brute linguistic fact about the Greek language. In other words, here the language teacher is already *confusing his own pedagogic simplification with linguistic reality*. And the propensity to that confusion has remained the occupational disease of the language teacher throughout the Western tradition. What has changed between Dionysius's generation and ours is not the linguistic difference between 'correct' and 'incorrect' but the ideological imperative that commands the pedagogic application of that distinction.

* * *

Where do we go from here? Are there, in principle, methods of language teaching that do not fall foul of these traps? I think there are such methods; but few language teachers have the resources or the authority to adopt or adapt them consistently, even if they wished to, because official examinations and qualifications are still predicated upon very traditional assumptions about what a language is. In practice, this results in a pick-and-mix approach, where the ideas behind the 'Reform Movement', the 'Direct Method' and 'Communicative Language Teaching', as well as appeal to a genetically programmed 'Language Acquisition Device', are all rolled into one, but no coherent strategy emerges. The resultant chaos is sometimes dignified by calling it 'pragmatic flexibility'.

An eclectic approach to language teaching was made academically respectable in England by Harold Palmer during the interwar period. Palmer, originally a Berlitz teacher, rejected what he saw as the excesses of the 'Direct Method'. Although he appears to have had no particular philosophy of education, he based his own pedagogic approach on what he believed to be 'the nature of language'. Unsurprisingly, this turned out to be a latter-day version of the language myth, in which language was held to be 'the mirror of thought', even though thought was distorted by its own verbal reflection (Palmer 1917: 29). Palmer tried to introduce a pseudoscientific terminology for the teachers, in which we encounter such items as *monologs, polylogs, miologs, alogisms* and *ergons*. Fortunately this rebarbative metalanguage never caught on, but Palmer's eclecticism did, doubtless in part because it allowed the teacher to adopt whatever combination of methods seemed like a good idea at the time.

Since Palmer's day, language teaching has continued to be a free-for-all. The 'science' that Palmer thought he had founded never matured, and the fundamental lessons of the educational pioneers were never properly digested. It is interesting that some of them are not even mentioned in the long but myopic article on the history of language teaching that appeared in the *Encyclopedia of Language and Linguistics*, published in 1994 (R. Asher 1994). There we find one vague reference to Pestalozzi, but none to Tagore, or Montessori, or Steiner.

Another of the figures not mentioned in that article is one I have already referred to: James Asher. It is ironic that Asher never seems to have realized how close some of his ideas were to those of Tagore. Tagore insisted very emphatically on the importance of physical activity in the development of the mind. He objected to the way in which children were disciplined to sit still in class, because this repressed their spontaneous physical reactions, and forced mental responses into the channel of vocal utterance. Again, it is interesting how closely this relates to Nowakowski's notion of 'yessence'. According to Nowakowski, essential parts of a language are gesture, grimaces, touching, moving, seeing, vibrating, and all the other bodily concomitants of vocal utterance.

A pioneer less often overlooked was the founder of the 'Direct Method', Maximilian Berlitz, who anticipated Saussure's conception of each *language* as a law unto itself, and concluded that teaching foreign languages by translation was bound to distort them. Nevertheless, decades after Berlitz had elaborated this insight into a viable programme of language teaching, schools and universities were still basing their examinations on translation, and still do. Asher was even closer than Berlitz to integrationist thinking and to Tagore. He recognized the fundamental fact that verbal communication has to be integrated into nonverbal programmes of physical activity. Verbal instruction is not adequate as a strategy for language teaching. Asher found that the kind of bilingual drill to which I was accustomed at school is actually an *obstacle* to the pupil trying to cope with an unfamiliar language. Maybe that explains why I was such a hopeless language learner: I sat there in the classroom expecting that language was going to be delivered by the same means as 'physics' or 'geography'.

Asher's explanation of his findings refers us neurophysiologically to the specialized functions of the bicameral brain. I do not propose to go into that here. Whether the hypothesis is correct is another question again: but at least it has a biomechanical basis, as integrationists would expect. More important still, it also highlights what was wrong with most of the traditional methods of language teaching. They rely crucially on *decontextualization,* even at the most basic level.

A pupil who is asked to repeat a certain sound or spell out a certain word is being engaged in a task of decontextualization; that is, being invited to treat the item in question in a way that prises it out of any context in which it would occur in everyday communication situations. Indeed, unless the pupil understands the decontextualization required, the pedagogic process immediately breaks down. We do not usually go around repeating isolated sounds or spelling out words just for the sake of it. But those decontextualizations are a prominent feature of traditional language-teaching techniques. What they teach the student, implicitly rather than explicitly, is that words are bipartite entities, each with a form and a meaning. Furthermore, *the form of a word exists independently of its meaning.* And this is a denial of yessence. It confuses talking with speaking, and writing with inscription.

Once again we come back to the same question: if there are no languages, what is it that language teachers are teaching? For the integrationist, there is little doubt about the answer. They are teaching a myth conjured up by the institutionalized practices of language pedagogy, in response to ideological demands of the society in which the teachers live and teach. A 'language', in this sense, is a metalinguistic extrapolation that has become attached to a particular language name. It does not matter whether the name is *English, French,* or whatever. It does not even matter whether it has an army or navy. But there has to be a name. No name: no language. That is the higher-order metamyth under which the language-teaching profession operates.

* * *

In the West the society that supports such metamythical constructs has always been a *literate* society, and it would be impossible to exaggerate how profoundly that affects the whole enterprise of language teaching.

We know that for at least five millennia, going back to the first Sumerian schools, language teaching has been based on writing. We still have numerous bits and pieces of what was left behind by Sumerian children doing their classroom exercises. There is no tradition (at least, none that has survived) that tells of a form of language teaching based exclusively on oral communication. What does that show us?

Writing is an essential tool of linguistic decontextualization. The point was already made by Plato in unmistakable terms (Harris 2000: 17ff.). That decontextualization impacts on both the explicit and implicit dimensions of language teaching in a fundamental respect. There is no other way the units of speech can be 'represented' as existing in a nonoral medium. It is no coincidence that the emergence of grammar in the Western tradition corresponds, precisely, with the transition from an oral to a literate society.

If you have no alphabet, you cannot develop what Havelock called in a memorable phrase 'the alphabetic mind'. (You would not be able to understand Dionysius Thrax either.) But Havelock's point can be generalized further. If you have no writing system at all, then you cannot develop what I would like to call 'the scriptorial mind'. And it takes a scriptorial mind to devise any programme of language teaching. Why? Because without the support of writing, there is no basis for independent identification of the units of speech. Aristotle was aware of this, but he did not at first grasp its full implications. When he did, he shied away from them and tried to fudge the issue, because otherwise it would have undermined the whole basis of Aristotelian logic. That too required a belief that languages are fixed codes.

Grammar was originally the study of the *grammata,* the letters. The letters in turn were supposed to 'stand for' the individual sounds of speech. Already in antiquity this doctrine ran into difficulties, as we know from the discussions of grammarians. But no Greek or Roman ever considered scrapping it, for the very good practical reason that a literate society finds it extremely useful for social and political purposes to have records of the past that outstrip living memory. This is the whole point of the legend of Atlantis, as told in Plato's *Timaeus.* It is also the reason why Greek and Roman linguistic education began with the alphabet. And so did mine, more than two thousand years later. *Plus ça change* . . .

In short, the support that literacy gives to the language myth is inestimable. It makes it possible to use visual symbols for the purpose of identifying elements in an oral code. The moment you accept that *this* letter 'stands for' *that* sound you already have the basis for envisaging the whole language as a complex multilevel code. That this extrapolation can rarely, if ever, be accomplished rationally or consistently drops out of sight beside the utility of the fiction thereby embodied. For all that, however, a linguistic fiction is still a fiction, as integrationists have been pointing out for decades now.

* * *

The challenge for language teaching in the twenty-first century is to deal with semiological realities in preference to promoting old linguistic fictions or implementing political agendas. One can already see what kinds of reorientation would be needed. As my Nabokovian allegory suggests, the whole notion of a 'linguistic community' needs rethinking. For integrationists, any community in which individual and collective activities are integrated in part by means of verbal signs is *eo ipso* a linguistic community. But that immediately poses enormous problems for traditional language teaching. Why? Because such a community has no determinate membership and includes a vast range of disparate verbal and nonverbal abilities. Such communities overlap and intermingle: they do not divide up neatly, either geographically or grammatically. For purposes of classroom teaching, they are a nightmare, as Tagore well realized. So the traditional strategy adopted by language teachers has always been to ignore them: that is, to *reverse the natural priorities and define communities by reference to languages.*

Had he lived to see it, Tagore would have deplored the fact that of the three major articles devoted to language teaching in the *Encyclopedia of Language and Linguistics,* one—and it is not the shortest of the three: it takes up seven double-column pages—is concerned solely with the question of *how to test your students.* This cannot be an accident. It reveals more eloquently than anything else the extent to which, in recent decades, the language teacher's professional vision has focussed on marks and examinations rather than on understanding what is going on in the educational process. Whatever shortcomings Dionysius's famous grammar of Greek may have had, one thing can be said in its favour. It has no section on how to test anyone's command of Greek.

As an Englishman travelling abroad in an alien linguistic environment, I have often been surprised by how skilfully some foreigners manage to make 'a few words of English' go a very long way. If tested on their command of the language, they would doubtless have failed dismally ('Me speak English, sah!). Their pronunciation was rough-and-ready, and their grammar nonexistent. A well-constructed subordinate clause would have been as out of place in their speech as a top hat in a rugby scrum. But in communicational fluency they needed no lessons. And I have sometimes wondered whether it might not be better to try to teach one's students communicational fluency first—if it can be taught—instead of trying to teach them languages.

I am well aware, to be sure, that in the 1970s and 1980s a good deal was heard about something called 'communicative' language teaching. But, as far as I have been able to discover, what that boiled down to was adding a bit of speech-act theory on to a basically code-based approach. The language system was still the core of the programme, and communication was a variable extra. Whereas for the people who are exponents of the kind of polyglot communicational fluency I have in mind, it seems to be the other way round.

Communication is the core, and languages are the variable extra.

* * *

Are language teachers today perhaps more enlightened in this respect than the benighted language teachers of my schooldays? Have I set up for demolition purposes a professional Aunt Sally that no longer bears any resemblance to the views and practices of language teachers today? I don't think so, to judge by some recent publications.

The first I happened to pick up at random was entitled *Developing Materials for Language Teaching*. It was published in 2003. That turned out to be an extremely depressing read. It projected an image of the language teacher as a professional whose main concerns were (1) to develop even more intricate classroom formats of the kind I was already all too familiar with, and (2) to argue with colleagues who preferred using rival formats. In other words, there was no attempt to address the linguistic questions I have been raising here: it was as if only the *methodology* of teaching was of any importance. The objectives were somehow all taken for granted. It was like listening in on a meeting of civil servants convened to discuss the best ways of collecting taxes.

The second book that came my way contained more of the same. It was called *Teaching and Learning a Second Language*. Date of publication 2003. Among other gems, it included a discussion of the thought-provoking claim that giving grades to students' work acts as a deterrent to their progress. In other words, if you want to teach students a foreign language, don't let them know how they are doing. That was certainly not the strategy when I was at school. Perhaps I would have done better if it had been.

The third book I looked at had a more promising title: *Language Learning: A Lifelong Process*. This too was published in 2003. It sounded less professionally claustrophobic. Alas for my expectations. As soon as I opened the pages, my eye fell upon the following sententious pronouncement:

> When it is said that one person speaks Hokkien or another speaks Portuguese what in fact is being implied is that the person can use and

understand the rules of that linguistic system and has a pretty sound grasp of the rules of the system, at each level of linguistic structure.

No advance on Priscian there.

Maybe I chanced on an odd selection of pedagogic texts; but I have no reason to think that they were unrepresentative of the kind of thinking that goes on in some areas of language teaching today.

* * *

In a paper published in 1987 on 'Linguistic Utopias', Mary Louise Pratt argued that linguists are prone to postulating discrete communities and subcommunities in order to anchor some stable concept of what a linguistic system is (whether the system be referred to as a language, a dialect, a sociolect, or any other kind of lect). I think she put her finger on a very important point. These concepts of communality are mythical, or 'Utopian'. Instead, she urged, we need not a linguistics of communities but what she called a 'linguistics of contact'. She defined this as 'a linguistics that places at its centre the workings of language across rather than within lines of social differentiation, of class, race, gender, age' (Pratt 1987: 61). I wonder why she did not go one step further by adding *'and nationality'*. That extra step is essential from an integrationist perspective. But it is a step that threatens to undermine the traditional position of the language teacher.

It is at this crucial point that the language myth begins to reveal its ugly side. Once that reversal of priorities is accepted, by which communities are defined by reference to languages, and this reversal is propagated in the name of education to generation after generation, it straightaway feeds the taproots of ethnocentrism, nationalism, social discrimination and many of the nastier forms of politics; as well as the cultural imperialism that nowadays promotes the notion of a miraculously neutral 'world language' (coincidentally called 'English') already in place.

These shallow linguistic deceptions must not be allowed to flourish in the future. Somehow, the teaching profession must take a fresh grip on the problems of human communication. I think that integrationism offers a theoretical basis for doing so. I also think it is a basis of which Tagore, the clearest thinker of our age on such matters, would have approved. I come back to my opening epigraphs. We need an approach that recognizes the 'yessence' factor in verbal communication, that emphasizes the difference between talking and speaking, and that refuses to treat texts as raw material for linguistic exercises or exemplification of grammatical 'rules'. The task is to make sure that language teaching does not spread linguistic confusion rather than enlightenment, does not divide humanity rather than reunite us. To put it in simpler terms, we need teaching programmes that give *language* priority over *languages*.

REFERENCES

Asher, J. J., 2000. *Learning Another Language Through Actions*, 6th ed., Los Gatos CA, Sky Oaks.
Asher, R. E. (ed.), 1994. *The Encyclopedia of Language and Linguistics*, 10 Vols., Oxford, Pergamon.
Chomsky, A. N., 1986. *Knowledge of Language*. New York, Praeger.
Davidson, D., 1986. 'A nice derangement of epitaphs'. In: Grandy, R. E. and Warner, R. (eds.), *Philosophical Grounds of Rationality*, Oxford, Clarendon, pp.158–174.
Harris, R., 2000. *Rethinking Writing*. London, Athlone.
Havelock, E. A., 1982. *The Literate Revolution in Greece and Its Cultural Consequences*. Princeton, NJ, Princeton University Press.
Jones, D., 1945. *An English Pronouncing Dictionary*, 7th ed., London, Dent.
Nowakowski, R., 2003. *Why Do I Make My Books the Way I Do?* Dabrowa Dolna, Bodzentyn, Bookmakery Elephant's Tail.
Palmer, H. E., 1917. *The Scientific Study and Teaching of Languages*, London, Harrap.
Pratt, M. L., 1987. "Linguistic Utopias". In Fabb, N. et al. (eds.), *The Linguistics of Writing*, Manchester, UK, Manchester University Press, pp. 48–66.
Tagore, R., 1961, 'A poet's school'. In Elmhirst, L. K. (ed.), *Rabindranath Tagore, Pioneer in Education*, London, Murray, pp. 44–65.

2 Learning to Write
Integrational Linguistics and the Indian Subcontinent
Rukmini Bhaya Nair

INTRODUCTION

Roy Harris has always been recognized as an unusual thinker, a lone warrior battling against what he felicitously calls "the language myth in Western culture" but, today, his views seem poised for a comeback. The position long held by him that "words are not learnt separately from everything else, but as integrated and integrating elements in a whole continuum of acquiring knowledge" is now supported by several robust new studies in language acquisition (Bloom 2000; Lanza 2001; Tomasello 2003). At the same time, the implications for language teaching of his more controversial view, that the invention of writing systems provided the human species with "important mental resources that were not available previously" and so changed forever the understanding of spoken language in literate cultures, have been less thoroughly examined. This paper attempts to bring together these two apparently disparate theses in Harris's integrationist work by examining them in the light of the long history of written scripts in India as well as the equally complex multilingual scenario characteristic of spoken discourse in India.

Harris's invention of the term 'integrationism' is relevant to begin with, for we have to recognize that this is not just a word for Harris; it is a just word in the sense that it does justice to those multifarious energies of the human mind that other paradigms have done their best to tame and harness. According to Harris, the word 'language' itself has been abused in Western linguistics because it has been turned into a sacred cow of intellectual discourse, a "Baconian idol of the market," and thus has exerted a misleadingly homogenizing influence. Its use—not least within the reigning Cartesian paradigm—has tended to reduce the rich complexity of our mental processes to a boringly simplistic and tractable level. What Harris dubs the 'myth of telementation'—the illusory idea that language is a 'fixed code' that transfers 'meanings' efficiently from one mind to another—has as a result gained enormous authority, and Harris picks out three particularly villainous trends that underpin the notion, which an integrational view of language must combat. These are:

A. Surrogationalism, which, in its naïve version, maintains that words stand for things, resulting in the erroneous identification of word with object;
B. Contractualism, which confines words to the role they play in creating, furthering and sealing social contracts;
C. Instrumentalism, which visualizes words as a means to some end or the other.

To this Cerberus-like three-headed monster called Telementation, I'd like to add a fourth, to me, equally vicious head, which I will call *scriptism*. In this paper, I will argue that, from the perspective of the Indian subcontinent, the almost sacred status attached to script-learning may have troubling implications. For the sacred 'ownership' of scripts, traditionally the preserve of a particular community—the Brahmins—might not only have kept literacy skills from being widely shared among the Indian populace, but, even more dangerously, might actually have prevented a full appreciation of the rich oral and multilingual contexts within which language was—and is—acquired on the Indian subcontinent (one of the issues touched on in, e.g., Goody 1987).

The language-acquisition conundrum, common to all societies but especially complicated in India, is addressed with admirable directness by Harris: "How do words exist? What are the conditions for their existence?" and his short answer is one that is impossible for even the most contrary linguist to disagree with:

> Words are not learnt separately from everything else, but as integrated and integrating elements in a whole continuum of acquiring knowledge. Questions about language are among the first questions prompted in intelligent children by the communication situations in which they find themselves. ("What does that mean?" "What is that called?" "Why is it called that?") (Harris 1997: 257)

Words, that is, generate a reflexive understanding of their own metalinguistic status at the very moment that they are being operationalised in conversation. There is no prising apart the 'meanings' of words from their 'uses' as the Chomskyans wish to do; or their 'use' from their 'intentions' like the speech act theorists Austin and Searle; or their 'permanent' properties as exemplified in the iterable codes of writing from the 'deferred' meanings that words exhibit in speech, as Derrida and the deconstructionists imply.

In my own research, I have specifically argued that such an 'innate' tendency towards metalinguistic curiosity could well be accentuated in situations such as those which normally prevail on the Indian subcontinent, where a child usually acquires two or more languages simultaneously from birth.

In this paper I speculate that the scenario in India is complicated by the fact that there may be a deep-seated conflict between two kinds of metalinguistic 'stance'. The first of these 'stances' is fostered by the coexistence of languages within the 'natural', *oral* context of language acquisition. During such a process a child, acquiring, let's say, Bengali, Hindi and English all together may realize that a 'thing' may be called by alternative names and moreover the same phonetic shape may possess different meanings in different languages. For example, the word for 'thing' in Hindi is /chi:z/, pronounced the same as 'cheese' in English, and one can easily imagine a simple question such as 'Who stole my cheese?' having multiple cultural implications in a context where code-mixing as well as cross-cultural wordplay is as common as chalk—or cheese (discussed further in Bhaya Nair 1991).

The second 'stance' is engendered by the way in which scripts reflect and 'change' the way we perceive spoken language and our relationship to it. It is in the second area that Harris's provocative remarks about writing and iterability are well worth pondering. Writing changed forever the nature of spoken communication within the cultures that it entered. "There is", Harris states, "no such thing as a pre-literate linguistics."

Writing, in Harris's opinion, made possible the science of linguistics—an opinion certainly borne out in the Indian case, where the grammarian Panini wrote an empirically rich and theoretically rigorous description of classical Sanskrit as far back as the 4th century BCE. Nor was Panini's work *ab initio*; it came, rather, out of an established literate culture, preceded by the debates among other grammarians of his times such as Nirukta, Nighantu and the Pratishakhya philosophers, also produced as written documents. Panini's major work—the *Ashtadhyayi*—was also followed by an impressive series of key texts such as Patanjali's *Mahabhashya* in the 2nd century, Katyayana's *Varttika* in the 3rd century BCE and Bhartrhari's *Vakyapadiya* in the 4th century CE, as well as a continuing tradition of detailed scholarly commentaries on grammatical issues that would very likely have been impossible without the iterative attention to detail that writing enables.

Yet a committed integrationist such as Harris might also seek to confer on every speaker—literate or illiterate, child or adult, grammarian or layperson—the attitude of a theoretical linguist insofar as we all have foundational questions to ask about words. In the sections that follow, I will:

1. raise some of these basic questions in the context of language configurations in India;

2. provide a brief history of language scripts on the Indian subcontinent;
3. focus on the relationships between the Indic scripts and cognitive parameters such as learnability, emotional investment and self-perception;
4. foreground the cultural implications of having so many scripts in one country as well as the vexed relationship between the various syllabic Indian scripts and the alphabetic Roman script in which much of the official business of the state is conducted; and
5. discuss the future of the scripts of India including the technological interventions that make them more 'accessible' in a 'networked society'.

INITIAL QUESTIONS

According to the *Guinness Book of Records*, India is home to about 865 of the world's estimated 6,000 spoken tongues—a figure of one-sixth, which happens to roughly correspond to the Indian share of the world population. It is important to note that these counts, usually based on interpretations of census data, vary considerably, but even the most conservative estimate gives us about 325 languages (as identified and documented in, e.g., Singh and Manoharan 1993). Such pluralism is undoubtedly impressive, but the situation with regard to the scripts of India is even more striking. India, at the start of the 21st century, is almost unarguably the greatest script repository in the world; whereas most continents have reduced their script usage to two or three main writing systems—Arabic and Roman in Africa; Roman in the Americas; Roman in Australia; Roman, Cyrillic and Greek in Europe—the situation in Asia is instructive in that it offers us contrasting histories of script usage. In China, the other great literate civilization in Asia, we observe that a single format of ideograms *united* a vast Middle Kingdom with languages as distinct as Hokkien, Cantonese, Teochew, while India offers us a diametrically opposed trajectory. In India, it was just one single *ur*-script—namely, Brahmi—that morphed into numerous *different* forms over the last couple of millennia with most of these scripts still going strong today.

I shall argue here that certain radical—and very long-standing—alterations effected by these processes of script-morphing occurred over time in the structures of self-knowledge and learning across the subcontinent. Each of India's present regional literatures, that is, is supported by almost 1,500 to 2,000 years of script history; and the script-girt identities that Indian communities possess today are backed by centuries of script development and script memory. In India, one is never just a 'native speaker' of X language, but is either literate in, or an aspirant to literacy in, one or more scripts—in Hindi, in Oriya, in Gujarati, in

Tamil, etc., and one's cultural identity is indissolubly linked not only to the languages but to the scripts that one commands

Specifically, I want to suggest that the long history of India's scripts has had an impact not only on post-Independence national language policy but, as interestingly, on a second 'silent revolution' now taking place in the realm of computer e-scripts, and in those small-town, under-privileged, invisible classrooms where English today, with its stand-alone script, has become, as it were, an 'aspirational' language—not necessarily inspirational but certainly 'aspirational'!

At the top end of India's educational hierarchy, on the other hand, a strong context of cultural memory seems to have ensured that the youthful and go-ahead IT industry in India has been forced to address an age-old problematic—that of mediating between India's multiple scripts. Despite the global preference for the Roman script and their own almost exclusive dealings with this script and this script alone, the IT sector in India has, rather surprisingly, developed robust systems whereby one can type a word in, say, Devanagari Hindi and see it magically transformed into Tamil! Computer software indigenously invented can, moreover, achieve plausible *translations* between languages as diverse as Malayalam and Bengali. Cognitively, therefore, it may be contended that these technological innovations have served to radically revisualize and revitalize linguistic relationships on the subcontinent and allay deep-seated anxieties concerning divisive differences between the Indian languages.

Pragmatically, however, it is apparent that not all our scripts are equally privileged. In the aftermath of colonization, the Roman script continues to lord it over the other scripts of India. Expressions of feeling are implicitly still regarded as being in the domain of the 'mother tongue', while English dominates intellectual discourse as an elite 'father script'. Therefore, given the contemporary aspirations of Indian democracy where our still unrealized goal of universal education is inconceivable without effective, culturally acceptable writing systems—the conundrum presented by the multiple (and unequal) scripts in India is key to the understanding of the linguistic construction of 'self' and 'other' in India's extremely plural culture. In this chapter, then, I revisit a set of familiar philosophical questions with especial reference to the paradigm case of India, asking:

> *What relationship obtains between the oral and written forms of a language?*
>
> *How does this relationship affect the ways in which national as well as individual identities are formed in a multilingual, plural society?*
>
> *More generally, how do scripts influence the ways in which we 'see'?*

52   *Rukmini Bhaya Nair*

EVOLUTION OF THE INDIC SCRIPTS: A BRIEF HISTORY

The following table traces the history of the Indian scripts:

INDUS VALLEY SCRIPT (2500/1500 BCE)
(Of unknown origin and written in boustrophedon style, i.e. right to left and then left to right)

BRAHMI (7th C. BCE)   KHAROSHTI (5th C. BCE)
(Semitic? Origin—right to left)   (Aramaic Origin—left to right)

8 Different Scripts
Early   Late   Sunga
Maurya   Maurya
   Ashokan Brahmi   MEDIUM: STONE
   Script (6th C. BCE)

   Prototype Scripts of Northern India (1st C. BCE–1st CE)
      Gupta Period Script (4th C.–6th C. CE)

(Siddhamatrika Script [W. branch of the E. Gupta Script 6th C. CE] MEDIUM: PALM LEAF, TREE BARK)

(Variation: the Grantha Script [Developed in Southern India in the 5–6th C. CE during the Pallava and Chola Periods] was originally used only to transcribe Sanskrit texts but later to transcribe other texts from the Dravidian languages and to transliterate into Nagari and vice versa) MEDIUM: COPPER AND PALM LEAF

Nagari Script (Developed in Northern India during the 7th–9th centuries CE with about 10 to 12 major variations and has remained virtually unaltered until the present; still going strong in the 21st C.)

MEDIUM: PAPER, ELECTRONIC SCREENS

Some of the main scripts in contemporary India are:

SCRIPT/LANGUAGE	NUMBER OF SPEAKERS (1991Census)	
Bengali	68,007,965	
Gujarati	41,309,582	
Gurmukhi (Punjabi)	20,923,984	
Kannada	44,977,201	
Malayalam	29,098,518	
Marathi	78,937,187	
Oriya	31,659,736	
Sindhi/Kashmiri	80,18,700	(estimate)
Sanskrit (Hindi, Devanagari Script)	350–400 mil.	
Tamil	55,858,946	
Telugu	88,508,008	
Urdu (Arabic Script)	100,000,000	(estimate)
English (Roman Script)	50,000,000	(estimate)

Related scripts in Southeast Asia include the Sinhalese, Balinese, Thai and Burmese scripts, all of which share a rough systemics, in that:

1. The writing system is phonetic in nature; it maps the sounds of the *aksharas* (letters) to specific and unique shapes.
2. The basic set of *aksharas* for many of the languages that share this writing system consists of sixteen vowels and about forty consonants.
3. The actual rules for forming consonant-vowel (CV) combinations and conjunct characters, however, vary quite a bit from script to script. Thus, when two or more scripts are in use for a single language, one is expected to know the specific rules as well as the shapes that relate to particular conjuncts when reading text in each script.
4. Usually, a consonant-vowel (CV) combination is written by adding a vowel extension (*matra*) to the consonant. Conjuncts are generally written by concatenating half the shape of each consonant in Devanagari and its derived scripts or one-half of the consonant below the other in the South Indian scripts.
5. Some invented *aksharas* have also, though rarely, been added to some languages and in some cases, special symbols/diacritics are used to indicate 'foreign' sounds.

These shared characteristics of the Indic scripts appear to have an effect on the way this group of syllabic scripts is cognized in a manner quite different from the alphabetic Roman script. The charts below show the parallel organization of the Indic scripts in the major Indian languages.

Gut.	DEV	GUJ	PUN	BEN	ORI	TEL	KAN	TAM	MAL	SINH	URD	SIND
k	क	ક	ਕ	ক	କ	క	ಕ	க	ക	කා	ک	ک
kh	ख	ખ	ਖ	খ	ଖ	ఖ	ಖ	-	ഖ	ඛ	کھ	ک
g	ग	ગ	ਗ	গ	ଗ	గ	ಗ	-	ഗ	ග	گ	گ
gh	घ	ઘ	ਘ	ঘ	ଘ	ఘ	ಘ	-	ഘ	ඝ	گھ	گھ
ṅ	ङ	ઙ	ਙ	ঙ	ଙ	ఙ	ಙ	ங	ങ	ඞ	ں	ڱ

Figure 2.1. Velars.

Pal.	DEV	GUJ	PUN	BEN	ORI	TEL	KAN	TAM	MAL	SIN	URD	SIND
c	च	ચ	ਚ	চ	ଚ	చ	ಚ	ச	ച	ච	چ	چ
ch	छ	છ	ਛ	ছ	ଛ	ఛ	ಛ	-	ഛ	ඡ	چھ	چھ
j	ज	જ	ਜ	জ	ଜ	జ	ಜ	ஜ*	ജ	ජ	ج	ج
jh	झ	ઝ	ਝ	ঝ	ଝ	ఝ	ಝ	-	ഝ	ඣ	جھ	جھ
ñ	ञ	ઞ	ਞ	ঞ	ଞ	ఞ	ಞ	ஞ	ഞ	ඤ	-	ڃ

Figure 2.2. Palatals.

54 *Rukmini Bhaya Nair*

Ret.	DEV	GUJ	PUN	BEN	ORI	TEL	KAN	TAM	MAL	SIN	URD	SIND
ṭ	ट	ટ	ਟ	ট	ଟ	ట	ಟ	L	ട	ට	ٹ	ٹ
ṭh	ठ	ઠ	ਠ	ঠ	ଠ	ఠ	ಠ	–	ഠ	ඨ	ٹھ	ٹھ
ḍ	ड	ડ	ਡ	ড	ଡ	డ	ಡ	–	ഡ	ඩ	ڈ	ڊ
ḍh	ढ	ઢ	ਢ	ঢ	ଢ	ఢ	ಢ	–	ഢ	ඪ	ڈھ	ڍ
ṇ	ण	ણ	ਣ	ণ	ଣ	ణ	ಣ	ண	ണ	ණ	–	ݨ

Figure 2.3. Retroflexes.

Den.	DEV	GUJ	PUN	BEN	ORI	TEL	KAN	TAM	MAL	SIN	URD	SIND
t	त	ત	ਤ	ত	ତ	త	ತ	த	ത	ත	ت	ط
th	थ	થ	ਥ	থ	ଥ	థ	ಥ	–	ഥ	ථ	تھ	ٿ
d	द	દ	ਦ	দ	ଦ	ద	ದ	–	ദ	ද	د	د
dh	ध	ધ	ਧ	ধ	ଧ	ధ	ಧ	–	ധ	ධ	دھ	ذ
n	न	ન	ਨ	ন	ନ	న	ನ	ந	ന	න	ن	ن

Figure 2.4. Dentals.

Lab.	DEV	GUJ	PUN	BEN	ORI	TEL	KAN	TAM	MAL	SIN	URD	SIND
p	प	પ	ਪ	প	ପ	ప	ಪ	ப	പ	ප	پ	پ
ph	फ	ફ	ਫ	ফ	ଫ	ఫ	ಫ	–	ഫ	ඵ	پھ	ڦ
b	ब	બ	ਬ	ব	ବ	బ	ಬ	–	ബ	බ	ب	ب
bh	भ	ભ	ਭ	ভ	ଭ	భ	ಭ	–	ഭ	භ	بھ	ڀ
m	म	મ	ਮ	ম	ମ	మ	ಮ	ம	മ	ම	م	م

Figure 2.5. Labials.

Sem.	DEV	GUJ	PUN	BEN/ASS	ORI	TEL	KAN	TAM	MAL	SIN	URD	SIND
y	य	ય	ਯ	য	ଯ	య	ಯ	ய	യ	ය	ى	ي
r	र	ર	ਰ	র/ৰ	ର	ర	ರ	ர	ര	ර	ر	ر
l	ल	લ	ਲ	ল	ଲ	ల	ಲ	ல	ല	ල	ل	ل
v	व	વ	ਵ	-/ৱ	–	వ	ವ	வ	വ	ව	و	و

Figure 2.6. Semivowels.

Learning to Write 55

Sib/Asp	DEV	GUJ	PUN	BEN	ORI	TEL	KAN	TAM	MAL	SIN	URD	SIND
ś	श	શ	ਸ਼	শ	ଶ	శ	ಶ	—	ശ	ශ	ش	ش
ṣ	ष	ષ	—	ষ	ଷ	ష	ಷ	ஷ	ഷ	ෂ	—	—
s	स	સ	ਸ	স	ସ	స	ಸ	ஸ	സ	ස	س	س
h	ह	હ	ਹ	হ	ହ	హ	ಹ	ஹ	ഹ	හ	ه	ه

Figure 2.7. Fricatives.

Vowels	DEV	GUJ	PUN	BEN	ORI	TEL	KAN	TAM	MAL	SIN	URD	SIND
a	अ	અ	ਅ	অ	ଅ	అ	ಅ	அ	അ	අ	ا	ا
ā	आ	આ	ਆ	আ	ଆ	ఆ	ಆ	ஆ	ആ	ආ	آ	آ
æ	—	—	—	—	—	—	—	—	—	ඇ	—	—
ǣ	—	—	—	—	—	—	—	—	—	ඈ	—	—
i	इ	ઇ	ਇ	ই	ଇ	ఇ	ಇ	இ	ഇ	ඉ	ا	ا
ī	ई	ઈ	ਈ	ঈ	ଈ	ఈ	ಈ	ஈ	ഈ	ඊ	ای	—
u	उ	ઉ	ਉ	উ	ଉ	ఉ	ಉ	உ	ഉ	උ	ا	—
ū	ऊ	ઊ	ਊ	ঊ	ଊ	ఊ	ಊ	ஊ	ഊ	ඌ	او	—
ṛ	ऋ	ઋ	—	ঋ	ଋ	ఋ	ಋ	—	ഋ	ඍ	—	—
ṝ	ॠ	ૠ	—	ৠ	ୠ	ౠ	ೠ	—	ൠ	ඎ	—	—
e(s)	ऎ*	—	—	—	—	ఎ	ಎ	எ	എ	එ	—	—
e/ē	ए	એ	ਏ	এ	ଏ	ఏ	ಏ	ஏ	ഏ	ඒ	اے	—
ai	ऐ	ઐ	ਐ	ঐ	ଐ	ఐ	ಐ	ஐ	ഐ	ඓ	اَے	—
o(s)	ऒ*	—	—	—	—	ఒ	ಒ	ஒ	ഒ	ඔ	—	—
o/ō	ओ	ઓ	ਓ	ও	ଓ	ఓ	ಓ	ஓ	ഓ	ඕ	او	—
au	औ	ઔ	ਔ	ঔ	ଔ	ఔ	ಔ	ஔ	ഔ	ඖ	اَو	—
ḥ	अः	અઃ	ਅਃ	অঃ	ଅଃ	అః	అః	அஃ	അഃ	අඃ	—	—
aṅ	अं	અં	ਅਂ	অং	ଅଂ	అం	అం	—	അം	අං	ں	—
aṁ	अँ	અઁ	ਅਁ	অঁ	ଅঁ	—	—	—	—	—	—	—

Figure 2.8. Vowels.

56 *Rukmini Bhaya Nair*

Vowels	DEV	GUJ	PUN	BEN	ORI	TEL	KAN	TAM	MAL	SIN	URD	SIND
ka	क	ક	ਕ	ক	କ	క	ಕ	க	ക	ක	ک	
kā	का	કા	ਕਾ	কা	କା	కా	ಕಾ	கா	കാ	කා	کا	
kæ	–	–	–	–	–	–	–	–	–	කැ	–	
kǣ	–	–	–	–	–	–	–	–	–	කෑ	–	
ki	कि	કિ	ਕਿ	কি	କି	కి	ಕಿ	கி	കി	කි	کِ	
kī	की	કી	ਕੀ	কী	କୀ	కీ	ಕೀ	கீ	കീ	කී	کی	
ku	कु	કુ	ਕੁ	কু	କୁ	కు	ಕು	கு	കു	කු	کُ	
kū	कू	કૂ	ਕੂ	কূ	କୂ	కూ	ಕೂ	கூ	കൂ	කූ	کُو	
kṛ	कृ	કૃ	–	কৃ	କୃ	కృ	ಕೃ	–	കൃ	කෲ	–	
kṝ	कॄ	કૄ	–	কৄ	କୄ	కౄ	ಕೄ	–	കൄ	කෲා	–	
ke(s)	कॆ*	–	–	–	–	డె	ಕೆ	கெ	കെ	කෙ	–	
ke/ē	के	કે	ਕੇ	কে	କେ	కే	ಕೇ	கே	കേ	කේ	کے	
kai	कै	કૈ	ਕੈ	কৈ	କୈ	కై	ಕೈ	கை	കൈ	කෛ	کَے	
ko(s)	कॊ*	–	–	–	–	కొ	ಕೊ	கொ	കൊ	කො	–	
ko/ō	को	કો	ਕੋ	কো	କୋ	కో	ಕೋ	கோ	കോ	කෝ	کو	
kau	कौ	કૌ	ਕੌ	কৌ	କୌ	కౌ	ಕೌ	கௌ	കൌ	කෞ	کَو	
kaḥ	कः	કઃ	ਕਃ	কঃ	କଃ	కః	ಕಃ	க꞉	കഃ	කඃ	–	–
kan	कं	કં	ਕਂ	কং	କଂ	కం	ಕం	–	കം	කං	کاں	–
kaṁ	कँ	કઁ	ਕਁ	কঁ	କଁ	–	–	–	–	–	(kān)	–

Figure 2.9. Consonant-vowel combinations.

MISC	DEV	GUJ	PUN	BEN	ORI	TEL	KAN	TAM	MAL	SIN	URD	SIND
q	क़	–	–	–	–	–	–	–	–	–	ق	ق
kh	ख़	–	ਖ਼	–	–	–	–	–	–	–	خ	خ
ġ	ग़	–	ਗ਼	–	–	–	–	–	–	–	غ	غ
z	ज़	–	ਜ਼	য	–	ౙ	–	–	–	–	ز	ز
ṛ	ड़	–	ੜ	ড়	ଡ଼	–	–	–	–	–	ڑ	ڐ
ṛh	ढ़	–	–	ঢ়	ଢ଼	–	–	–	–	–	ڑھ	–
f	फ़	–	ਫ਼	–	–	–	–	–	–	ෆ	ف	ف
ṉ	ऩ	–	–	–	–	–	–	ன	–	ඞ්	–	–
ḻ	ऴ	–	–	–	–	ఌ	ಳ	ழ	ൾ	ළ	–	–
ṟ	ऱ	–	–	–	–	ఱ	ಱ	ற	ഠ	ඁ	–	–
ḷ	ळ	ળ	ਲ਼	–	ଳ	ఌ	ಳ	ள	ള	ළ	–	–

Figure 2.10. Miscellaneous consonants (part of an extended character set used mostly to capture the sounds of sounds of 'foreign' words).
(Source: Eden's Page: Scripts of All Asia at www.geocities.com/athens/academy/9594/)

As the preceding charts graphically illustrate, the writing systems developed in India have a systematically different 'cognitive feel' from the Roman. A preliminary set of positions and questions with respect to some of these putative cognitive parameters is set out below.

COGNITIVE PARAMETERS BEARING ON THE USE OF INDIC SCRIPTS

Ever since Levy Bruhl in the early decades of the 20th century several hypotheses have been presented on the cognitive impact of script literacy on individuals and cultures. I have summarized, rather ruthlessly, the points of view expressed in half a dozen such key texts; they might include the following:

- L. Levy Bruhl in *Primitive Mentality* (1923) and *How Natives Think* (1926): Writing is a characteristic feature that distinguishes 'civilized' societies from 'primitive' ones.
- Marshall McLuhan in *The Gutenberg Galaxy* (1962): Writing technologies were a major force in changing social and other relations between individuals in the modern West. The medium affected the message.
- Jacques Derrida in *Of Grammatology* (1976): Writing is more arbitrary, symbolic and conventional than speech and hence illustrates our 'humanness' even more strikingly than oral discourse.
- Scribner and Cole in *The Psychology of Literacy* (1981): Knowledge of writing *does not* directly impact on memory, rational thinking and other cognitive functions
- Walter J. Ong in *Orality and Literacy* (1982): By changing the medium of intellectual inquiry from the spoken to the visual, print technologies underwrote the move from the arts of rhetoric and disputation to those of 'silent' internalized inquiry and interpretation.
- David Olson in *The World on Paper: The Conceptual and Cognitive Implications of Writing and Reading* (1994): Writing as a tool for learning about the world enables self-perception and provides a new set of categories for thinking about oneself, both as an individual and a social being, in relation to the world around one.

Turning from these theoretical perspectives to the Indian example, we find that they are replicated in the language debates on the subcontinent. Of the many crucial questions asked with regard to cognitive factors and their effect on individual choices and public policy, I will briefly indicate three here in order to demonstrate how complicated the analysis of this terrain could be in India:

How Learnable are the Phonetically based Indian Syllabaries in Comparison with the Alphabetic Roman System?

Olson, Ong and Scribner and Cole address these concerns which, in the Indian context, translate into a question about the relationship between what we might call the 'information-heavy' Indic syllabaries versus the 'information-light' Roman alphabet: meaning that, in English, as we know, 26 letters developed in a quite unrelated cultural context, were pressed into service to represent, roughly, the 47 sounds of the language; while in Hindi, for example, there are 47 unique shapes that stand in for each of the 47 phonemes of the language; and, although this is somewhat of an oversimplification, the alphabet charts from the Sanskrit-based writing systems should provide some proof of the general plausibility of my argument. The following sorts of subquestions about the cognitive difference between the Roman and the Indic scripts follow, therefore, from the main question about 'script learnability' posed earlier.

1. Is error proneness in the Roman alphabet (i.e., in novices' matching of sounds to letters) compensated for by the potential it offers for quick guess-work through fast visual recognition and faster mental-processing speed?
2. What evidence is there that children and/or adult learners find one or the other system more robust?
3. Do dyslexics and 'slow learners' find one or the other script systems easier to master and to what extent is this affected by their prior knowledge of speaking their own mother tongues and multiple languages?
4. How might the 'visual illusions' engendered by the systematic 'phonemic gaps' in the representational system of the Roman script be analyzed, especially when a learner is already familiar with a system that displays far fewer such 'gaps'?
5. Can the Roman script in fact be 'improved' and adapted for the language systems of India and at what emotional cost?

How are Indian Languages that do *Not* have a Written Script to Negotiate the Move into Literacy?

(See Levy-Bruhl and Derrida in this connection and consider subquestions of the type posed next):

1. Should language without written scripts choose the script of a neighbouring language that most resembles their own?
2. Should they choose the script belonging to the national language (i.e. Devanagari) because it offers greater country-wide mobility?
3. Should they choose the Roman script (i.e. the power and money language on an international stage)?
4. Should they devise their own completely independent writing systems and, if so, on what basis?
5. Which of the choices listed previously is (a) practically feasible and (b) cognitively attractive?

How Easy is it to Transliterate between one Indian Syllabic System and the Other and What Gains Accrue from the Process for Translation and Interlanguage Communication? (McLuhan, Ong and Olson are Relevant in this Connection.)

Answer: It has become relatively easy to *transliterate* between the Indian scripts now actually using a regular Roman alphabet keyboard, given the advances in computer technologies and various software packages that facilitate exchanges between the Indian languages. These technological advances seem in fact to have contributed greatly to boosting confidence in the functional efficiency of the Indic scripts in the 21st century; it has, for example, become relatively simple to produce school and college textbooks on a mass scale very fast and to transfer 'texts' from one language to another. However, the impact of these groundbreaking technological inventions on the vexed matter of *translations* between the Indian languages remains unclear—a crucial question to which I return in my last section on the future of the Indian scripts.

Script is, and has always been, language made visible, permanent and powerful. Unlike speech, which is innate, part of our biological inheritance, scripts are invented, part of our cultural repertoires. This is perhaps why Jacques Derrida suggested that one of the best sites to observe the intersection of culture and cognition is the written word. Writing, as he puts it, signifies "the great adventure of hand and eye." It is an epistemic exploration in which a different set of modalities—touch, and grasp and vision—takes over the territory of the verbal.

It is obvious, though, that in the Indian case not all scripts typically have the same status in real-life situations. In the aftermath of colonization, elite education on the subcontinent still depends crucially upon the entextualization of English, a language variously estimated to be spoken by anything between 5% and 35% of the population but handled with ease and creativity by perhaps fewer that 2%. In this sense, English in India can be accurately described as the language of the new Brahmins of India. At the end of this section on cognition, then, we must ask: how do these cultural factors of power and hegemony that inevitably affect the way in which we view the 'problem' of multiple scripts intersect with the cognitive conundrums I've just posed? It is to this question that I turn in my next—penultimate—section on:

THE CULTURAL AND POLITICAL DIMENSIONS OF INDIAN SCRIPTS

A whole slew of issues about the management of extreme linguistic diversity in a context where adhering to the idea of a deeply institutionalized 'common' identity has been the *sine qua non* of the Indian polity since

60 *Rukmini Bhaya Nair*

Independence was declared in 1947; about the preservation of minority rights; and about the very idea of 'basic literacy' in a situation where several 'native scripts' seek to coexist along with English in its 'nonnative' Roman guise arise whenever the sociopolitical aspects of India's scripts are discussed. A couple of illustrations, the first visual and iconic and the second anecdotal, might serve to clarify:

1.

Figure 2.11   Recto of ten-rupee banknote.

2.

Figure 2.12   Verso of ten-rupee banknote.

From its very first printing, as shown, the paper currency of India has had a similar format. One of the faces of the note carries a picture symbolizing a unified 'India' (Mahatma Gandhi, for example); the other face (fortified by images of the Bhakra Nangal dam, which ushered in India's 'Green Revolution', or the peacock, which is the national bird of India) is flanked to its right by a list of scripts symbolizing India's linguistic pluralism. Thus, a 'unity in diversity' message is clearly conveyed by both faces of any Indian currency note; what is noteworthy (no pun intended), however, is that the list of 'Indian scripts' *does not include* the Roman script standing in for the English language. The other side of the note—the legal tender side, as it were—*does* include English; it is, in fact, the sole 'other' language taking its place alongside the national language, Hindi. From which evidence we may surmise that English is- and has always been an elite language of power in India, keeping Indians 'integrated' economically and officially while occupying a far more ambiguous position in the cultural sphere. English and the Roman script are, in this sense, represented as simultaneously being both Indian and 'alien' in the national consciousness—a conundrum which still plagues India in the 21st century despite the worldwide success of Indian writers in English and the impressive growth rates recorded by Indian industry in the last two decades as the country has rapidly 'globalized'.

1. An interview with a student from Nagaland in JNU in the 1990s. When asked what his mother-tongue was, this student replied, chillingly: "In my state, we have no language."

It was, of course, easy to guess his meaning: Nagami, his native language, is written in the Roman script. Consequently—so great is the violence done to oral traditions in the modern Indian state—an intelligent young person at the end of the 20th century can still hold the entirely erroneous belief that he does not really have a 'language' because it is written in a borrowed *script*.

Paradoxically, it is exactly this sort of false consciousness that the 'fingertip consciousness' brought about by e-scripts and, ultimately, e-speech synthesizers might help erase. But I shall come to this point a little later. At the moment, if we return to the matters of culture and 'cultural currency' to which this section is devoted, we could recall a provocative observation made by the sociologist Jack Goody. Goody argues that the Brahminical hold over learning has meant that, despite India's long-standing traditions of textuality, literacy never acquired a mass base on the subcontinent. Neither was individual enterprise in terms of investment in literacy ever promoted among the masses of India. Gutenberg's printing presses may have initiated an unstoppable 'democratization of learning' from the 15th century on in Europe, but Goody's argument contends that literacy in India was never similarly democratized (Goody and Watt 1968). Even today India's poorest citizens—about 20% to 30%—remain to date without access to the most basic literacy, prompting uncomfortable questions about the hegemonic role of writing as a cognitive tool for the exercise of power on the Indian subcontinent.

Languages, we know, enter into stages of self-annihilating denial when submitted to intellectual neglect. If the intelligentsia of India turn to English books, papers, journals and vocabulary whenever difficult conceptual terrain is being traversed, then the Roman script does in fact hold the 'vernaculars' (a word which literally means 'the language of the slaves'!) still in thrall. This is a feature of academic discourse that is often debated within the country and the argument made that it is not enough for a language to be confined to the emotional domain alone. For this division itself is a hegemonic and gendered one—expressions of feeling, kinship terminology and oral discourses are implicitly seen as all 'mother-tongue' speech acts, while English remains the unquestioned 'father tongue', the language of science and government. And this is precisely where the Roman script seems to win out presently over the other scripts of India. Few would deny, after all, that the organization of modern institutions, especially in India, where clerkdom remains all-powerful, is predicated upon writing. When India gained freedom from colonialism in 1947, within the first few years of becoming independent, it made three or four important moves with respect to literacy, which continue to have major cultural consequences. First, it adopted the principle of Linguistic States. Secondly, it adopted English (and the Roman script) as an interim language, for an initial period of fifteen years, until Hindi and the 'other languages' of India became sufficiently 'strong' (the Eighth Schedule of the Constitution of India lists specifically these languages). Thirdly, it adopted, by just one casting vote, Hindi (and the Devanagari script) as the National Language of the country; and, finally, it adopted the three-language formula, which meant that every child who passed through the schooling process in India had to learn three languages and three, or at least two, scripts.

Today, we are in a position cautiously to reassess the results of these decisions taken over fifty years ago, and they offer, as is to be expected, cause both for regret and rejoicing. On the one hand, having states that in part self-identify on grounds of linguistic distinctiveness has meant that each state sees its language in opposition to the language of other states and battles for a script identity of its own (Bengal and Assam, for example, whose scripts differ by only two letters). Hence, what Jawaharlal Nehru called the divisive 'passion for building a wall round a language' has been reinforced. At the same time the state languages have indeed been strengthened and now have robust literary establishments of their own (e.g. the Sahitya Akademis).

English, too, has gone from strength to strength. Rather than being given up after fifteen years, it is now acknowledged to be on a par with Hindi as the 'other' official language of the nation, and its status as a power and aspiration language is naturally further shored up by the forces of globalization. As a result, we no longer realistically talk in India about 'giving up English'. Rather, our questions concern the specific role that English and a mastery over the Roman script is to be given vis-à-vis the other languages of India. As for Hindi, our 'national language' still faces stiff resistance in the southern states of India, and indeed from other states as well, which resent the hegemonic role of this dominant language and script. Here, it should also be noted that, ironically, much more seems to have been done for the cause of Hindi by entertainment media like 'Bollywood' cinema and television than by any official state organ so far.

A further consideration is that India's adoption of a three-language/three-script literary formula for school education has meant that the very structure of our educational system seems to decree that a linguistic subject must translate herself constantly into different registers. In effect, then, a child passing through a regular Indian school is conceptualized as possessing three different layers of selfhood: she has a 'core' self symbolized by her mother tongue, a 'national' self represented by Hindi and an 'international' self represented by English or another 'library' language. It is true that such a picture is ideal and that in real life the situation in India continues to be both gravely unjust and terribly complicated because so many of India's children are still denied their rights to primary education. Even so, it could be argued that this 'formula' is, at least in principle, an enriching one, since it significantly multiplies linguistic opportunities for "the presentation of self in every day life" for those Indians who in fact manage to master all three (or more) of the languages/scripts on offer. Each of these cultural and historic factors also comes forcefully into play when we assess the future of language policy in India in the light of current technological developments in IT—which brings me to my last section, concerning:

THE E-WRITING ON THE WALL

To end by looking at the future, we might recall once again that, of the six thousand or so languages in the world, only about a hundred or so have scripts, and still fewer have scripts guaranteed to survive in the aggressive e-century to come. As Derrida, who, as I have mentioned, has controversially affirmed the greater 'humanness' of script over speech since language is at its most arbitrary and conventional in a written form, might put it—the linguistic states of modern India literally *reinscribe* these traditional perceptions of difference. Indeed, the fact that language is at it most conventional in its written form is one that Indians have been familiar with for a long time. Compare the two following statements, for example, the first from the Arab historian Al Biruni in the 11th century and the second from a paper on 'Scripts and Language Planning in India'

(1981) by the linguist D. P. Pattanayak. In the early 11th century, Biruni complains:

> The Indian scribes are careless, and do not take pains to produce correct and well-collated copies. Consequently, the highest results of the author's mental development are lost by their negligence, and his book becomes already in the first or second copy so full of faults, that the text appears as something entirely new, which neither a scholar nor one familiar with the subject, whether Hindu or Muslim, could any longer understand. It will sufficiently illustrate the matter if we tell the reader that we have sometimes written down a word from the mouth of Hindus, taking the greatest pains to fix its pronunciation, and that afterwards when we repeated it to them, they had great difficulty in recognizing it.

What Al Biruni may have failed to recognize is that the 'Indian scribes' were actually using *different* scripts. These scripts bore a 'family resemblance' to each other because they derived from the same source—but they had evolved to suit the structure of different Indian languages. Hence, the pains that Biruni took to 'fix the pronunciation' of the words he heard went unrewarded not so much because the 'Indian scribes were careless' but because they were producing individual scripts with different protocols of pronunciation.

Nor have the problems that Biruni faced quite gone away a millennium later, for in the 20th century D. P. Pattanayak observes:

> So much religious and emotional significance is attached to script that it is really difficult to talk in rational terms about script and script reform. Scripts are no more permanent than fashions in clothes. But in a traditional society, where the instrument of writing was a clod of clay, a piece of chalk, an iron stylus, the feather of a bird, or the medium of writing was either a birch leaf, a palm leaf or a rock face, the number and shape of letters in the writing system had to be meticulously preserved . . . Writing [was] popularly endowed with magical power. This had led to the belief that the script was the soul of a language . . . [But] today a new script is created in India almost once every six months either for a specific language, or by way of suggestion to be accepted as a pan Indian script or a Universal script. This indicates the direction of change in thinking in this regard.

The 'integrationist' task faced by linguists and planners is in fact to predict these changes in thought of which Pattanayak writes—the next turn of the language wheel, so to speak, in India, which might, I suppose, be termed the Ashokan Brahmi Chakra. Symbolically, this ancient *chakra* or 'wheel of dharma', which is to be observed carved on many 4th century Ashokan inscriptions in early Brahmi script, also occupies pride of place at the centre of the flag of independent India (see following).

Figure 2.13 Illustration of the Indian national flag containing the Ashokan wheel.

Each Indian script currently in use could be seen to function as an essential spoke in this sturdy old wheel—and I am not unmindful here of the pun inherent in 'spoke' as the past tense of 'speak'! E-commerce, e-cars, e-mail lead inevitably to the notion of *e-scripts*. Indeed, the lexicon of the present century could well be said to begin with the letter *e*. India, in particular, has an obligation to organize itself in this respect, for it has more than its fair share of the world's written languages. There is, therefore, an urgent need to ask how—and whether—the advent of new technologies currently on offer in IT-savvy India can intervene in that difficult historic debate over identities exemplified by the multiple scripts of India.

On the one hand, as I have maintained, these fecund 'mother-tongue' scripts connote vibrant literary traditions that are relatively independent; on the other hand, the argument has been made, not without justification, that the impetus of mass education has been painfully slowed down not only because of the lack of political will but by the fact that every single basic text has had to be printed over in a dozen different scripts. *Translations* between the Indian languages (*bhashas*), as a corollary, are plagued by the spectre of inadequacy. It is in this context that we can ask our last fraught question: *What exactly will the languages of the Indian subcontinent look like in the next millennium?*

Such an enquiry concerns not what these several languages might *sound* like in the future, nor even their impact upon our hearts, but specifically what they will *look like*—even if the question seems absurd at first glance.

One might answer with appropriate scorn—why, they will look exactly as they have looked throughout the centuries. So, what's new? But if we were, for a moment, to be quite literal-minded in our rereading of the query, a more interesting perspective might emerge.

I believe that the technologies already on offer in India could offer new solutions to the major problem of producing quality translations on the subcontinent, provided it is accepted that *transliteration* may offer strong foundations for *translation*. This is a major insight gained from studying the multiplicity of scripts that still flourish across the length and breath of India. It is reasonable, of course, to object that differences between languages are not captured by matching letter to letter or phoneme to phoneme. Shape and sound exemplify only the gross, material forms of language. What matters in translation is grammar, syntax and above all— semantics or meaning—what Harris calls the very 'conditions of existence' of words. It is to address this basic question of Harris that we may turn to the claims made by the Akshara Bharati group of software engineers who worked initially at Indian Institute of Technology, Kanpur, and later moved to the 'IT-city' of Hyderabad. These engineers are not merely conducting a routine software task; rather, we find them talking of 'overcoming the language barrier' in India precisely by combining basic notions of script literacy with what they call a 'Paninian grammar'. They write:

> This machine-translation "Anusaaraka system . . . makes text in one Indian language accessible in another Indian language". At the present time, it can do a rough translation between languages as apparently diverse as Telegu and Hindi.

The Aksara Bharati group point to the enormous social advantages of their script-based 'anusaaraka' in the not too distant future, and we could similarly draw attention to other important innovations made in this field by the government-sponsored 'C-DAC' organization. C-DAC's 'Leap' software for the Indian scripts is based on systematic research carried out during the 1980s and 90s and, as someone who has personally used the Inscript keyboard, I can vouch for the 'miraculous' effects produced. Typing a word in, say, Devanagari and seeing it transformed instantaneously on-screen into its Tamil shape suddenly allows one to imagine the dynamic processes that created the different forms of the Indic scripts. So far, our eyes were fixed only on the stable, static forms of these scripts as we saw them in the here and now, but when one witnesses the ceilinged shapes of Assamese, Hindi and Bangla, where a straight line runs across the roof of the linguistic universe, change in a trice to the curvilinear forms of Telegu, Malayalam or Kannada, new research questions suddenly seem possible. With the present innovations in technology we may be able to study the evolution of the scripts with new eyes, as it were—and even perhaps to conceive of a research program that tracks their morphological changes across time. For, if we are so inclined, we can now use present technology to visualize not only how each letter of the Sanskrit syllabary resembles its siblings across languages but also how by rotating and mixing the elements of a particular letter around defined axes, the regional languages of India were able to lay claim to different script identities that, in turn, also conferred on them cultural and political power.

Moreover, software such as the Inscript is relatively 'smart': type in, for example, a short-*i matra* to the right of a letter and it changes over automatically to the left. Obviously, too, you can run a spell-check on your words, and en route, you may learn fascinating—presumably statistically verified—'facts' such as the most frequently used 'letter' across all the Indian syllabaries being /r/.

Psychologically, then, I'd like to reinforce a point I made at the beginning of this essay, namely that, for potential translators and learners, the awe, not to say anxiety, engendered by our perception of the deep-seated differences between languages could be significantly reduced through the series of visual seductions on offer on-screen today and Ashokan Brahmi, the ur mother script, now seems to speak to Indian readers again across the centuries. A combination of the 'anusaaraka' translation software developed by Akshara Bharati and the 'Inscript' of C-DAC today seems almost to signal a *qualitatively* new kind of literacy because they so clearly highlight the *relationship* rather than the much-discussed *differences* between the Indian scripts. These systems hold some promise for the Indian subcontinent and indeed may do so for the rest of the world—one notes that Google has already installed this software on all its Indian sites!—because the most heartening feature about them is that they are no vague imaginings. They are up and running and have already been extended to phonemic English. The next research task is to stretch them to include the Arabic-Urdu and other scripts and to effect other subtle improvements.

None realize better than the denizens of a postcolonial society, however, that gung-ho prophesies about the reach of new technologies are to be viewed with scepticism. To write futuristic messages on the graffiti walls of a culture is a risky business, and anything one scrawls is bound to be overwritten by more prescient fists. Although the Cambridge anthropologist Marilyn Strathern has envisaged a 'Universal Personal Translator' that will soon enable effortless travel between languages, we are still justified in asking uncomfortable political questions about exactly who will benefit from these easy rides. For, to return in these closing moments to Jack Goody's pessimistic thesis, it is apparent that even the most inexpensive, 5,000-year old, pen-and-paper or chalk and blackboard technology of handwriting has failed to reach a good proportion of the world's population. Nevertheless, it would be fatal to underestimate the industry, skill and vision that have gone into the making of the e-paradigms of translation via transliteration designed so specifically for over a billion subcontinental users of the future.

Finally, in considering the framing 'script' which has historically been assigned to English in India, I must return to the beleaguered role of English and teachers of English in Indian classrooms and ask a question that constantly haunts us, even now, throughout the length and breadth of India:

> What is the identity of the English teacher, who writes her enigmatic messages in the visually and culturally distinctive Roman script; what role is she expected to fulfil in an India where the 'digital divide' only reflects other kinds of more basic divisions between the haves and the have-nots?

The ambiguous ancestry of the English teacher in India needs little elaboration. A single example will suffice to draw attention to her ironic predicament: 1857, as we all know, was the year of the Sepoy Mutiny—now renamed the First War of Indian Independence—but it was in this very year that the 'Indian Universities Act' also established universities in Calcutta, Bombay, Lahore, Allahabad, and Madras, where the medium of instruction was without question—and remains without question—English. In other words, I'm suggesting that the teaching of English and the revolutionary anticolonial impulse have existed side by side in a sort of difficult but creative tension in the history of colonial and postcolonial India, where Macaulay's famed Minute on Education of 1835, followed by the Universities Act in 1857, more or less ensured that an English education and an English education alone represented the paradigm case of 'being educated' for the elite of India, while the 'other languages' of India, both united and divided by their several linguistic scripts, were inevitably corralled into a highly homogenized 'mother-tongue' enclosure. In post-independent India, English was then retained by an Act of Parliament as our 'transitional national language', which we were supposed to give up after fifteen years. That never happened, of course; instead, the English language has today changed, ironically, from being a colonial language to a conduit language, through which all the thoughts of the world pass.

In a unipolar 20th century, America has emerged as a dominant superplayer and the demand for English has reached unprecedented proportions. Indeed, in India, English is often casually referred to as a 'killer language' eating up or cannibalizing all the other 6,000 languages of the world; and although the hunger for 'communication skills' in English grows by the minute, we could also with perhaps with equal truth assert that 'communication kills' when it is confined to English education alone. For it is undeniable that most Indians still live under conditions where, far from having open access to English, almost 40% of our population is still functionally illiterate in any language. So if we admit that literary and critical activity grows in a specific eco-environment and sustains itself on the soil of cultural memory, then we have a problem on our hands. My earlier question, then, more directly put is: *What is the next revolution that we can forecast for English studies from the Indian perspective?*

On the one hand, the large-scale bureaucratization and commodification of literature in the postcolonial Indian nation-state has, for reasons of complex history, created a terrifying attitudinal indifference to the variety of voices, texts and languages in the subcontinent; on the other hand, in the words of Salman Rushdie, "The India that came into being in 1947 is rapidly changing into something else". One of the more hopeful aspects of this 'rapid change', as I see it, is that all those powerful and long-excluded forces contending for the space of literacy may, in the next couple of decades, redefine the traditional contours of the English literature-led critical enterprise as it was earlier laid down.

This is one major ethical revolution that English in India may hope to play a part in. Paradoxically, in this 'revolutionary' situation, it could be that our English departments will be more themselves by being less themselves in the coming decades—by opening up to other languages, other disciplines and other scripts. And here we cannot forget that India, unlike China, Europe or America, will in the next fifty years be a predominantly below-forties young nation. For the first time in India we have a generation nurtured on television and products of a visual culture patently impatient with homilies from us staid and complacent pundits who have hitherto controlled the literary establishment. It is quite likely that in this 'Young India' (to use a Gandhian phrase) of the 21st century, many of which generation are in the vanguard of a global IT industry, the age-old contest between oral and literate cultures of India will be redefined in terms of various forms of visual and tactile representation.

As a result, one of the most important concerns of English teachers all over India in the next decades could be to work at establishing connections between the individual pleasures of literature and social programmes of literacy for all—in other words, we need to work at building connections between the isolated elitism of English, symbolized by its stand-alone Roman script, and the other tongues of India, so differently scripted. Speaking for myself, I believe that the most exciting ethical issues in Indian education in the near future will arise out of the struggle of various groups—such as women, Dalits, Adivasis and so on—to enter the literacy stakes and to insert their own texts and, even more importantly, theories of text into the traditional canon as they increasingly gain power through literacy. An attendant opening up of new areas like translation studies, script studies, cross-cultural studies, cognitive studies and so forth will inevitably follow—and it is here that we may need to lean on Roy Harris's integrationist insights to combat the old errors of Indian 'scriptism' as well as '*pre*scriptivism' in order to extend our conceptions of the scope of both linguistics and literary studies.

Linguists, as Roy Harris has repeatedly emphasized, have far too much invested in words to perceive these mental objects without a hugely distorting bias in their favour:

> The trouble with words, as Samuel Butler once observed, is that we expect them "to do more than they can"; and no one has greater expectations of words than the linguist has. The very highest expectation that a linguist has in this regard is that words will make it possible to explain what language is. And this will indeed be more than words alone can do. That incapacity is the fundamental paradox of linguistics. (Harris 1997: 242)

Harris's syllogistic reasoning here, to my mind, resembles Gödel's exemplary proof of the incompleteness of mathematics. One cannot, in effect, use the methods of logic to prove the premises of theorems—that would be circular, paradoxical. Similarly, "words alone" cannot explain what Harris calls "the fundamental questions"—a thought which to me suggests that questions about language in an India highly stratified at the top and vital but chaotic below may actually require us to revive some of those revolutionary questions that have long been part of India's cultural repertoire but have been pushed entirely to the margins of serious intellectual discussion in our schools and universities. These questions derive from a variety of sources and include, for example:

- Gautama Buddha's *sarvam dukham* question: 'Why is there suffering in the world?' transcribed in the Pali script in the 6th Century BCE.
- Aristotle's question: 'What is the nature of tragedy?' transcribed in the Greek Script in the 4th century BCE.
- Confucius's Question: 'With coarse rice to eat, with water to drink, and my crooked arm for a pillow—is not joy to be found therein?' written in the Chinese Script in the 1st century CE.
- Akbar's *din-i-illahi* question: 'Can there be a single syncretic faith that brings together all people?' transcribed in the Arabic script in the 15th century CE; it is, incidentally, worth noting that of all the Great Mughals, Akbar was the only illiterate or scriptless one, yet his words survive as part of the literate conventions of the Mughal courts, which routinely recorded the 'Life' of the reigning emperor as a part of the court records.
- Kabir's *kahu ke man ki ko jaanat* question: 'Who can know the mind of another?' transcribed in the Devnagari Script in the 15th century; Kabir was a near contemporary of Emperor Akbar.
- Karl Marx's question: 'How does one change the world to enable fair economic relationships?' Roman script, 19th century.
- Sigmund Freud : What does a woman want? Roman script, early 20th century.

And to this series, we might, if we choose, add another at the start of the 21st century:

- How can a teacher who educates her students in the most powerful language the world has ever known use this language to truly empower rather than to exploit?

The point about such questions is, of course, that they entirely resist 'final solutions'. That, indeed, is what makes them 'fundamental'; they stimulate debate, not still it. I began this paper with Roy Harris's invention of 'integrationism' as a concept that invited such debate, and I end now with another word of his: 'panchronism'. I have argued in this essay that in language studies in India today, we sorely need 'panscriptism' as well. More generally, we would do well to heed Harris's warning that a commitment to raising fundamental questions, almost by definition, also precludes a 'blind' commitment to any kind of 'pre-scripted view' or 'perspective' whatsoever:

> A perspective is a corridor with invisible walls. Or rather, walls that give the illusion of transparency. All that looking "through" them yields is a reflection of the wall opposite. In order to escape this illusion, it is necessary to make the effort to discover or develop other perspectives. That effort is the proper domain of linguistic theory. (Harris 1997: 241)

Amen to that!

ACKNOWLEDGMENTS

Indic scripts of the major Indian languages from 'Eden's Page: Scripts of All Asia' at www.geocities.com/athens/academy/9594/.
British Indian Rupee Note from Google Images from 24x7interestingfacts.blogspot.com.
Indian National Flag via Google Images, from http://www.wonderfulinfo.com/ocs/India/indian_flag.jpg.

REFERENCES

Bhaya Nair, Rukmini. 1991. Monosyllabic English or disyllabic Hindi? Language acquisition in a bilingual child. *Indian Linguistics*, 52, 51–90.
Bloom, Paul. 2000. *How Children Learn the Meanings of Words*. Cambridge, MA: MIT Press.
Goody, Jack. 1987. *The Interface between the Written and the Oral.* Cambridge: Cambridge University Press.
Goody, Jack, and Ian Watt. 1968. The consequences of literacy. In Jack Goody, ed., *Literacy in Traditional Societies.* Cambridge: Cambridge University Press, 27–67.
Harris, Roy. 1997. From an integrational point of view. In *Linguistics Inside out: Roy Harris and His Critics* (Current issues in *Linguistic Theory*, vol. 148), eds. George Wolf and Nigel Love (Amsterdam: John Benjamins, 229–310.

Lanza, Elizabeth. 2001. Bilingual first language acquisition: A discourse perspective on language contact in parent-child interactions. In J. Cenoz and F. Genesee (eds.), *Trends in Bilingual Acquisition*. Amsterdam: John Benjamins, 201–229.

Singh, K. S., and S. Manoharan. 1993. *Languages and Scripts: Names and Titles*. Delhi: Oxford University Press.

Tomasello, Michael. 2003. *Constructing a Language: A Usage-Based Theory of Language Acquisition*. Boston, MA: Harvard University Press.

3 Language Learning, Grammar, and Integrationism

Daniel R. Davis

Harris (1998:1) defines integrationism as 'a view of human communication', and integrational linguistics as 'the application of integrationism to the specific case of language', in order to 'change the way people think about language'. Toolan (1996: 321) closes with the following definition: 'The integrational stance is not itself a method or model but such a reconsideration of utterances in their contexts as indicates the limitations or incompleteness of any analytic methodology one might apply to them.' One cannot blame language teachers for shying away from these statements and the approach they represent, despite Widdowson's undoubtedly correct defense of teachers' theoretical interests (1978: 163). After all, students are trying to learn 'a language', not to change the way they think about language in general. And how can a 'reconsideration of utterances' occur without a first consideration of utterances, that is to say, their grammatical form and possible meanings? The simple response to these rhetorical objections is to say that the experience of learning a language involves the consideration and reconsideration of utterances, quite possibly in terms of grammatical form and meaning, and with reference to context. This experience can very well change how students think about language. One only has to consider the difficulty of composing a grammatical and appropriate letter in a language one has attempted to learn to see that language study forces students and teachers to reconsider their language assumptions. The open and critical reader will find much in integrationism that corresponds to and in some cases explains her experiences of language learning and teaching.

Integrationism consists of a number of linguistic, communicative, and semiotic principles. In relating two language-learning experiences, I hope to illustrate some of these principles and how they may be applied to language learning in general. I am aware that, within the field of applied linguistics, a range of research models are available to the investigator, and that empirical evidence for good reasons holds greater weight than personal experience, which is seen as anecdotal. However, one purpose of integrationism is to develop ways of analysing experience, in such a way that it can be brought to bear on research questions pertaining to language. Although this kind of analysis often points to ideological and political issues, these need not be construed in simplistic terms. Bolton (2005: 73–78) warns against oversimplification of the politics of language: 'The big picture here is that there is no one big picture, but a number of them'. Kachru (1990: 6) outlines a balanced approach to political issues in world Englishes, and by extension, applied linguistics:

> I believe that 'social concern' refers to the responsibility of a discipline toward relevant social issues, and application of an appropriate body of knowledge to seek answers to such issues. The term 'social issues' naturally opens a Pandora's box: what is a social issue? And, how can a profession be evaluated on its response to such issues? These are, of course, controversial questions, and as Bolinger (1973: 539) rightly states, the answers to these questions have to be rediscovered by each generation.

The open-endedness of this particular approach to applied linguistics and the politics of language resonates well with an integrationism dedicated to the careful examination of experience.

THE IMMERSION CLASS

I began the conference version of this paper with an example of learning Welsh, based on my experiences in Welsh, French, German, Cantonese, and Mandarin/Putonghua language classes. I introduced greetings in context, calling out participants by name, greeting them in Welsh, and encouraging them to answer me in Welsh. I made it clear that each person in turn had to submit to my will as a teacher—no individual would be allowed to opt out, even though this 'language class' was just a game being played out in the context of a conference paper.

The point of the class session is that within academic culture we share a conception of what a language class is, and willingly enter into this conception, almost without thinking. This may not be true of language teachers, for whom consideration of teaching method is built into their training and experience. Nevertheless, one can argue that the general educated population has an unreflective understanding of what types of behaviour may be encountered in a language class, and the methods of language teachers depend to a certain extent on the methods to which their students have been acculturated. Of course, there are a number of conceptions of what a language class is, and these varying conceptions map quite neatly onto successive approaches and methods in the history of second-language teaching (see Richards and Rodgers 2001: 4–15 for one example). Earlier versions of the language class are to be found near the beginning of the Western grammatical tradition, and emphasise the written word and correctness of construction and interpretation (Harris and Taylor 1997: 51–52). What I term here 'the immersion class' enters the language teaching tradition with first, the recommendations of the nineteenth-century Reform Movement, which criticized the techniques and emphasis of the earlier Grammar-Translation method, and second, the introduction of the Direct Method (Richards and Rodgers 2001: 11–12). Both of these innovations advocated the use of the target language as the classroom language, and the inductive teaching of grammar. Despite the immersion class's introduction as a reform or alternative to the grammatical tradition, much of our conception of a language class still depends on the grammatical tradition and its concept of grammar (which will be taken up in the next section).

What are the characteristics of the immersion class, more specifically? First, the immersion class removes the student from everyday life. The interactional rules are different, and the outcomes and outputs are different from those in other forms of experience. The teacher, usually standing at the front but also moving, faces the students, who are usually sitting. The teacher manages classroom activities, setting the topic, direction, and speed, and opening and closing the session. Students comply with the teacher's requests to the best of their ability, participate, pay attention, take notes, or divert from the subject matter inwardly, passively, and silently. Often participation is constructed in turn taking. In these respects the immersion class is much like a game, self-contained, structured, arbitrary, but not abstract (Harris 1988: 24 and 39). Despite the separateness from the world entailed by the games analogy, nevertheless (as in the games analogy) it is also assumed that the skills acquired in the immersion classroom transfer to and can be integrated in the world outside the classroom.

The immersion class subjects the student to the will of the teacher as both linguistic and behavioural authority. The teacher defines the objectives and the methodology. The student surrenders or at least defers control to the authority of the teacher. This surrender affects the agency of the student.

The third characteristic is that the student is expected to play the role of a constructed native speaker. The student behaves passively (in deferring to the teacher's authority), but also actively, in trying to acquire native speaker norms, for the purpose of interacting with "native speakers". The model student suspends her own judgements about the language and culture under study, behaving as if she were someone else. In the immersion class she is Student X, speaking Language Y, with native speakers. I do not mean that the teacher is necessarily a native speaker, but that the student plays the role of a person interacting with native speakers. The teacher models this role for the students as well, although sometimes also plays the role of native speaker. The student does not model her behaviour on native speaker behaviour, nor does she behave as herself in a possible context of interaction. If real-world contexts of interaction are brought in, they are stereotypical and not individual. The student plays out a role, that of a hypothetical language student, neither her own individuality, nor that of individual members of a real language community. Each of these three characteristics of the immersion class will have an effect on the politics of the anticipated language contact situation, when the student comes into contact with speakers of the language under study.

Just as Student X is a theoretical student, one without specific limiting characteristics or personality traits, Language Y here implies an interchangeability of languages, as if there were no sociolinguistic or cultural baggage. Kachru (1990: 15) illuminates the difference between expected roles and sociolinguistic realities when he says of applied linguistic observations on English in the Outer Circle:

> First, there is an idealization of contexts of use; second, the focus is on static categories of the lectal range as opposed to the dynamic interactional nature of the functions; third, the observer isolates the use of English from the total repertoire of the user; and fourth, the researcher does not recognize the confusion between the performance and the model.

In the reality of actual language classrooms throughout the world, for cultural and/or political reasons, a speaker might show recognition, respect, and solidarity in different ways. Language attitudes and the symbolic value of different languages influence individuals' language choices in a classroom context, from a range of possibilities including languages and varieties that can be characterized as standardized, academic, "world", access, lingua franca, vernacular, heritage, or minority-status. Individuals might see a particular language as worthy of attention only through the lens of a particular educational or linguistic philosophy (such as the acquisition of literacy skills in that language, or the construction of a standardized grammar of that language). Canagarajah (1993: 602) gives specific instances in which 'the classroom is a site of diverse discourses and cultures represented by the varying backgrounds of teachers and students such that the effects of domination cannot be blindly prescribed'. The role of the norm-acquiring Student X of Language Y does not of necessity emerge from the reality of language students and their language behaviour.

This attack on the artificiality of the "Student X of Language Y" construct corresponds to the integrationist position on languages. In integrationism, individual languages do not emerge from interactants' language behaviour, nor does that behaviour consist in the medium of individual languages. For integrationists, language, not languages, is the first-order behaviour and focus of attention. Our linguistic behaviour is an integral part of our other human interactive behaviour. Languages, for their part, are second-order cultural constructs by which we organize and conceptualize privileged components of this first-order interactive behaviour. "Language Y" is a culturally contingent way of picking out only certain components of linguistic interaction. In the *Language Makers* (1980), *Language Myth* (1981), and *Language Machine* (1987), Harris argues that linguistics does not have privileged scientific access to the nature of language, but rather inherits a set of approaches to language that developed in the course of the Western philosophical and grammatical tradition. Our view of language reflects our culture's approach to language, which emerged in the development of philosophy, grammatical instruction, and standardized national languages depending on the social and literary institutions of written grammars and dictionaries. Further work in integrationism has explored the shape which our views of language take: Hutton (1990) analyzes the use of the type-token relationship in linguistic theory, more specifically, how this arises from our language practices in everyday life, but is generalized into a theoretical account of language that ignores the function of memory in our linguistic behaviour. Love (1990) examines what role "languages" play in shaping our language views. Taylor (1992) treats the history of language views in philosophy and linguistics as rhetorical positions. Toolan (1996) deals more generally with the interaction between integrationism and philosophical and critical approaches to language. Hayley Davis (2000) treats words as a social and cultural construct, and considers how interactants use them metalinguistically, that is, to guide and shape their language behaviour.

Integrationism makes the case that individual languages are not language, but are instead a construct upon language. Similarly, the immersion classroom is not the totality of language contexts nor even a representation of those contexts, but instead a constructed cultural institution. This apparently perverse statement and its accompanying sceptical viewpoint have the potential to inform a reconsidered approach to language teaching and to bring together or contribute to movements which have already emerged within applied linguistics and teaching methodology. If readers can get over this hurdle and the bind it places them in (after all, we have devoted our lives to these same particular aspects of language now being called a myth), what awaits them is not a solution to language problems, but a reevaluated set of principles, or a way forward. This means a way out of ideological dilemmas and awkward moments in education and a way toward helping students and teachers. The first integrationist principle is that our way of seeing language is culturally conditioned. Its application to language learning is that the language classroom is a distinct cultural context from the many possible contexts of language use, and that the language classroom as cultural context is idiosyncratic in its practices with respect to these other contexts. This application highlights the fundamental problem of the language classroom: How to integrate in-class language activity with language use outside of class.

My initial experiences of French (1974–1977), Welsh (1979, 1986, 1999), German (1980–1982), and Mandarin (1996–1997) took place in the context of immersion classrooms of this type. In each I learned important things about each of these languages, and was not in any way struck by the constructed nature of languages as second-order entities. The immersion classroom is an excellent introduction to pronunciation, for those students who can allow themselves to perceive and adopt the teacher's phonetic and phonological norms. (I say 'allow themselves' to emphasise the ideological nature of language learning. Resistance comes from within, and is a greater stumbling block than hearing or fine motor control.) Basic vocabulary and grammar can be introduced. Perhaps best of all, the class creates a temporary community of speakers at the same level.

Set against these benefits, one can identify a number of drawbacks (cf. Richards and Rodgers 2001: 12–14 on Direct Method difficulties and limitations). The temporary community, so helpful at first in establishing a context of use for the language, can become a limitation, ultimately contributing to isolation from the main community of language users. The limitation on grammar and vocabulary acquired can result in a simplified but also koinéized form of the language in question. There may be a kind of prestige associated with speaking a trans-dialectal form of the language, especially if it happens to correspond to a literary standard. On the other hand, this can isolate one from native-speaker practices. In my various experiences of these courses the functional value was primarily phatic: One could not understand native speakers in public conversation, or read and discuss literature, or take care of daily needs. I was struck by the difficulty of implementing what I had learned in the classroom with what I encountered in communities where these languages were spoken. French speakers in Quebec and France proved unwilling to accept my French as French; Welsh and German speakers were unwilling to switch from English to their vernacular in order to interact with a foreigner speaking their vernacular language. One could argue that these difficulties stem from a number of educational and sociolinguistic factors (the first being one's own learning limitations), but underneath all of these one can see that, even in an immersion classroom in which behaviour is intended to model that of the language community, there is insufficient awareness of the limitations of that model (while allowing its strengths), its rootedness in other education traditions, and its inability to reflect all communicationally relevant aspects of the language contexts it purports to model. The strength and difficulty of the integrationist position is that it asks linguists and teachers to reconceptualize their work and their interactional context. It makes sense of these critiques but unlike them does not impose another construct as "the next big thing". Simply having the awareness of the classroom as a distinct space points to methodologies that emphasise integration and empowerment. The problems of the immersion class stem in part from its reliance on and compromise with earlier grammatical methods. Given the cultural lie of the land, the expectations of the language learners and teachers often lead to activities drawn from the grammatical tradition.

GRAMMATICAL STUDY OF A MINORITY LANGUAGE

As an undergraduate in the United States studying the Welsh language (1980–1985), I was unsatisfied with grammatical descriptions of Welsh. Rather than describing the language behaviour of the few Welsh-speaking people whom I had encountered, they seemed to describe the grammatical tradition, that is, they reported how one form of Welsh can be parsed. It was hard to relate such descriptions to meaningful communication in a social context. They didn't help me to speak, write, or read, nor to understand conversation, nor to feel comfortable in a Welsh medium. By this I mean no criticism of the teachers or their course design, which, in the case of the intensive and academic courses I took, left me with lasting linguistic and cultural memories and skills. My criticism is directed at the set of assumptions with which I approached my learning, and which was encouraged by the texts I used.

This point is related to the sociolinguistics of the Welsh language, in that the spoken dialects differ significantly from the literary standard, and those studying Welsh as a second language are often taught a recently constructed compromise language which differs from the standardized form and the regional dialects. However, there is more to it than that. From the available descriptions I was already aware that there were different forms of Welsh, varying according to region and register. I knew that part of learning the language would be to learn when to use which form of it. I was not aware of the extent of linguistic variation in the spoken language, and of the social, cultural, and communicational implications of bilingualism. Love (1990: 79) mentions this issue in connection with Welsh, although his further characterizations of Welsh as 'dying' and the use of code-switching in Wales as marking 'semi-speakers' do not reflect current thought on the sociolinguistics of Welsh. I felt as if the grammars enabled me to produce sentences of Welsh that were correct, but not real, and not mine. This is in part because I had no connection to their context of use, except by analogy with the contexts of other languages I had studied. Since these other languages were Latin, French, and German, they gave me very little idea of how and when to use a minority language, in Wales or anywhere else.

But the other problem was that, even allowing for an improved, sociolinguistically aware grammar, the task of the text seemed to be to state the obvious. It is not easy to illustrate what I mean by this. On the one hand, an introductory language text should give some sense of the patterning encountered in the language studied, and these patterns must of necessity assume very limited preexisting knowledge on the part of the learner. On the other hand, oversimplification can lead to sociolinguistic isolation. A further problem seemed to me to lie in the way that Welsh second-language learning had to fit in with second-language learning in general. As mentioned in the previous section, the language was taught by immersion, in isolation from multilingual contexts. As mentioned earlier, the somewhat simplified form of *Cymraeg Byw* (Living Welsh) did have the effect of sociolinguistic isolation. On top of this, the form and content of metalinguistic discussion and grammatical description were dictated by external discourses: second-language textbook (Rhys Jones 1977 is a good example), traditional grammar (Williams 1980), or linguistic theory (Jones and Thomas 1977). Each of these texts provided examples serving its own ends, understandably, but with the result that three different languages emerged, each with its own grammatical characteristics and description, and each answering an implied argument, that Welsh is like any other language. A good example is statements on word order. In a discussion of sentence types, Williams (1980: 167) states, "The normal order of the simple sentence in Welsh is verb + subject + object + extension of the predicate". This traditional but also structural grammar is the source of the typological claim that Welsh has VSO order (although this is usually qualified as allowing SVO order in certain cases). Jones and Thomas (1977), making allowance for a different notation, would give this order as auxiliary verb + subject + verb + object + extension of the predicate, but they derive this from an underlying SVO order. Rhys Jones (1977: 29) introduces the same auxiliary verb sentences with the note, "Note that the verb comes first in these sentences . . ." (Manning 2004 discusses the politics of the ways in which various linguistics traditions describe word order in Welsh.) My point here is not that these descriptions are wrong, or in need of a super-description that coordinates them. It is rather that the grammatical description does not reflect or relate or matter to the interactive behaviour of speakers of the language, as one might naively suppose. Instead, grammatical descriptions reflect and relate and matter to the respective publishing discourse, for the purpose of proving that Welsh can be described in the same way as other languages (dictionary entry, paradigm, phrase structure, transformation, or whatever unit of analysis is required). This amounted to a justification of the power of a particular model of linguistic theory to reduce Welsh to the same pattern as other languages, or, alternatively, a political statement of the viability of Welsh as a foreign language. I must point out that each of the books cited was extremely valuable and useful in its own terms and purposes, and each gave me access to different aspects of Welsh; also that more recent grammars and textbooks (see Thorne 1993; King 1993, 1996; and Thomas 1996) have paid greater attention to the sociolinguistic problem of variation between registers.

Let me repeat that I am talking about the impact that these texts had on my assumptions about language, in that they contributed to a notion that all languages are not only equal, but essentially the same, both in the details of their grammar and in their social position. I held these assumptions uncritically, and was not aware of them as a problem (socially, yes, as explained in the preceding section, but grammatically, no). The problem was the boredom factor of the statements in the grammar. I do not mean that grammar is boring in the traditional sense (as is said of Latin, "first it killed the Romans, and now it's killing me . . ."), but instead, that I saw descriptive linguistics and the demands of language teaching as conspiring to produce statements about Welsh that showed that it could be described like any other language, and learnt like any other language. This created input for the machinery of linguistic theory, as well as documents for the learner that looked like foreign language instruction books, at the cost of removing or downplaying complexity, uncertainty, and indeterminacy. The only way to make Welsh predictable (and therefore learnable) was to reduce it to safe generalizations. As early as 1899, Henry Sweet warns of the 'arithmetical fallacy', 'If languages were perfectly rational . . . we should be able to handle words like the nine digits in arithmetic, and combine them into sentences at pleasure by applying a few simple grammatical rules' (Sweet 1964 [1899]: 70). Naturalness and idiomaticity are casualties of this approach, 'The result is to exclude the really natural and idiomatic combinations, which cannot be formed a priori, and to produce insipid, colourless combinations, which do not stamp themselves on the memory, many of which, indeed, could hardly occur in real life . . .' (Sweet 1899: 72). Sweet goes on to give humorous examples, outdoing himself (and possibly clouding the argument) with 'The philosopher pulled the lower jaw of the hen'. The humour of this sort of sentence is beside the point, as is the degree of realism. The more serious problem is that these sentences are not interesting, not memorable, and do not integrate with lived cultural experience.

I did not have much access to "lived cultural experience" of Welsh at the time (nor do I have much now, for that matter), but I became aware of this problem because the grammatical statements emerging from linguistics and second-language teaching felt wrong to me, and I came to realize that this was because neither of these discourses suited the politics of my programme of study at the time. My mythology required that Welsh be constructed as the "other". This mythology presupposed an essential cultural difference that was lost when my (hypothetical) Welsh-speaking ancestors migrated into English-speaking communities (see Coupland, Bishop, and Garrett 2003 for a related discussion of ideologies of North American Welsh identity). I did not want to accept the limitations of a descriptive rule, especially if that rule downplayed or concealed the essential cultural difference of the "other". I wanted to represent my experience of the Welsh language as something not representable. In short, my motivation for acquiring Welsh was incommensurate with the available means of acquiring Welsh.

I became interested in the patterns of use of Welsh prepositions. These were attractive in a number of ways. On the page they seemed regular and irregular, straddling the boundary between lexical and grammatical description. Sweet's comments on grammar and dictionary illustrate this descriptive ambivalence:

82   Daniel R. Davis

> Grammar, like all other sciences, deals with what can be brought under general laws, and relegates all the other phenomena of language to that collections of isolated facts which we call the dictionary. It need hardly be said that there is no absolute line of demarcation between the two; thus the prepositions and many other particles belong both to the grammar and the dictionary. (Sweet, 1964 [1899]: 73)

When it comes to the relevant components of a linguistic approach to language study, we are still very much inhabitants of the same cultural house as Sweet. Even though an integrationist would not accept uncritically his characterization of grammar as a science, Sweet's words can be read as a map of our metalinguistic tradition. Prepositions can be described as rule-governed (it often makes sense to talk of them as occurring within constructions), but they can also be described as arbitrarily deployed with particular words or lexical items.

The first four lines of the famous poem 'Hon' ('This') demonstrate the attraction and mystery that prepositions held for me:

> Beth yw'r ots gennyf i am Gymru? Damwain a hap
> Yw fy mod yn ei libart yn byw. Nid yw hon ar fap
> Yn ddim byd ond cilcyn o ddaear mewn cilfach gefn,
> Ac yn dipyn o boendod i'r rhai sy'n credu mewn trefn.
> (Parry-Williams 1963 [1949]: 12)
> Translation (by Daniel Davis):
> What difference does Wales make to me? Accident and chance it is
> That I live in its boundaries. On the map it is
> Nothing but a lump of earth in a back corner
> And a bit of punishment for those who believe in order.
> Literal gloss (with apologies to integrationists and Welsh speakers alike, and glosses of prepositions in bold):
> What is the odds **with** me **about/for** Wales? Accident and chance
> Is my being **in** her yard pt living. Not is this **on** map
> pt nothing but lump **of** earth **in** nook
> And pt bit **of** torment **to/for** the those that pt believe **in** order.

Some of these prepositional usages are familiar to English speakers: partitive: 'lump of earth', 'bit of torment'; locative: 'in her yard', 'in a nook', 'on a map'; and postverbal complement: 'believe in'. Others, such as 'with me', are not familiar, and are explained as idioms. Welsh grammars and textbooks identify a possessive construction:

> (1) Mae car 'da Michael (Southern dialects)
>   Gloss: Is car with Michael
>   'Michael has got a car'

(2) Mae gan Michael gar (Northern dialects)
Gloss: Is with Michael car
'Michael has got a car'
(Examples from King 1996: 62)

This construction is not entirely regular (in the Welsh grammatical tradition not every preposition can form sentences of this type) but occurs very frequently in spoken and written Welsh, and it is not associated with a particular lexical item (in the way that the preposition *mewn* 'in (indef. object)' is associated with the verb *credu* 'believe' in line 4 of 'Hon'). As for *ots* 'matter', etymologically derived from English 'odds', grammars identify another idiom, *does dim ots gennyf i* 'I don't care; it doesn't matter to me', which takes a prepositional complement/argument *am* 'about'. The metalinguistic appeal of these is that they are simultaneously lexical and grammatical; they involve arbitrary associations with particular words, but also semantically and syntactically regular patterns that never quite consolidate into reliable classes and categories. They form a part of a cultural kind of knowledge simultaneously irritating and valuable to the learner, and of very little interest to a universalist and autonomous approach to syntax (though semantically centred approaches such as Fife [1990] have distinguished themselves in providing a meaning-motivated description of Welsh prepositional usage).

In the foregoing discussion of prepositions I have sought to demonstrate why prepositions were interesting to a "Welsh" American learning Welsh, and how that interest has its roots in cultural politics. The danger of entering into a detailed discussion of prepositions, grammar, and the Welsh language is not that of boring the reader, who has the freedom to skip ahead. The danger is that it confers a reality on "prepositions" and on "a language" which integrationism would not be prepared to condone. As we have seen, integrationism argues that the ways in which we see language are provided by our culture. This principle in itself is not disputed by mainstream linguistic theorists, who set it aside as the nonscientific understanding of the lay public. Sociolinguists and anthropological linguists take the problem more seriously, but by and large do not extend it to elements of language structure. Integrationism would ask the following question (and indeed, this question was put to me by Roy Harris, Hayley Davis, and Stephen Farrow in 1987): Why should it be the case that "a language", or a grammatical category, "preposition", have any first-order existence? The orthodox answer might be, because prepositions form part of a linguistic system that is necessary to communication (see Taylor 1992 for full details of this and similar discursive positions). The integrationist reply is that this linguistic system is a cultural construct (and specifically, is an artifact of theory), and that communication occurs, not through, but around (and at times, in spite of) language. What, then, is a preposition? And what is a part of speech?

84 *Daniel R. Davis*

The integrationist answer is that this is part of a tradition about language that arose for cultural and historical reasons. This tradition is grammar. A technological adaptation (phonetically based alphabetic writing) allowed a number of tasks to be achieved by means of a language-related semiotic activity. Reliance on this technology, and the elaboration of an educational programme to support it, brought about the transformation of our conception of language. The administrative demands of a newly founded Alexandrian Empire created a demand for a literate class of administrators and scribes, and grammar was developed in order to provide training in literacy skills for this class. The parts of speech embody a building-block approach to language and enable students of reading to engage in word-for-word parsing (Harris 1980: 119–123; also Harris and Taylor 1997: 53–54).

These ways of seeing language survive because they are embedded in social and cultural politics. Grammar is more than a means to literacy; it is a way of containing and controlling literacy. Rather than defining prepositions as the component of language systems that enables them to incorporate and identify relationships between objects and actions, the integrationist position is that we rely on the concept of a preposition more because it allows us to specify what sort of speech or writing is "correct" vs. "incorrect" or "native" vs. "foreign" (although it must be said that there are other acts of normative control that individuals exercise to achieve the same linguistic and social ends). Toolan (1996: 175) describes this isolation and correction of language as a kind of police work, taking place in a culture which adheres to a "commonsense" (that is, political) consensus about a standardized form of its language. Cameron (1995: 218–219) applies integrationist thinking to sociolinguistics when she explains that grammatical rules (based on parts of speech) and other forms of verbal hygiene serve to 'tidy up messy or troublesome realities', and further, that these are supported by 'the fear that the meanings which anchor your own view of the world are not, after all, shared by everyone . . .' James and Lesley Milroy (1999: 45–46) represent the consensus in sociolinguistics when they state, 'Language attitudes stand proxy for a much more comprehensive set of social and political attitudes, including stances strongly tinged with authoritarianism, but often presented as "common sense" '. Within orthodox linguistic theory it is an article of faith to say that we have unconscious control of a linguistic system, the parts of which we cannot name. The integrationist position is somewhat more world-weary: The perennial confusion of the words *pronoun* and *preposition* by nonlinguists is not a sign of their miraculously unconscious grasp of a language system as vehicle of communication, in spite of their inability to apply metalinguistic terminology to that system. It is rather a sign that the accuracy of this terminology is of secondary importance to the authority and political aims of the one wielding it. These political aims include compromises as well as acts of exclusion. (Lippi-Green 1997 explores the nature and significance of these exclusionary acts in the United States.) A similar case is the layperson's frequent confusion over mathematical terms such as *median* and *mean*: The rhetorical and political impact of statistical terminology overwhelms and even conceals the accuracy with which this terminology is deployed. However, we do not take confusion between these words to be evidence of innate, unconscious ability in statistics.

The first principle is that our ways of seeing language are historically and culturally contingent. Grammar arises in a specific historical and cultural context, as a way of dealing with the specific language problems posed by a new language technology. The second principle is that as members of a culture we participate in activities dependent on these ways of seeing language because they have enduring and current political utility in our society. Grammar has survived because of its normative and political uses. The third and most basic principle is that these ways of seeing language, and the activities based on them, can only be understood through examining one's experience of language as honestly as possible. The problem is, how do we communicate if not through a linguistic system? How do we redefine linguistics, its components (including prepositions), and its concepts (including languages)? The only way to begin is by situating the problem in the context of one's own experience; that is, to come to terms with one's experience. For the purposes of a description of Welsh prepositions, my response to this problem was to emphasise the constructed nature of prepositions within the Welsh and related grammatical traditions, the multiple analyses of prepositional usage and meaning within the Welsh grammatical tradition, and the indeterminacy involved in assigning interpretations to folklore texts. In order to achieve this without framing it as an attack on the assumptions of the Welsh grammatical tradition, I completed my thesis without claiming authority over "the language". I tried to show that any structural analysis of prepositions was a political interpretation of experience in terms of available grammatical traditions. In my case, the important experiences were the assertion (or construction) of a Welsh-American identity in a North American cultural context, and the acquisition of Welsh as a second language. As I moved through these experiences, how was (Welsh) grammar redefined? Grammar went from being the imitation of native-speaker norms to the communication structure of language (bridging sound and meaning) to a cultural construct with sociopolitical uses.

The preceding sections presented a narrative of what I learned about grammar as I learned Welsh: that learning a language is NOT the same process across languages, and also that grammar is very much abstracted from this process and is at best a hermeneutic. In the course of this study I could not adopt a Welsh identity, though this was often the assumption underlying the norm-acquiring process.

Integrationism might be read as proposing that teachers teach students to become "linguists" themselves: to construct and test their own rules and norms (Davis 1994), but to recognize that this is not tapping into some preexisting, preordained language system "out there" (and therefore conferring "knowledge" of the object), but is merely an ad hoc construction to achieve an outcome in a particular cultural and communicative situation. We are nearer to a solution to the problem mentioned at the beginning: How can integrationism help language teachers, or say something relevant to the language-teaching classroom? It can help by suggesting that language teachers ask themselves the following questions:

1. How do your own language experiences and those of your students shape the learning context and the object of study (i.e. the language in question)? How do your language experiences differ from those of your students?
2. Can you analyze the language ideologies that are involved in how context and object of study are shaped? These are more easily identifiable through differences in experience.
3. How are the functions and items that we see as constituting language and the methods based on these constructed by the social, cultural, and political ways that we see language? Can you contextualize items that are valuable or useful to the task at hand, but redefine the rest so that they do not consume scarce resources?
4. Social roles and political empowerment: Can you teach your students to create their own rules, for their own purposes? What will inspire students to recognize and analyse the politics of their language situations?
5. How would it change your teaching if you saw language structure (or any models of language, for that matter) as intellectual history, and saw this history as a kind of politics?
6. How is this politics anchored in reality, whether that is biomechanical, macrosocial, or experiential?
7. What part do you play in creating your own role and authority? What are you using it for? What will your students use it for?

REFERENCES

Bolinger, Dwight. 1973. "Truth Is a Linguistic Question". *Language*, 49: 539–550.
Bolton, Kingsley. 2005. "Where WE Stands: Approaches, Issues, and Debate in World Englishes". *World Englishes*, 24.1: 69–83.
Cameron, Deborah. 1995. *Verbal Hygiene*. London; New York: Routledge.
Canagarajah, A. Suresh. "Critical Ethnography of a Sri Lankan Classroom: Ambiguities in Student Opposition to Reproduction through ESOL". *TESOL Quarterly*, 27.4: 601–626.
Coupland, Nikolas, Hywel Bishop, and Peter Garrett. 2003. "Home Truths: Globalisation and the Iconising of Welsh in a Welsh-American Newspaper". *Journal of Multilingual and Multicultural Development*, 24.3: 153–177.
Davis, Daniel, R. 1994. "Teaching American English as a Foreign Language: An Integrationist Approach". *Who Owns English?*, ed. by Mike Hayhoe, Stephen Parker, and Anthony Adams. Buckingham, UK: Open UP. 68–76.

Davis, Hayley G. 2000. *Words—an Integrational Approach*. London: Curzon.
Fife, James. 1990. *The Semantics of the Welsh Verb: A Cognitive Approach*. Cardiff. UK: Univ. of Wales Press.
Harris, Roy. 1980. *The Language-Makers*. Ithaca, NY: Cornell University Press.
Harris, Roy. 1981. *The Language Myth*. London: Duckworth.
Harris, Roy. 1987. *The Language Machine*. London: Duckworth.
Harris, Roy. 1988. *Language, Saussure, and Wittgenstein: How to Play Games with Words*. London; New York: Routledge.
Harris, Roy. 1998. *Introduction to Integrational Linguistics*. Kidlington, UK: Elsevier.
Harris, Roy, and Talbot J. Taylor. 1997. *Landmarks in Linguistic Thought 1: The Western Tradition from Socrates to Saussure*. London; New York: Routledge.
Hutton, Christopher. 1990. *Abstraction and Instance: The Type-Token Relation in Linguistic Theory*. Oxford; New York: Pergamon Press.
Jones, Morris, and Alan R. Thomas. 1977. *The Welsh Language: Studies in Its Syntax and Semantics*. Cardiff: University of Wales Press for the Schools Council.
Kachru, Braj B. 1990. "World Englishes and Applied Linguistics". *World Englishes*, 9.1: 3–20.
King, Gareth. 1993. *Modern Welsh: A Comprehensive Grammar*. London; New York: Routledge.
King, Gareth. 1996. *Basic Welsh: A Grammar and Workbook*. London; New York: Routledge.
Lippi-Green, Rosina. 1997. *English with an Accent: Language, Ideology, and Discrimination in the United States*. London: Routledge.
Love, Nigel. 1990. "The Locus of Languages in a Redefined Linguistics". *Redefining Linguistics*, ed. by Hayley G. Davis and Talbot J. Taylor. London; New York: Routledge.
Manning, H. Paul. 2004. "The Geology of Railway Embankments: Celticity, Liberalism, the Oxford Welsh Reforms, and the Word Order(s) of Welsh". *Language and Communication*, 24.2: 135–163.
Milroy, James, and Lesley Milroy. 1999. *Authority in Language: Investigating Standard English*. London; New York: Routledge.
Parry-Williams, T. H. 1963 [1949]. *Ugain o gerddi*. Llandysul: argraffwyd gan J.D. Lewis, Aberystwyth, Wales: Gwasg Gomer.
Rhys Jones, T. J. 1977. *Living Welsh*. Sevenoaks, UK: Teach Yourself Books.
Richards, Jack C., and Theodore S. Rodgers. 2001. *Approaches and Methods In Language Teaching*. Cambridge; New York: Cambridge University Press.
Sweet, Henry. 1964 [1899]. *The Practical Study of Languages: A Guide for Teachers and Learners*. London: Oxford University Press.
Taylor, Talbot J. 1992. *Mutual Misunderstanding: Scepticism and the Theorizing of Language and Interpretation*. Durham, NC: Duke University Press.
Thomas, Peter Wynn. 1996. *Gramadeg y Gymraeg*. Caerdydd: Gwasg Prifysgol Cymru.
Thorne, David. 1993. *A Comprehensive Welsh Grammar*. Oxford, UK; Cambridge, MA: Blackwell.
Toolan, Michael J. 1996. *Total Speech: An Integrational Linguistic Approach to Language*. Durham, NC: Duke University Press.
Widdowson, H. G. 1978. *Teaching Language as Communication*. Oxford: Oxford University Press.
Williams, Stephen Joseph. 1980. *A Welsh Grammar*. Cardiff: University of Wales Press.

4 Grammaticality and the English Teacher in Hong Kong
An Integrationist Analysis

Christopher Hutton

This paper attempts to set out the issues and theoretical complexities that surround the subject of the teaching of English today, with special reference to the debates within Hong Kong. The question of Standard English and the teaching of English both within the so-called native-speaker countries and globally has given rise to massive debate. Integrationists, unusually, seem to find themselves in accord with the critical edge of this literature, which is suspicious of the reification of language within linguistics, and of a pedagogy based on a concept of decontextualized rules. However, integrationism is also a 'lay-oriented' inquiry, committed in some sense to the lived reality of language users as 'language makers'. As I understand this position, it involves a rejection of the tripartite distinction generally made in linguistics between (i) the language system as an abstract set of communicative rules, (ii) the use of the system for communication through voluntary acts of individuals in particular contexts, and (iii) opinions, understandings, conceptualizations of language associated with all kinds of language users, both lay and expert. This opens up a series of methodological and political dilemmas, which are illustrated in this paper from my experiences as a teacher in Hong Kong.

A number of sample experiences:

1. A wealthy member of the Hong Kong elite and benefactor of the university rings me up in my capacity as head of the University of Hong Kong English Department and asks me whether I or one of my colleagues can review teaching material for a friend of his who is preparing English course material for primary students. He wants someone to say whether the pronunciations on the tape are correct of not. I pass him onto the Linguistics Department, after complaining that our post in English phonetics and phonology has not been renewed.
2. A distinguished retired chief justice sends me a letter lamenting declining English standards in Hong Kong: 'We are all very concerned about the standard of English in Hong Kong'. He attaches material from a Web site about a method for teaching English pronunciation recommended by the British Council, in which relevant comments have been highlighted in yellow marker pen.

3. My fellow students and I are invited to dinner at the house of my Cantonese teacher. Her husband, a senior manager in one of the major Hong Kong companies, prefaces the first course with the statement: 'What are we going to do about the standard of English in Hong Kong?'
4. A friend writing the minutes for a government committee asks me to look through them and check the English. Many sentences in the document have structures of this kind: 'X suggested the committee to pursue the matter further'. After some hesitation, I correct these to 'X suggested the committee pursue the matter further'. A few days later I am told that my friend's boss reinserted the deleted 'to' in each context. In the same text is an expression 'for steer', as in 'The matter would be referred to X for steer'. I query this and suggest 'for guidance' as an alternative. We decide to leave the expression in the text on the grounds that it is institutionalized in the civil service culture, but I do point out that I have not encountered this expression before.
5. I get into the lift of my building and a young child, after prompting from the parent, begins counting off the floors in English as the lift ascends.
6. A sign outside a building where renovation work is being carried out: 'We regret any inconvenience course'.
7. I receive a document from the university in which the word 'would' appears where I would have written 'will', as in: 'The university would continue to pursue its goal of attaining world class status'.
8. One of my former students now teaching English in secondary school e-mails me with a grammatical problem put to her by her students which requires a yes/no answer, i.e. not one which includes a notion of context, as in 'it depends what you are trying to say . . .'
9. I get into any lift in Hong Kong and look at the sign, prominently displayed: 'When there is a fire, do not use the lift'. On occasion, I point this out to visitors as an example of institutionalized HK English.
10. I go through an essay and find that many paragraphs begin with the word 'besides'. I cross out one or two of the 'besides' and write in the margin: Don't begin a paragraph with 'besides'.

In Hong Kong, talking about English and standards of English is fundamental to public or civic discourse. The prevalent discourse of decline reflects two contradictory modernization processes in post-1960s Hong Kong. The first was the popularization/democratization of access to English driven by compulsory education, increasing social mobility and affluence, and the shift from a manufacturing to a service economy, in which people increasingly worked in offices rather than factories, and knowledge of English became essential for a whole range of medium- and low-status jobs. The second was the rise of a quasi-national identity based on the spoken Chinese variety in Hong Kong, Cantonese, which promoted Cantonese to the language of much of the informal public sphere (media, entertainment, civil associations). The discourse of decline is also prevalent in the United Kingdom. The chair of the English Association, Professor John Batchelor, was reported as lamenting straight-A students' 'shaky grasp of the basics' (Batchelor 2004: 7): 'Often it is the nuts and bolts that they really need: the right use of the colon and semicolon, the right use of the apostrophe—distinguishing between "it's" and "its" and so on'.

Linguists have generally been suspicious of this rhetoric of declining standards, and have attributed it to elite cultural pessimism and suspicion of wider access to literacy and education. There is clearly some truth in this, as the most vocal critics of declining standards of English in Hong Kong are drawn from the ruling business elite. This elite displays at best ambivalence about the rapid expansion of the tertiary sector in the early 1990s, which has widened social access to university education in English. But anxiety about standards is a more complex phenomenon than this allows. The anxieties of the users of English reflect also the complexities of this widening access to English which is not accompanied by any discernible shift towards speakers 'making the language their own', to use the words of Harris's inaugural lecture at the University of Hong Kong (Harris 1989: 46).

In the immediate aftermath of the 1997 retrocession of sovereignty to the People's Republic of China, the Hong Kong government issued a so-called 'firm guidance' policy which was designed to reduce the number of schools teaching through the medium of English, and reemphasize mother tongue as the educationally most effective medium of instruction. This was a continuation of a policy initiative launched in the final stages of the British colonial administration. Schools which wished to continue teaching through the medium of English had to demonstrate that they could operate at the required standard (http://www.emb.gov.hk):

> Educational research worldwide and in Hong Kong have shown that students learn better through their mother tongue. . . . The educational benefits of mother-tongue teaching include: mother-tongue teaching has positive effects on students' learning; most students prefer learning in the mother tongue; students learning in the mother tongue generally perform better than their counterparts using English as medium of instruction (MOI); and students of traditional Chinese-medium schools consistently achieve a higher pass percentage than the territory-wide average in both Chinese Language and English Language in the Hong Kong Certificate of Education Examination. This shows the positive impact of mother-tongue teaching on the learning of Chinese and English as a subject. It is therefore Government's policy: to encourage secondary schools to use Chinese as MOI; and to discourage the use of mixed code, i.e. a mixture of Chinese and English, in teaching and learning.

Although this move might have been understood as a rejection of colonial norms in education policy, it also reflected an originally Western philosophy of education which stressed the necessity of an organic unity between the language of the home sphere and that of public institutions, in particular the school: 'With the use of Chinese as MOI lifting language barriers in the study of most subjects, students will be better able to understand what is taught, analyse problems, express views, develop an enquiring mind and cultivate critical thinking. Mother-tongue teaching thus leads to better cognitive and academic development. Our students can also have more time to concentrate on the learning of English' (http://www.emb.gov.hk).

Contrary to a widespread public perception, which erroneously associates mother-tongue education with adherence to traditional Chinese culture, the colonial government itself had attempted at various times in Hong Kong's history to promote mother-tongue education. The current postcolonial Hong Kong government's own documents recognize this, stating that:

> [t]his policy has been re-affirmed over time: In 1984, Education Commission Report (ECR) No. 1 established a clear policy to encourage secondary schools to teach in the mother tongue; In 1986, Government introduced support measures to schools using Chinese as MOI; In 1990, ECR4 endorsed the principles for MOI and recommended regular reviews to monitor progress and stronger measures to encourage Chinese-medium instruction and minimise mixed-code teaching; In 1994, Government started to advise schools on the language proficiency of their Secondary 1 intake to assist them in choosing an appropriate MOI; In 1994, Government announced a Policy Commitment to issue firm guidance to all secondary schools on MOI by 1997/98; and In 1996, ECR6 re-affirmed the policy of mother-tongue teaching, supported the publication of advice on the appropriate MOI in 1997 for adoption by individual schools in 1998 and asked for clear indications of sanctions for non-compliance.

In the history of the European empires, missionaries often preferred to use vernacular languages as the medium of instruction. These had the virtues of circumventing traditional knowledge structures and texts in classical languages, and the corrupting, commercial modernity of English. Missionary schooling in early Hong Kong had also made use of vernacular languages or the local Chinese dialects, and one of the leading Chinese-medium schools in Hong Kong today, Pui Ching Middle School, is the creation of a Baptist foundation.

Macaulay's Minute on Education ([1835] 2001: 20), which is frequently quoted as illustrating the iniquities of the imposition of English on India, is actually a blueprint for modernization/Westernization through the vernacular languages:

> It is impossible for us, with our limited means, to attempt to educate the body of the people. We must at present do our best to form a class

who may be interpreters between us and the millions whom we govern; a class of persons, Indian in blood and colour, but English in taste, in opinions, in morals and in intellect. To that class we may leave it to refine the vernacular dialects of the country, to enrich those dialects with terms of science borrowed from Western nomenclature, and to render them by degrees fit vehicles for conveying knowledge to the great mass of the population.

Vernacular language policy and English were actually two sides of the same colonial coin, and Macaulay's minute describes the language situation as it evolved in colonial Hong Kong.

The colonial government's initiatives had foundered on the resistance of the public, who saw an education through the medium of English as key to the social mobility of their children. Given that English was required for jobs in the government, law, education, medicine, this was not surprising. The argument—then and now—that English-medium does not translate into good English has failed to convince the public, who are well aware that the elite schools in Hong Kong are English-medium, as are in general the universities. The problem from the government's point of view was that many so-called Anglo-Chinese schools in Hong Kong were actually teaching in mixed mode, described pejoratively as Chinglish. This language mixing was the result of the increasing availability of English-medium education. In particular after the signing of the joint declaration in 1984 which set a timetable for Britain's withdrawal from Hong Kong, education in English-medium was also seen as highly desirable as it allowed for the possibility of being educated abroad, at the secondary or tertiary level. The middle classes, and increasingly all classes with disposable family income, aspired to the same privileges as the Hong Kong Chinese elite, namely, to give their children an international education in English. The class of high-ranking bureaucrats and business leaders who offered firm guidance on mother-tongue teaching after 1997 would themselves never consider exposing their own children to it. It also gradually began to dawn on the new leadership of Hong Kong that mother-tongue education was not the policy of the new sovereign power, which had a strong centralizing tradition of language planning involving the promotion of a normalized national pronunciation, Putonghua. By promoting mother-tongue education, the Hong Kong government was in effect emphasizing a regional rather than a national identity within the People's Republic of China.

A postcolonial panic about declining standards of English triggered aggressive action to bring secondary English teachers up to standard, by making those without formal qualifications in English (i.e. a degree majoring in English) submit to a so-called 'benchmark' examination. In addition, the so-called Native-speaking English Teachers (NET) scheme, originally set up in 1987, was reinvigorated for the school year 1998/9 (http://www.ed.gov.hk). This scheme aims to assign 'native speakers' to Hong Kong primary and secondary schools. The duties of NETs include the following:

To be responsible for classroom teaching and assessment; to provide support to the English Panel Chairperson, including assisting in curriculum development and preparation of teaching materials; to assist in conducting extra-curricular activities related to the English language, e.g. speech, drama, debates, choral speaking and extensive reading; to assist in running oral activities for students after school; to assist in setting up an English corner in the school where students can come together to practise oral English and read English books under their guidance; and to act as an English language resource person for other teachers in the school.

The sensitivity of the term 'native English speaker', with its racial connotations, led to its replacement and applicants were required to be 'native-speakers of English' or to have 'native-speaker English competence'. This was not defined further, however. The scheme in its original form and its current manifestation is also widely resented by in-service Hong Kong teachers, not least because of the implication—which is not the official interpretation of the scheme at all—that native speakers (which is understood within Hong Kong society to mean white people) make better teachers of English than the Hong Kong Chinese. The politically correct view from applied linguistics rejects Randolph Quirk's position that 'contempt for standards' has undermined the teaching of English in the native-speaker countries and that the exportation of this to EFL and ESL countries is to be resisted (Quirk 1985: 6, quoted in Widdowson 2003: 44). Instead, the applied linguistic view is that native speakers are not *ipso facto* qualified to teach English and even if qualified as teachers, lack the Hong Kong nonnative speaker's advantage of having an insider's views of the particular, local linguistic and cultural barriers that stand between the learner and the 'target language'. Thus, McKay (2002: 44) talks of the 'native speaker fallacy' and the 'strengths of bilingual teachers' in EIL (the teaching of English as an international language), as well as rejecting the idea that bilingual users of English should be required 'to accommodate to the rhetorical patterns of the Inner Circle country in which they are studying, or if they should be allowed—or even encouraged—to organize their written texts according to the rhetorical patterns of their first language' (McKay 2002: 77). Since 'an international language is one that by definition belongs to no one country or culture, then there are valid reasons for promoting local cultural topics and ways of learning' (2002: 79).

Commenting on this issue of 'ownership of English', Widdowson (2003: 43) argues that this gives rise to a 'problem for pedagogy'. Since we are no longer following the native-speaker model, we are faced with a 'diverse plurality' of competing models and no way to choose between them. To this one could say that there is no given native-speaker standard in the inner circle countries which simply presents itself for use. To the once fashionable concern for class, dialect and accent in the schools, we have now simply added race, culture or ethnicity.

Ironically, in other language subjects in most contexts, the politically correct view is that the native speaker is the most qualified person to teach a language, since it is assumed that no one else is qualified to speak on behalf of the culture that is associated with the language. Can one imagine a teacher of Arabic or Chinese producing musings equivalent to these from a university teacher of English in Germany when contemplating the status of the structure 'I learn English since ten years'? (Erling 2002)

> I am no longer convinced that the production of such a sentence is simply a '*typical* German error'. After reading about certain features of New Englishes—the Englishes of post-colonial countries like Ghana, India, Nigeria, and Singapore—I noticed that several features of the so-called New Englishes were the same as those manifesting in my classroom. Such linguistic features, which are apparently gaining ground in their native contexts, are judged as errors when made by German students. In other words, according to the research, certain grammatical formations are now considered part of the standard in India, for example, but are still dismissed as incorrect in Berlin. Once I had realized this, I started to ask myself why, if standards of English are supposedly expanding, I should still be correcting a student when she writes, for example, 'The story was touching me deeply'?
>
> My moral quandary about what to count as correct or incorrect in my students' papers is a perfect example of the debate about standard English rearing its head in the second-language classroom—the so-called 'widening standard language debate' (Bex and Watt 1999). The expansion of English and the continual recognition of other varieties of English make questions about correctness more problematic than ever before. What should we consider correct or incorrect in a world where more and more varieties of English are gaining institutionalized legitimacy? What form of the language should we be teaching to students who use English internationally? And, more pressing, where should I use my red pen? (Erling 2002: 8–9)

Erling observes that, after completing the course, students often return to using tenses incorrectly when judged against the standard, 'and this does not seem to affect their communicative competence' (Erling 2002: 11). The piece concludes with a plea for the student body and the use they make of English to be further analyzed within 'a broader interpretation of the standard to include the sociolinguistics of English in a world context' (Erling 2002: 12).

The Hong Kong government's benchmark examination (for English teachers without formal qualifications in English) reflects no such moral qualms. In its report on the Language Proficiency Assessment for Teachers (March 2003, http://www.emb.gov.hk), the examiners noted that markers had commented 'on the poor language standard of some weaker candidates as well as overall limitations in terms of lexical structure and structural variations. Lower-order grammatical errors were also common, such as subject-verb agreement, countable and uncountable nouns, and singular-plural forms' (p. 4). Reflecting the influence of terminology from linguistics, the report also noted that candidates needed to focus more on register:

> When writing, they need to consider the distance and relationship between the writer and the reader, which in turn determine the tone and style of the text. In this year's Writing Paper, adopting a tone of politeness and cooperation would have been most appropriate. Many scripts, however, sounded condescending. . . . The overuse and misuse of 'should' such as 'Parents should seek help from teachers' . . . displayed a lack of sensitivity to the text and to the reader. Scripts such as these were marked down on Organisation and Coherence.

One section of the examination concerns the correction of errors and problems in student writing. The report noted candidates often wrongly categorized the type of error, even if they managed to correct it successfully. Thus, the structure 'He look like' was not a 'tense problem' as a number of candidates had suggested: 'The error in this item is that the verb "look" should be changed to "looks" in order to agree with the third-person singular subject form' (p. 5). Presumably the candidate could also change the pronoun from 'he' to 'they'. In the sentence 'He likes play TV game', the bare infinitive form 'play' is incorrectly used and should be replaced by either the gerund 'playing' or the infinitive with 'to' as in 'to play'. Interestingly, the answer that 'the preposition "to" should be added before an action' was categorized as wrong. Greater confusion was created by the structure 'it was excellence'. The following answers were rejected: 'Wrong use of adjective and noun'; 'Wrong use of adjective'; 'The noun excellence should become excellent'; 'Excellence is a noun, not an adjective'. Answers such as 'first language interference' or 'Chinese-English' were not acceptable.

The 'native-speaker' question lurks uneasily in the background to this test. The listening comprehension was based on a recording which was 'natural sounding and delivered at normal speaking speed in standard accents (native English speakers and Hong Kong Chinese second language speakers)'. Candidates are recommended to listen to the way texts 'are read aloud by competent speakers'. The classroom language assessment section for the September 2003 report noted that (p. 9):

> While perfect enunciation for every single word uttered is not expected, language teachers should aim to be accurate in their speech and articulation. Language teachers should serve as models for their students as far as language acquisition is concerned. Efforts should therefore be made by teachers to present themselves as such. Taking the final consonant as an example, while it is natural to drop the final consonant in

authentic speech, especially when it is fast-paced and informal, there are occasions when a missing final consonant can bring about a change in meaning, thus resulting in communication being impeded. 'Please dine with me' can easily turn into a request of a very different kind when it is uttered as 'Please die with me'.

On the question of correct grammar, it is interesting to compare some of these answers with those kindly provided by the ever-vigilant if somewhat dense grammar-checker supplied by Mr Gates. 'He look like' was diagnosed as having a problem with 'subject-verb agreement' and the form 'looks' is offered as a correction. If requested, a paper clip with Groucho Marx eyebrows pops up to offer an explanation: 'The verb of a sentence must agree with the subject in number and in person'. Interestingly, the paper clip also seems to be suffering from moral qualms about bossing the computer user about. Although the verb 'must' agree, the user in the examples offered to illustrate this point is invited politely to 'consider' using 'What were Steven and Laura like as schoolchildren' instead of 'What was Steven and Laura like as schoolchildren'. Instead of 'Tom watch the snowy egret stab at the fish', we are invited to 'consider' the sentence 'Tom watches the snowy egret stab at the fish'. However, grammatical anarchy breaks out when confronted with 'He likes play TV game'. This elicited no negative comment at all; nor did 'it was excellence'. However, if the checker is widened to include 'both grammar and style', the phase 'was understood' was identified as 'passive voice' and the suggestion, now sounding quite authoritarian, offered that the writer should 'consider revising'. This is because the active voice may give rise to a 'livelier and more persuasive' sentence. Loyal to the traditional notion that a sentence expresses a complete thought, the line from Erling quoted earlier, 'And, more pressing, where should I use my red pen?' is designated as a fragment which the writer is asked to 'consider revising': 'If the marked words are an incomplete thought, consider developing this thought into a complete sentence by adding a subject or verb or combining this text with another sentence.'

One of the more striking aspects of the benchmark test in Hong Kong is the set of meta-messages that the exercise sends. One text chosen for reading comprehension (a letter to the newspaper in the September 2002 examination) includes strong criticism of 'memorization of content' as fostered by 'the present examination culture': 'Research has conclusively shown how useless this is as a goal in education when most of what is memorized is forgotten two weeks after the examination.' Almost all the texts chosen concern language education, so that the examination is also a means for the imparting of specific messages about education. The examiners' notes also exhort teachers to read more and listen to or read different kinds of English. However, in one of the speaking exercises, a poem entitled 'A Levels' by Spike Milligan is included in which children 'laughing and playing in the Sun' are contrasted with those in the shadows being fed 'Algebra-Science-Syntax' (Guidance notes for candidates, p. 102).

In the new syllabus for English majors who wish to qualify as teachers, the government has now mandated that World English and Hong Kong English be taught, but it is unclear how Hong Kong English is to be integrated into the teaching of English in the classroom.

The idea that a language is a system of rules obviously permeates this exercise and the wider set of metalinguistic beliefs and practices in which it is embedded. Many teachers fail this test and are thus prevented from teaching English until they manage to pass. The high failure rate feeds directly into the discourse of declining standards. After the results of the latest examination were released, the *South China Morning Post* trumpeted: 'English teaching skills plummet' (Tuesday, June 10, 2004, p. C1), based on the observation that scores in some of the five areas tested—writing and listening—were lower than the previous year. The fact that the cohorts of students taking the test were not comparable in this simplistic way was ignored in favour of an eye-catching headline.

Clearly, the exercise is predicated on the notion of standard English, however liberally interpreted, and of notions such as 'competent speaker'. Within integrational linguistics, the notion of standard English has been characterized as 'a remarkable example of a self-fulfilling prophecy', a myth 'which had been invented to serve the purposes of a typically Victorian brand of national idealism' (Harris 1988: 1, 26). Davis characterizes the concept of standard English as 'a confused and confusing one' (1999: 86), blending the theoretical-philosophical objections of Harris, i.e. in pointing to the 'muddling of speech and writing' and the problematics of the fixed-code fallacy with the political objections of Crowley, in that prescriptivism 'is used to the benefit of specific social interests and against other such interests' (Crowley 1987: 199; Davis 1999: 85). This critique can be found in Harris's recent piece 'English: how not to teach it'. Harris attacks the idea of teaching English on the basis of the so-called rules of English grammar. This approach is not only inadequate to the subject but is additionally guilty of 'muddling' the students' minds:

> The reasons why this misguided practice is so popular among teachers of English are not difficult to discern. In the first place, it is much easier to teach English grammatical rules than to teach English (easier not only for the purposes of exposition, but for purposes of conducting simplistic 'tests' and marking 'examinations'. If there are rules, you either get it right or you get it wrong, just as in arithmetic. In the second place, the teaching of rules vests authority, and hence social and political power, both in the teacher and in the institutions which sponsor this authoritarian approach to linguistic instruction (Harris 2006: 15).

Harris distinguishes between 'precepts' and 'rules'. Precepts for language learners include familiar instructions such as 'an adjective must agree with its noun in gender, number and case' (Harris 2006: 16). While there are precepts associated with English, or the teaching of English, it is a mistake to conflate these with rules. The highway code reflects legally codified rules; a cookery book offers precepts for the activity of cooking.

As I mentioned in the introduction, this is one area in which integrationism can look to a substantial body of writing which echoes, or appears to echo, political scepticism about the discourse of standards. For Watts, standard English arises out of a deeply entrenched tradition, which in his own linguistic experience was realized in the 'tedious exercise of parsing English sentences and texts' in grammar school in the early 1950s. Standard English is a 'social institution', revealing in Berger and Luckmann's terminology 'reciprocal typifications of actions'. It is the product of 'social construction' which involves 'a powerful language ideology' supporting the concept of 'legitimate language' (Watts 1999: 66). 'Correct English' and 'proper English' connote the superiority of 'perfection', 'excellence', 'unity', 'unchangeability' over the notions of 'variability', 'development and change', and 'alternative standards' (Watts 1999: 41).

Trudgill (1999) defines Standard English initially by a series of negatives: it is neither a language nor an accent; it is not a style, nor a register. Having cleared the field in this way, Trudgill acknowledges that 'we are obliged to say what it actually is'. The answer is that Standard English is a 'dialect', since it is merely one among many of the subvarieties of English. One of the supporting arguments for this position is that 'most British sociolinguists' agree on this point. Standard English is a purely social dialect, 'spoken as their native variety, at least in Britain, by about 12 per cent–15 per cent of the population' who are concentrated at the top of the social scale. This social dialect is defined not by pronunciation or lexis, but by grammatical features. These features are characterized as 'grammatical idiosyncrasies', when compared with the other dialects. Thus, 'Standard English has an unusual and irregular present-tense verb morphology in that only the third-person singular receives morphological marking: *he goes* versus *go*. Many other dialects use either zero for all persons or *-s* for all persons' (1999: 125).

One of the many problems with Trudgill's discussion is the lack of clarity about the distinction between speech and writing. The idea of people speaking standard English as their 'native variety' reflects the grip the concept of native speaker—one derived essentially from European Romanticism—has on modern linguistics.

The denial by integrationists and others that Standard English exists, and the evident confusion among those who argue for the importance of this concept yet cannot agree on its scope or definition, might be thought to sit awkwardly with the lived experiences of language users, not least those English-language teachers in Hong Kong faced with the benchmark examination. Yet, these teachers might plausibly be presented as victims of a language politics which has come to define—one might say reduce—English to a set of normative rules, in a sociocultural context in which the teachers have no authority. Their resentment of the NET scheme reflects this. But, what is one to make of a teacher of English who has trouble correcting the 'missing' -s for the third-person-singular verb? Is one not tempted to say that this teacher is somewhat like a mathematics teacher who thinks that 2 + 2 = 5?

Discussing the relationship between language education and linguistics, Widdowson notes that the complex formulations of generative grammar might well encourage us in the belief that linguistics has nothing to say to the language teacher. But, on the contrary,

> the remoteness and partiality of linguistic descriptions does not invalidate them. On the contrary, such descriptions are revealing precisely *because* they are partial and informed by a particular perspective. If linguistics could provide us with representations of experienced language, it would be of no interest whatever. Linguistic accounts of language only have point to the extent that they are detached from, and different from, the way in which language is experienced in the real world (2003: 7).

Widdowson defends the specialized terminology of linguistics from the perhaps trite charge that it is a language of deliberate mystification. The representations of language offered by linguists 'can be used as frames of reference for taking bearings on such realities from a fresh perspective. This involves a process of mediation whereby the linguist's abstract version of reality is referred back to the actualities of the language classroom' (2003: 8). Against the contemporary trend of demanding relevance and usefulness for academic inquiry, Widdowson contends that 'it is not within the brief of linguistics to make useful theories' (2003: 10). This falls to a separate task of mediation, and 'the linguist, qua linguist, is not in a position to judge what use might be made of linguistic theory and description' (2003: 11).

On the global spread of English, Widdowson proposes that we think of this 'not in terms of the spread of a stable and unitary set of forms, but as the spread of a virtual language which is exploited in different ways for different purposes' (2003: 50). This notion of English as a virtual language is used to counter 'the conspiracy theory that the language itself has powers of suppression, that it is the English language which colonizes, using the English people simply as a medium, as a means of transmission' (2003: 50). This conspiracy view of English is associated primarily with Robert Phillipson (1992: 47), who defined what he termed English linguistic imperialism where 'the dominance of English is asserted and maintained by the establishment and continuous reconstitution of structural and cultural inequalities between English and other languages'.

Mainstream applied linguistics and Widdowson's approach to English teaching and world English have been characterized by Alistair Pennycook as 'liberal ostrichism' (2001: 30). It is held to deny 'both its own politics and the politics of language'. Pennycook maps applied linguistics as a critical space or as a 'problematizing practice position'. He terms this 'critical applied linguistics', a framework within which language is viewed as 'fundamentally bound up with politics', articulating a profound scepticism about science, truth claims, and the possibility of an emancipatory position outside ideology'. This position 'draws on poststructuralist, postmodernist perspectives, viewing language as inherently political, understanding power more in terms of its micro operations in relation to class, race, gender, ethnicity, sexuality, and so on' (2001: 167).

What do Widdowson and Pennycook have to offer the language teacher or the learner of English? This is unclear. What is one to make of an applied linguistics which demands of linguistics that it remain self-consciously detached from the real world? Pennycook, in moving beyond the Marxist concept of political emancipation, to embrace the possibilities of difference, looks to a concept of 'postcolonial performativity' to carry his argument forward. Performativity is intended to stress the classroom as a site of 'transformative critical work' rather than mere 'rational discussion' or 'critical awareness' (2001: 163):

> Narrative or memory work in pedagogy and research isn't just about telling stories but is about accounting for how our bodies and desires got here. This is why, in a critical applied linguistics class I taught in Melbourne a few years ago, we had to stop at a certain point in our discussions of CDA, of language politics, of different sorts of feminist pedagogy, of multiliteracies and we had to tell our stories, relate our own discursive and corporeal critical histories, recreate how it was that we came to be and see ourselves as critical. This, therefore is another crucial element of engagement: As we work to engage critically, poetically, historically, hermeneutically, and narratively . . . we need to find ways of engaging with lives, bodies, and desires.

But suppose as a student I feel less than enthusiastic about sharing my bodily history with the teacher, does that mean that I am denied access to an understanding of the politics of language standards? Are political conservatives not allowed to be language teachers?

The fundamental issue is one of authority, or 'ownership'. Modern linguistics understands its scientific task as self-consciously distinct from, and superior to, normative grammar. Whereas in normative grammar, authority resides in the grammarian, or a tradition, or in a particular examination procedure, in modern linguistics the arbiter of grammaticality was the 'native speaker'. The irony was that the self-avowedly scientific, rationalist-objectivist generative movement was grounded in the Romantic-organicist concept of native speaker. What was never clear was how it could be scientifically determined to which language the data (the example sentences which were put before the informant) belonged. Ideally, the informant would be one uncorrupted by knowledge of normative grammatical categories and traditional precepts. The attempt to build a universal, context-free science of language was built on the organicist assumptions of Romantic identity theory.

The concept of native speaker has been widely critiqued in applied linguistics, and this reflects the problem of authority for the nonnative speaker or learner of English. One way around this problem was simply to declare that English was no longer the property of its native speakers, and to affirm the rights of ownership of all its global users. The problem was that nobody really believed this—least of all the end user, the nonempowered teacher of English in a Hong Kong secondary school. The paradoxical politics of this was to affirm that English was the exception, i.e. that all other languages belonged to their native speakers. The Romantic concept of native speaker was actually strengthened, in that the case of English was an example of *ad hoc* political adjustment to a situation which could not otherwise be reconciled with the Herder-Humboldt ideal of a world linguistic ecology of mother tongues. The assumption was that native speakers of English had some kind of privileged access to Standard English, reflecting the conflation of speech and writing which is implicit in the political use of the native-speaker model. Ironically, concern with standard English, both as an attempt to develop a standard and from a politically critical standpoint, has been as much a concern of those located at the edge of the expansion as of those at its imagined centre. Thus, to give a few examples, Swift was an Irish Protestant, Murray was a Scot, Kachru, an Indian from Kashmir; English studies developed in northern Europe (Otto Jespersen) and in the British empire as much as in the United Kingdom. It was a German philologist, Jacob Grimm, who made an early prediction of the global rise of English (Grimm 1852).

A Romantic native-speaker model from northern Europe has been generalized as the universal, panchronic natural state of affairs. We should note that in Islam the language of primary identity, the so-called classical Arabic of the Qu'ran, is not conceptualized as a mother tongue. Nor was the concept part of the worldview of the Chinese literati who dealt with a written form which was not conceptualized as deriving its legitimacy from authentic speech. These traditional language ecologies are open to the objection that they were grounded in elite knowledges and rote learning: the Romantic theory incorporates a substantial element of Protestant politics of linguistic transparency. But a modern or even postmodern politics of language can I believe make use of these alternative formations in thinking more productively about global English. Nor should rote learning be dismissed out of hand—as memorization can be empowering.

Like the various critics of Standard English, integrationism, in asserting its lay-centred or lay-oriented nature, offers a potential starting point for an understanding of the politics of authority and ownership in relation to issues of language standards. One promising avenue is the possibility of new forms of reference materials, grounded in an integrationist critique of the dictionary and the reference grammar. New possibilities are being opened up by the rise of the World Wide Web and of increasingly sophisticated corpus-based reference tools. The World Wide Web is in effect a gigantic corpus and all kinds of users can look to it for information, not as a replacement authority over usage but as access to linguistic experience, including all kinds of metalinguistic discussion and information. The question of authority remains, but it is devolved substantially onto the user. If the user is a homophobic, racist, sexist believer in the one true Standard English and the need to restore a golden age, that person needs to make judgments about the kinds of sites or authorities he is going to access and emulate. If the user is a Japanese punk rocker, then different concerns arise.

This is not to idealize the Web as an ideal space of universal equal access—not everybody has access to computers, literacy, and so on. Nevertheless the Google string search seems to me a powerful tool for integrational linguistic analysis and for the language learner—precisely because the 'English' that is the English language on the Web is unbounded and undefined. Issues of standardization are played out in the mechanism of the search itself—this is a reflexive process, without a determinate end point. I have observed that creative-writing courses offered in my department, at least for some students, create a different attitude to writing in English, since there is a need to confront style and word choice and grammar as a personal issue, for which one must take responsibility and which must also address the issue of an audience. The problem with much student writing is that the only imagined addressee is the teacher, who is assumed to be already possessed of the ideal form of the knowledge that the student is seeking to impart. My concluding thoughts are that while we may not be able to derive a new method of language teaching from integrational premises, integrationism can point to new language technologies as powerful illustrations of what it is saying about everyday mundane human interaction; and integrationism helps us historicize and relativize the 'native-speaker' model of language ownership, which underlies many of the more pernicious assumptions of linguistic ideologies in the Western tradition.

REFERENCES

Batchelor, John (2004). 'Shaky grasp of the basics'. *English Association Newsletter*, no. 175, Spring 2004, p. 7.

Bex, Tony and Richard J. Watts (1999). *Standard English: The widening debate*. London: Routledge.

Crowley, Tony (1987). Description or prescription? An analysis of the term 'Standard English' in the work of two twentieth-century linguists. *Language and Communication*, 7: 199–220.

Davis, Hayley (1999). Typography, lexicography and 'Standard English'. In eds. Tony Bex & Richard J. Watts, *Standard English: The widening debate*. London: Routledge, pp. 69–88.

Erling, Elizabeth J. (2002). 'I learn English since ten years': The global English debate and the German university classroom. *English Today*, 70, 18(2): 8–13.

Grimm, Jacob (1852). Über den Ursprung der Sprache. *Abhandlungen der Königlichen Akademie der Wissenschaften zu Berlin aus dem Jahre 1851*. Berlin.
Harris, Roy (1988). Murray, Moore and the myth. In *Linguistic thought in England 1914–1945*. London: Duckworth, pp. 1–26.
Harris, Roy (1989). 'The worst English in the world?' Supplement to the *Hong Kong University Gazette*, 36(1): 37–46.
Harris, Roy (2006). English: How not to teach it. *Integrationist notes and papers 2003–2005*, No. 2. Devon, UK: Tree Tongue Press.
Macaulay, Thomas B. (2001). Minute on education in India. In Antoinette Burton (ed.), *Politics and empire in Victorian Britain: A reader*, pp. 18–20. New York: Palgrave. Minute dated February 2, 1835.
McKay, Sandra Lee (2202). *Teaching English as an international language*. Oxford: Oxford University Press.
Pennycook, Alastair (2001). *Critical Applied Linguistics: A Critical Introduction*. Mahwah, NJ: Lawrence Earlbaum.
Phillipson, Robert (1992). *Linguistic imperialism*. Oxford: Oxford University Press.
Quirk, Randolph (1985). The English language in a global context. In R. Quirk & H. Widdowson (eds.), *English in the world*. Cambridge: CUP.
Trudgill, Peter (1999). Standard English: What it isn't. In eds. Tony Bex & Richard J. Watts, *Standard English: The widening debate*. London: Routledge, pp. 117–128.
Watts, Richard J. (1999). The social construction of standard English: Grammar writers as a 'discourse community'. In eds. Tony Bex & Richard J. Watts, *Standard English: The widening debate*. London: Routledge, pp. 40–68.
Widdowson, Henry (2003). *Defining issues in English language teaching*. Oxford: Oxford University Press.

5 Integrationism, New Media Art and Learning to Read Arabic

Sally Pryor

The foundation of the work discussed here is provided by my own experience of informally learning some written and spoken Arabic. I applied this experience to the creative production of two innovative new media artworks: *Postcard From Tunis* (Pryor, 1997) and *Postcards From Writing* (Pryor, 2004). The artworks express an integrationist theory of communication, language and writing while also extending the theory into new media, in this case, interactive multimedia. The artworks creatively demonstrate that dynamic, multidimensional and reflexive signs can be created through human-computer interaction, particularly rollover interaction. These signs combine auditory, pictorial and scriptorial forms of communication and have great potential for language teaching and learning activities, particularly those involving reading new scripts.

Figure 5.1. Still from *Postcard From Tunis*; the white asterisk indicates the location of Tunis.

AN ACCIDENTAL INTEGRATIONIST

I learned Arabic informally when I lived in Tunis, the capital of Tunisia. English is only the third language of the country, and I spent most of my time in the home of the Kousri family, where it was not spoken at all. Most members of the family spoke the country's second language, French, but at home this was used only in order to talk to me. Thus, almost all of the time I lived in an environment of Tunisian Arabic, which I barely understood. I did a lot of watching and listening and I began to learn this language informally, appearing to the family to be a sweet girl who was not very bright and, more distressingly, had no sense of humour. However, this immersive language learning experience was as fascinating as it was humbling. I am very grateful for the generosity, kindness and patience I encountered in Tunis; I gained a great deal from the experience. Of interest here is the valuable opportunity it gave me to explore communication and language learning in real life and from first principles. In particular, I was able to study language learning without framing it within the formal apparatus of a structured teaching environment and a conventional view of a language as a code. I arrived in Tunis as a new media artist, not a linguist, but these language experiences ultimately turned me into an integrationist, especially, as will be described below, when I searched for ways to express them artistically in interactive multimedia form.

At the risk of losing clarity by mixing metaphors, I have to say that issues of communication and language hit me between the eyes in Tunis. I'd never really thought deeply about them while living in English-speaking countries. But here, the outsider's perspective opened my eyes. Initially my perceptions were at a nonverbal level, that is, I understood things that I could not express verbally, especially as someone who is more a visual artist than a writer. Actually articulating this new understanding in words was a slow process and first involved the creation of an interactive new media artwork.

A number of aspects of communication had become clear to me in Tunis. Firstly, verbal and nonverbal activities are not separate from each other: spoken languages do not exist in isolation from other forms of communication. Secondly, one can communicate quite well at times with nonvocal forms, for example, facial expressions, gestures, touch, body orientation, gifts, and so on. As an example, I had to change the way that I expressed my sense of humor, changing from quick wordplay to pantomime. And thirdly, I began to notice the crucial importance to communication of both time and context.

In terms of spoken language learning, the following story is typical:

> Najiba Kousri, the mother of the family, is at home, seated at a table in the dining room and in front of a bowl of food. I know that she doesn't speak French or English.

> She says to me: [attinimralfa] [my phonetic transcription] and looks meaningfully at the kitchen.
> I have heard the first part of this sound, i.e. [attini], before. Through observing previous activities in daily life, I guess that she means something similar to "give me ..." or "get me ...".
> I think that she would eat her meal if some practical problem wasn't making her hesitate. I guess that she wants some cutlery in order to eat the thick stew.
> I go to the kitchen, and I pick up a fork and look at her inquiringly.
> She shakes her head at me and says: [attinimralfa].
> I pick up a spoon and look at her.
> She nods and smiles.
> I bring it over to her.
> She scoops some food.
> I am pleased, believing that I have done something useful. I am very fond of her and look for ways to be helpful.
> This successful activity gives me a great sense of achievement, which also recalls dimly remembered childhood experiences.

Naturally the story described previously would not be sufficient to teach me to confidently handle such requests for spoons. A certain amount of repetition and variation would be required. However, there are useful observations that can be made on examination of the story. Firstly, let us look at it from the perspective of a conventional view of communication. This is one that explicitly or implicitly assumes

- a sender-receiver model of human communication,
- a fixed code view of language, and
- the centrality of speech to any understanding of language and communication.

In this view, the story above simply describes me learning a code, which would be something like:

[mralfa] = *spoon*

This interpretation makes many assumptions. An obvious one is that Tunisian spoons have the same cultural meanings as do the spoons that English speakers are familiar with. A less obvious assumption is that the English word *spoon* has a fixed meaning itself and represents the 'mental idea of a spoon' (whatever this may be). Thus, in a conventional view of language, the code I learned could be expressed more fully as:

Form = spoken word [mralfa]
Content = 'mental idea of a spoon'.

Thus, from this point of view, I could confidently communicate about spoons in Tunis by saying [mralfa].

An integrationist perspective is quite different. The basic idea is that human communication is designed to integrate past, present and future activities, with time providing the main axis along which these activities are integrated. Of central importance are the claims that communication is itself an integration of activities, rather than something that is additional to those activities and that, as Harris describes it, "the product of that integration as well as its enabling mechanism is the sign" (Harris, 1995, p. 5). As a result, it is not possible to separate an integrationist sign from the context in which it is created; that is, there is no abstract invariant form or meaning of the sign that is separate from *actual* episodes of communication. In other words, there is no code; there is only what Harris has called the sign-in context, "an integration in which sign and context reciprocally and uniquely define each other" (Harris, 1998b, p.124). This is true whether the sign is verbal or nonverbal; therefore, there are no abstract invariant meanings in spoken language either. Thus, in the integrationist view, a linguistic sign is something that is created by an integration of activities, rather than a code that is invoked *in addition* to those activities. And, there are no fixed boundaries between language and nonlanguage, either for the language learner or for anyone else.

Integrationism can be extremely difficult to understand and I have certainly found this to be true. Part of the problem is that merely reading the word *sign* evokes cultural associations with a named thing or atomic unit and an implicit division into a distinct and specifiable form and a distinct and specifiable content. Integrationism requires a paradigm shift in our thinking, such that we challenge the (pervasive) idea that the form of a sign (for example a [mralfa] in the preceding example) has a fixed content. Instead, we understand that it cannot mean anything at all *except* when integrated in a communicative context. Meaning resides in temporal relationships, rather than in (labelled) atomic units. As I understand it, an integrationist sign resembles a momentary set of active connections that integrate activities together across time and space. It may occupy one point in time and space but it is also utterly and contextually linked to what came before, what is and what comes next. As George Wolf explains, "the integrational sign integrates in two senses, 'passive' and 'active': (i) it itself is an integral part of the communicational context, and (ii) it brings aspects of the communicational context together" (Wolf, 1999, p. 27). Crucially, the integrationist sign cannot be separated into form and content at all. We may think we can separate signs like this. However, as Toolan points out,

> Interactants, for their own purposes, can do this [conceive of particular signs as comprising a specifiable form and content], and even agree with each other about such 'separations'. A might on some occasion say "You just made that hand gesture at me and you meant 'whatever'

didn't you?" and B might on that occasion reply "Well, yes, I suppose I did." But these contextualized determinations, that particular bits of verbal or non-verbal material are a 'form' with a particular 'meaning', are occasion-specific; they cannot be generalized and set down in a codebook or grammar or dictionary that can serve as guide for all occasions and through shifts of time (Toolan, personal communication).

Several aspects of my [mralfa] story clearly reflect an integrationist point of view. Firstly, it is immediately obvious that language does not exist in isolation from communication and that there can be no language without communication. The story supports the integrationist contention that communication 'comes first' or guides language, not the other way around: Najiba might well have succeeded in getting me to bring her a spoon by means of pointing to the kitchen and gesturing with a scooping motion. The story also supports Harris's observation that "in face-to-face communication vocalization is only one component in an integrated series of activities which include gesture, gaze, facial expression, and bodily posture" (Harris, 1998a, p. 12). It also seems clear that language learning involves successfully integrating activities within a context, and for the language learner there are no fixed boundaries between language and nonlanguage: the boundary shifts from moment to moment.

How might an integrationist explain what I was learning in the preceding story? What was happening as I apparently learned the spoken word [mralfa]? I was learning a language but, from an integrationist viewpoint, I wasn't learning one element in a fixed-code vocabulary made up of (suspiciously) neat pairs. Instead of learning a code, I was learning to make contextualised connections between activities (speaking, listening, fetching, and so on). I was narrowing down a range of possibilities by excluding irrelevant ones. I was learning local patterns of behaviour, that is, relationships. The meaning of a sign involving [mralfa] would always be created anew. As an obvious example, for me the meaning of the second auditory sign involving [mralfa] was not identical to the first, despite the fact that it sounded similar, because the second sign was influenced by the activities previously integrated by the first. I certainly would not have picked up the fork twice. This 'newness' of a sign involving [mralfa] would always be the case, even after I apparently 'knew' the word as evidenced by successful integration of activities. Harris explains it this way:

> All words begin, in our experience, as words of "unknown meaning" ... "meaning" is the value we seek to attribute to words so as to make some kind of sense of this or that episode of communication in which they feature ... our search for the "meaning" stops when we have discovered how to integrate the occurrence of the word into enough of our linguistic experience to satisfy the requirement of the case ... [and] our search for "meaning" is articulated to a large extent metalinguistically (by asking questions, consulting dictionaries, etc.), i.e. is essentially dependent on the reflexivity of language" (Harris, 1998a, pp. 69–70).

Integrationism, New Media Art and Learning to Read Arabic 109

In this case I didn't ask a question or consult a dictionary, but I think that Najiba understood that my inquiring look integrated with my fork presentation signified something like "Is this fork what you want?" Of my description, Toolan has remarked (personal communication):

> We don't have much of an explanation of how Najiba understood you and vice versa. It helps that your guess (the fork) was a pretty good one: you didn't go into the other room and turn on the cooker, for example, or open a window, or bring back a tea-towel. Integrated sign-interpreting perhaps relies on a general principle of mutual focussing of attention.

It is also quite possible that I actually did do some of these things on even earlier occasions and shame has made me forget them!

Thus, the meanings of any sign involving [mralfa] is the contextualized integration of communicative activities that the sign makes possible, which may or may not involve actual spoons. These activities occur in time and space and in specific contexts that have various macrosocial characteristics. The meaning is influenced, but not fully described, by macrosocial conventions, such as vocabularies of the Tunisian Arabic language. To return to the apparently banal English word *spoon*, we need to distinguish the spoon itself, that is, the object that sits as a tool in the cutlery drawer waiting to be brought out and used, from the meaning of a word *spoon*, which has no such qualities. However, further discussion of this issue is beyond the scope of this paper and the reader is referred initially to Toolan, 1996, and Harris, 1998a.

POSTCARD FROM TUNIS

Despite my evolving integrationist understanding of language and communication, I continued to have trouble eradicating the pervasive concept that learning a language involves learning a code until I began actually creating the interactive multimedia expression of my language-learning experiences. Back in Australia and within the ease of my mother tongue, I sought to artistically express them in a form that offered similar experiences to users. The process of actually conceiving, designing and creating an interactive CD-ROM made me think very practically—not just theoretically—about what a successful method of language learning and teaching must require. It was then that the validity of the integrationist view became clearer. Once stripped of the metalinguistic apparatus of a formal language lesson, it was obviously impossible to create, for example, an expression of the apparently neat form + content pair discussed earlier: how to directly connect an auditory sound [mralfa] with the user's mental idea of a spoon. It was impossible. I could only make it possible for the user to create a relationship by integrating the activities of listening to a sound [mralfa] and looking at a *picture* of a spoon, which is not the same thing at all. More generally, then, rather than presenting apparently fixed linguistic meanings, it was only possible to offer relative relationships created by the integration of activities within specific contexts.

After a great deal of experimentation and programming, the result was a personal CD-ROM portrait of Tunis, *Postcard From Tunis*, a work that introduces users to the sounds and written forms of some elementary Tunisian Arabic words. *Postcard* is presented as a series of linked postcards, each with its own background soundtrack. As a user traverses these postcards by moving and clicking the mouse, s/he creates a unique audiovisual combination of images, writing and sounds, much of which was actually recorded in Tunis. The work is multidimensional, combining graphics, photographs, animation, spoken and written words, sound recordings and music. There is almost no spoken or written English and very little French, which reflects my own experience. The work is also interactive: there are multiple hyperlinked pathways through the material. However, its unique quality is the extensive use of rollovers. A rollover is the activity that occurs when the user moves the mouse (without clicking it), resulting in the on-screen movement of the user cursor and a variety of audiovisual responses. The unique rollover design of this artwork enables a gestural and immersive experience for users, who, as they explore the artwork, create in real time a collage (layered in space) and montage (juxtaposed in time) of images, sounds and texts. Thus, the uniqueness of the communicational signs in *Postcard From Tunis* comes from the combination of

- an integrational approach to language, writing and language learning
- multidimensional sounds, visuals and scripts; and
- human-computer interaction activities that develop the communicational potential of the rollover.

The creation of this artwork formed a research method. The result was the development of dynamic and multidimensional signs having great potential for language teaching and learning. As will be explained next, these include written Arabic signs that indicate in writing, but not in words, how the user is to read them. The artwork demonstrates the powerful communicational possibilities of the dynamically reflexive and multidimensional signs (pictorial, scriptorial and auditory) that can be created in new media by the integration of human-computer interaction activities. Moreover, these signs cannot adequately be theorised *without* an integrationist semiology

INVESTIGATING WRITING

It is extremely difficult to think clearly about reading and writing when we live in cultures that place so much social, political and cultural importance on written words. Thus, we tend to make barely perceptible assumptions about the separation of writing from pictures and to conflate the term *writing* with *written words*. Harris's integrationist theory of writing provides a vigorous solution that manages to clearly tease writing apart from the transcription of speech, which is just one of writing's possible uses. Instead, writing is (re)aligned with spatial configurations in general (Harris, 1995). *Postcard From Tunis* presents an integrationist exploration of writing and its possible transformations at the human-computer interface. Pictures are not dominated by writing, as is so often the case in language learning and elsewhere, but instead the two are treated as complementary facets of one integrated form of communication, that is, spatial communication.

Postcard is a playful, affectionate, interactive and audiovisual portrait of Tunis with writing as one major theme. The artwork has an interwoven vocabulary of eight Tunisian Arabic words. These reflect the themes of the portrait and are interleaved as various combinations of visual and auditory forms of communication, rarely linked to English or French. The artwork is designed so that, just as during an actual visit to Tunis, a user might learn a few spoken words and, possibly, learn to read them in Arabic. As the user moves through the work, rollover activities mean that s/he is repeatedly and unintentionally exposed to the words in various contexts. The aesthetic of the artwork is one of exploration, repetition and the pleasure of informal language learning, expressed as the gradual building of connections through integration of activities.

The communicational space of *Postcard From Tunis* is made up of a number of differently structured spaces. A simple space is presented in a number of screens, one for each featured word, in which there is a moving cursor that is not controlled by the user. This cursor continually traces written Arabic words from right to left, starting from the far right-hand side, as shown in a static form in Figure 5.2.

Harris points out that once a written sign has actually been formed, it is a static sign and gives no indication of the kinetic process of its formation. Thus, simply looking at a written Arabic sign will not tell a non-Arabic-literate reader the order of its formation. In *Postcard,* however, this moving screen cursor gives a clue: in integrationist terms it traces (and exposes) the order of formation of the static written sign. Here, the combination of the kinetic cursor and the static written sign creates a new kind of kinetic written sign in which the formation *can* be reprocessed. This may seem a small point but it is significant because a fundamental aspect of the written sign has been transformed. This new written sign tells the reader how to start processing it, that is, where to start scanning and in what direction, and it does so without using words.

باب

Figure 5.2. The moving screen cursor in *Postcard From Tunis.*

112 *Sally Pryor*

Other significant types of communication spaces in *Postcard* are provided by rollover activities. There are a number of active sites within the screens such that when the user rolls over one of them the following generic responses are integrated:

- the graphic (image or text) changes visually in some way, for example, a written form changes colour or/and a picture transforms;
- audio plays, for instance, a spoken Arabic word;
- the background sound track level drops; and
- the cursor changes to indicate whether this location is also clickable.

This rollover functionality is very powerful. Neumark notes that "[w]hen sound and image suddenly meet at the moment of the user's interaction, users can experience an intimate engagement and pleasure distinctive to CD-ROM" (Neumark, 2000, p. 4). Each screen has its own background sound composition, so a user's rollover movements also generate a unique soundtrack made up of these rollover responses montaged and collaged together and layered over the background composition.

In this artwork, speech is decentered from its usual dominant position: an auditory sign plays only when the user rolls over a picture or script. For example, rollover on graphic forms similar to those in Figure 5.3 would transform them visually and trigger the sound [felooka; my phonetics], which also creates a meaningful link between them.

The image in the left-hand panel is a (simple) picture of a boat. The image in the right-hand panel is a written Arabic word, similar to *boat/ yacht*. The user's cursor rolling over both images triggers a [felooka] sound and creates a relationship between them.

The generic rollover routine described previously also varies, so that the four components (graphics, audio, background audio adjustment, and cursor changes) are sometimes joined by other responses. In these communication spaces, additional graphic forms also appear on rollover. It is here that dynamically reflexive written signs are created that indicate in writing, but not in words, how the user is to read them. An example of such screens is illustrated in static form in Figure 5.4. Upon entering the screen, the entire written word highlights at the same time as the related spoken word (a [felooka]) plays. Then, one at a time and moving right to left, individual alphabetic letters (or combinations made up of a consonant joined with a

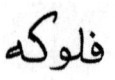

فلوكه

Figure 5.3. An example of graphic forms in *Postcard From Tunis* that trigger the same sound through rollover interaction.

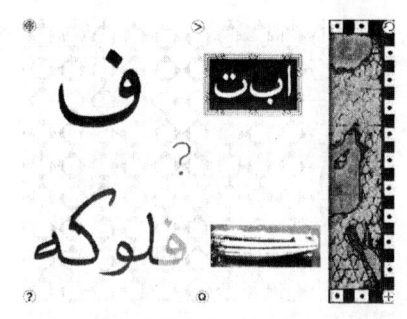

Figure 5.4. Still from *Postcard From Tunis* showing a screen containing dynamically reflexive written signs.

long vowel) are visually highlighted (and hence separated from the written word) and the integrated pronunciation is heard. At the same time, any vowel marks are displayed and the equivalent individual alphabetic letter(s) appear(s) above the written word. After this sequence has played, a similar set of activities is integrated whenever a user rolls over any part of the written word, thus creating a dynamically reflexive written sign that indicates how to read it. In the example illustrated next, rollover activity on the far right side of the written Arabic word is integrated with seeing that portion of the word highlight and hearing a sound [fff, my phonetics] begin to play. At the same time, a graphic sign appears immediately above it, which is the corresponding alphabetic letter, *Faa*. Subsequent rollover activity on the alphabetic letter is integrated with the spoken name of the letter and a mouse click would take the user to a postcard containing an interactive Arabic alphabet.

These dynamically reflexive written signs take advantage of the wider range of communicative possibilities in interactive multimedia systems. They are *Postcard*'s primary achievement in terms of language-learning activities. They also provide a material example of the fundamental spatiality of writing. Even though the Arabic script is integrated with speech communication, this new form of writing tells the user how to read it by using writing, but not words.

Harris's view of writing involving nonkinetic spatial configurations integrating biomechanically diverse activities is more apparent when encountering a previously unknown form of writing. When one cannot read a script, it becomes much clearer that writing is strongly linked to pictures and involved in graphical relationships. *Postcard* offers this experience to non-Arabic-literate users via a form of writing that they cannot read. For such a user, the script may initially appear to be uninterpretable graphic squiggles or curvy lines. As this user continues to interact with *Postcard*, s/he begins to make links between these "squiggles" and auditory and pictorial forms. Mouse-clicking the increasingly familiar and meaningful "squiggles" eventually takes the user to screens containing the dynamically reflexive signs described earlier that indicate how to correlate portions of these "squiggles" with speech sounds and letters of the Arabic alphabet. Thus, as the user interacts with the artwork, the perception of what is writing and what is not is continually affected by previous and subsequent activities. This perception will differ for the same user from moment to moment (as well as from user to user), illustrating the integrationist claim that there are no fixed boundaries between writing and pictures.

The traditional approach to communication assumes that signs in general behave like spoken words, as the paradigmatic form of linguistic sign. Because we cannot speak two words at the same time, it tends to be assumed that we cannot ever invoke or process two signs at the same time, but must concatenate them one after the other, as in speech. Thus, a dualist notion of the sign (one form and one content at a time) cannot describe or explain the kinds of multidimensional rollover signs described previously. What is the form? What is the content? How can these be separated and how can you isolate such a sign in time and space? In contrast, the integrationist sign allows us to describe what *Postcard* shows can actually be created through rollover activities at the human-computer interface, that is:

- combinations of static written signs and kinetic screen cursors,
- combinations of kinetic auditory and static scriptorial signs, or
- the dynamically reflexive written sign described earlier.

In fact *Postcard* uniquely supports integrationist theory because it demonstrates, in a way that cannot easily be done with words on paper, the idea that meaning is created through the integration of activities. Most of these signs can only be created through the integration of rollover activities; there is simply no way that they can be considered to be signs already created and ready in advance of an actual, material episode of communication. In fact, the business of 'making' a sign (triggering the speech segment and/or seeing the graphic form) by moving the mouse over a particular image or symbol on the screen is emblematic of the actual fusion of signification and signal in the use of signs. The sign isn't fully there (isn't sounded and/or seen) until you move the mouse appropriately, and the sounding is wedded to the image or text, one 'on top' of the other like Saussure's two sides of a single piece of paper.[1]

LANGUAGE LEARNING IN REAL LIFE

Formal language-learning activities can have limited relevance to real life. As Michael Toolan observed, "one of the things everyone recognizes is the strange gulf between language instruction on how to cope 'at the railway station' in a book or on a course, and experiencing 'the real thing,' as when one is stuck in Madrid-Chamartin railway station, scratching around with one's twenty words of Spanish, trying to get to Salamanca. Or indeed in Najiba's kitchen. The former processes are obviously artificial, inauthentic . . ." (Toolan, personal communication, 2006). Why is this so? As an integrationist, I must answer that compared to formal instruction, different activities are contextually integrated by linguistic signs in real life. Here we might also recall a familiar integrationist maxim: linguistic signs do not have abstract invariant meanings that can be separated from the contexts where they are created; they are not 'plug and play' units. Toolan also observed that another important difference in formal instruction might be the relative importance given to vocal signs compared to other (integrated) signs of communication. Integrationism reminds us that speech is not always of central importance in communication, and perhaps that is what one experiences in real life. My experience certainly supports this suggestion. I vividly recall straining my brain to the limit in order to take in, integrate and make sense of all that was going on in any episode of communication. On reflection, is this really so different from communication in one's mother tongue? An integrationist would answer that it is not.

Can language learning in the digital world get away from this problem of inauthenticity in formal language learning, or does it just draw on more modalities to mitigate the artificiality? I would argue that despite the opportunities offered by a wider range of forms of communication, success depends on the assumptions built into the design of the digital system itself. To take just one example, *Free Light Arabic* offers users pictures to click. A mouse-click on a picture leads to hearing a corresponding spoken Arabic word and seeing a written Arabic form. This activity implicitly presents both a coded and conventional view of language and an artificial encounter with it. In a sense, speech is presented here as the dominant modality, as the label of the picture. There is also an artificially structured and controlled quality inherent in the user's choice to select a specific graphic location on the screen, move the cursor over it and click the mouse.

My rollover solutions do not completely solve these problems; however, they do move things forward. In my artwork, the user simply moves the screen cursor in any manner over the screen, which initiates the range of rollover events previously described. For the user, this makes the interaction seem exploratory, open to chance and unexpected or random events, somewhat closer to real life. The interaction is multidimensional and involves making connections and noticing patterns, rather than learning codes. It is clearer that signs are something we *create*, rather than tools that we use. Verbal and nonverbal forms of communication are of equal importance here and are integrated with rather than isolated from

Figure 5.5 Still from *Postcard From Tunis*.

each other. Thus, speech is decentered from its usual dominant position and the model of communication expressed is integrationist rather than coded. These characteristics reflect my own experience of language learning, and extend it into a similar experience of the written sign. In fact, I made a system that would help me to learn to read Arabic myself. I took advantage of the potential of interactive multimedia to create new forms of writing. I developed forms of writing that help you to read it, without using words, and I offer this experience to users.

MORE POSTCARDS

Postcard From Tunis is an internationally award-winning artwork that offers a prototype of an integrationist approach to learning spoken and written languages at the human-computer interface. It is also an integrationist exploration of writing and its possible transformations at the human-computer interface. It is contextualised within an expressive and personal portrait of Tunis and its ancient scripts and symbols. *Postcard* argues for the usefulness of a new approach to language learning that does not try to separate language into tools and their use in action. *Postcard* points out the many communicational and educational possibilities of the signs that can be created in new media and it demonstrates just a few of them. Pryor (2003) offers a more detailed analysis of these topics.

Integrationism can be rather difficult to understand when expressed as written words, especially as the theory challenges the central importance of words themselves in communication. *Postcard* offers non-Arabic-literate users an experience of the integrationist view of language and writing via a form of spoken language and writing it is assumed that they cannot understand. The artwork does not include any verbal explanations of integrationist theory itself. In contrast, my subsequent work *Postcards From Writing* (2004) uses the Roman script, which it is assumed users are quite familiar with, and it offers a great deal of verbal explanation in English. It then supplements these forms of communication with the kinds of multidimensional signs described earlier. Like *Postcard From Tunis*, the primary rationale behind *Postcards From Writing* is creative expression rather than instructional design. Thus, it offers a heuristic exploration of a quite difficult theory and an experience of it that is as interactive, kinaesthetic, and audiovisually pleasurable as possible.

The visual style of *Postcards* is also playful and features writing and drawing by young children, suggesting a reconsideration of conventions of literacy. The work is presented as an intellectual road movie, an interactive journey set in Tunis, Oxford, and Ballarat (Australia), during which I travel to Oxford to interview Professor Harris. The starting point is an investigation of the idea that the concept of *picture writing* might provide a way of thinking about writing within the human-computer interface, as some suggest (for example, Bolter, 2001). As a user moves through the artwork, it becomes clear that the concept of picture writing has a very weak foundation and is a meaningless and rather ethnocentric term. Instead, an integrationist theory is offered as an alternative way to think about writing at the human-computer interface.

Like *Postcard From Tunis*, *Postcards From Writing* is multidimensional, combining graphics, photographs, animation, spoken and written words, sound recordings, and music. Like *Postcard From Tunis,* the user creates a collage and montage of sounds and images, leaving graphic traces resulting from user activities. Like *Postcard From Tunis*, the work is interactive: there are multiple hyperlinked pathways through the material. And once again, the particular quality is the extensive use of creatively designed rollover activities. Through interacting with the work, users create a variety of different signs, which, like those in *Postcard From Tunis*, offer an *experience* of the integrationist view of writing, rather than simply information about it. Despite being expressed in a familiar script, the work again offers users an experience of the view of writing as spatial configurations and of no fixed boundaries existing between writing and pictures.

118 Sally Pryor

Figure 5.6. Still from *Postcards From Writing* where rollover activity differentiates a written sign from a written form.

WHY POSTCARDS?

Both these interactive artworks are presented as digital postcards because the postcard is a communicational space where writing and pictures have had a more equal relationship and because the writer's perspective is personal. The works are also postcards because the postcard reminds us that while the card itself may travel from sender to receiver, its meaning does not. Equally importantly, the works are postcards because, as an etiquette tip in 1900 pointed out, "a little card will suggest what we cannot put into words" (Meadows, 1900, cited in Carline, 1971). In other words, as an interactive artist I find that words can often be a clumsy means of expression for me, and I'm sure many musicians, for example, would agree. I urge readers of this chapter to also explore my artworks themselves, in addition to reading what I have to say about them.

I would like to gratefully acknowledge the assistance from Michael Toolan and Roy Harris with this paper.

NOTES

1. I am indebted to Michael Toolan for this observation.

REFERENCES

Bolter, J. (2001). *Writing Space: The Computer, Hypertext, and the Remediation of Print*, second edition. Mahwah, NJ: Lawrence Erlbaum Associates.
Carline, R. (1971). *Pictures in the Post*. London: Gordon Fraser.
Free Light Arabic. Free Light Software, 3, rue des Primeveres. 91380 Chilly-Mazarin, France.
Harris, R. (1995). *Signs of Writing*. London: Routledge.
Harris, R. (1998a). *Introduction to Integrational Linguistics*. Oxford: Pergamon.
Harris, R (1998b). 'Three Models of Signification'. In Harris and Wolf (Eds.), *Integrational Linguistics: A First Reader*. Oxford: Pergamon.
Neumark, N. (2000). 'Making Contact with Artful CD-ROMs'. *IEEE Multimedia*, Jan-Mar 2000, Volume 7, Issue 1 (4–6).
Pryor, S. (1997). *Postcard From Tunis*, demo and order information at http://www.sallypryor.com/tunis.html.
Pryor, S. (2003). *Extending Integrationist Theory through the Creation and Analysis of a Multimedia Work of Art, Postcard From Tunis*. Unpublished doctoral thesis, University of Western Sydney, available at http://www.sallypryor.com/thesis.html.
Pryor, S. (2004). *Postcards From Writing*, full copy at http://www.sallypryor.postcards.html.
Toolan, M. (1996). *Total Speech. An Integrational Linguistic Approach to Language*. Durham, NC: Duke University Press.
Wolf, G. (1999). 'Quine and the Segregational Sign'. In Wolf (Ed.), *Language & Communication, 'Integrational Linguistics in the Context of 20th-Century Theories of Language'*, Vol. 19, No.1.

6 Teaching a Foreign Language
A Tentative Enterprise
Edda Weigand

THE INTEGRATIONAL CHALLENGE

Having finally arrived at a point in the history of science where we feel strong enough to face complexity, we recognize that *integration* is an inherent feature of it—be it the complexity of the external world or of the inner world of human beings. Cosmology has to tackle this problem as well as neurology, economics as well as linguistics. There is no simple starting point; on the contrary, already the presumed simple—be it neurons or quarks—turns out to be a complex integrated phenomenon (Weigand 2002a). Whereas for more than two thousand years not only modern linguistics but Western thinking in general shied away from addressing the complex and restricted itself to compositional models (Harris 2002), in recent times we can observe something like the opposite, namely, a 'flight from science and reason' (Gross et al. 1996) towards a search for a *new extended way of addressing the integrational complex*.

In this sense, we feel strong enough to relate integrational linguistics to teaching, an endeavour which multiplies the complexities of language by the complexities of an activity called teaching whose nature is still rather arcane. In the first instance, teaching can be grasped as a communicative activity which is carried out by an expert and which aims at enabling other human beings to achieve new or more proficient skills. It becomes immediately obvious that such an attempt to change human skills will be a highly complex process which is dependent on a multitude of variables, general and individual ones. Purely listing such variables in a compositional schema can only be a first heuristic step. What is needed is to see how these variables are integrationally connected in the process of teaching a foreign language.

After this still totally provisional approximation to a complex issue, we will first take a brief look at the current state of research on language teaching and learning before trying to make a fresh start in addressing the activity of teaching and its relationship to foreign languages.

SOME REMARKS ON THE STATE OF THE ART

In applied linguistics there is a vast literature on language teaching and learning which amounts to a rather confusing *puzzle of multiple aspects*. An underlying understanding of the whole is, however, missing. *With respect to teaching*, the issues relate to the goal of teaching and to how teaching and learning are conceived. Usually teaching is considered to be informing, the transmitting of knowledge (Gass and Selinker 2001: 2, 12). Even Coulthard (1977: 101), in the first edition of 'Discourse Analysis', describes teaching as *informing and instructing*, while in the second edition (1985²) he no longer touches on this precise point. Certainly, teaching is something like instructing but this tautology is of little help in understanding the phenomenon. On the other hand, teaching has to do with informing, but nevertheless teaching and informing have two basically different goals.

With respect to the process of *teaching and learning*, we are confronted with the concept of so-called *interlanguages* (e.g., Gass and Selinker 2001: 12). Everybody knows that language learning advances from simple to more complicated and varied structures and is inevitably accompanied by making mistakes. If these mistakes fossilize and hinder or even stop the learning process, this will certainly raise a serious problem, but I would doubt whether it can be avoided or overcome by experimentally documenting different levels of 'interlanguage'. For applied linguists, however, the point about interlanguages is that they may tell us something about how learners learn and indicate whether some kind of language acquisition process is taking place, which may be universal and may also apply to foreign-language learners.

As far as I see there is only one type of approach to *learning* that can claim to cope with the issue of integrated, mutually dependent variables, namely, the *connectionist perspective on development*, described, for instance, by Elman and others (1996) in their book on 'Rethinking Innateness'. Integration means interaction. Change of abilities, according to this view, 'arises through the interaction of maturational factors, under genetic control, and the environment' (p. 1f.). Until recently this position, which goes back to classic developmentalists such as Piaget, has lacked a solid theoretical basis. Recent developments in the neurosciences and in computational modelling, however, suggest that a 'theory of emergent form may be within our grasp'.

With respect to language, the situation in applied linguistics is even worse. Again, a solid understanding of the phenomenon is lacking. But this does not seem to cause problems; on the contrary, it seems to be fostered by applied linguists because it offers the chance of creating and maintaining a new discipline. Thus, for instance, Widdowson (2003) puts forward a linguistic view of language as a sign system that is simply out-of-date. The language myth was unmasked more than twenty years ago. Moreover, he seems to assume that he has the authority to tell linguists what they have to do, e.g. (pp. 7 and 10f.):

> If linguistics could provide us with representations of experienced language, it would be of no interest whatever. Linguistic accounts of language only have point to the extent that they are detached from, and different from, the way language is experienced in the real world.
>
> To my mind, then, it is not within the brief of linguists to make useful theories. . . . So the linguist, qua linguist, is not in a position to judge what use might be made of linguistic theory and description. Their usefulness potential is for others to realize.

For such a distinction between theory and practical use, Widdowson refers to physics and the construction of the atom bomb and ignores the fact that this case is quite different from the relationship between linguistics and applied linguistics. The construction of the atom bomb did not change the laws of physics but was based on them. On the contrary, what Widdowson has in mind amounts to influencing and changing linguistic theory. He emphasizes the gap between theory and practice in order to attribute the goal of 'appropriation of linguistics for educational purposes' to applied linguistics. 'Appropriation', according to him, 'involves a process of mediation whereby the linguist's abstract version of reality is referred back to the actualities of the language classroom. And this essentially is what applied linguistics seeks to do' (p. 8). Rather than attempting any 'appropriation of the language myth', we abandoned the myth a long time ago (Harris 1981), and with it appropriation or mediation.

Besides Widdowson's thesis of a self-determinating pan-syllabus of mediation, there are multiple other partial syllabuses for almost every linguistic type of approach, e.g., focusing on knowledge of rules and the human mind according to generative guidelines (Gass and Selinker 2001), or focusing on form versus meaning (Ellis 2001) according to the basic structuralistic dichotomy, or the lexical syllabus being based on different lexical models (e.g., Lewis 1993, Sinclair 1998). Communicative aspects are mostly dealt with separately and added to the grammatical syllabus, e.g., by Gumperz (1996), who focuses on the sociocultural context. A new perspective is offered by the use of corpora in language teaching (e.g., Sinclair 2004).

A few researchers are aware of the fact that language-in-use or dialogic interaction does not result from an addition of sign system and communicative factors but represents an integrated whole. Consequently, a teaching syllabus has to start from a communicative or dialogic basis (e.g., Lorenzen and Taborn 1983). In this respect, 'communicative grammars' or 'grammars-in-use' can be considered a promising step though they often lack a consistent theoretical basis and focus on single expressions such as modal verbs (e.g., Murphy 1994, and Leech and Svartvik 1975; cf. also Weigand

2003²). Wilkins' notional syllabus (1977), however, is an outstanding exception with a solid speech act theoretical basis.

The most confusing features of the current state of research in applied linguistics are, on the one hand, the arbitrariness of the puzzle and, on the other hand, the complacent claim of applied linguists that they know better than linguists what linguistics is about. Instead of relegating linguistics to the abstract field of artificial theory and creating a new discipline of mediation between theory and practice, reflection on the nature of the phenomena language and teaching are required. What we need are not polemical remarks but interdisciplinary cooperation on the basis of a solid linguistic theory of language use which starts from the nature of the phenomenon and is applicable to practice. It is only the nature of the phenomena of language and of teaching which is capable of disentangling the *puzzle* and making the underlying *mosaic* transparent.

THE PHENOMENON OF TEACHING

In an article which appeared about fifteen years ago on 'Fundamentals of the Action Game of Instructing' (Weigand 1989), I described teaching as a specific action game like other action games such as informing or arguing. Rethinking teaching again, I believe we can no longer regard teaching as an action game like others. Certainly, it is an action game but a very specific and complex one.

Let us first pose the question whether transcriptions of authentic school lessons can be our starting point on this issue. In the linguistic literature, mainly of sociolinguistic and conversation analytic provenance, authentic discourse of school lessons is taken as discourse of teaching and minutely analysed. For a few seconds of speaking more than twenty pages of transcription and description are needed. In the end, it becomes obvious that the authentic text does not really deal with teaching but, for instance, with disciplinary problems or with planning the next school party or the like. The alleged methodological exigency of starting from so-called empirical 'data' turns out to be a methodological fallacy insofar as it is not at all clear what 'data' really are. There is no empirical evidence as such. The only starting point has to be the attempt to understand the phenomenon (Weigand 2004b).

For professionals of language teaching and for applied linguists, however, analysis of classroom interaction can provide valuable insights into how teachers really see the teaching process, i.e. how they put a methodology that they have learnt theoretically into practice. It can also show up differences of approach and point to good classroom practice and procedures which will facilitate the language-learning process. Moreover, it demonstrates how learners respond to language learning situations and how they interpret various types of teaching techniques, communicative, functional, grammatical ones.

Teaching undoubtedly is some sort of intentional activity. I do not touch here the highly problematic point of teaching aims as laid down by the teaching and educational establishment in school and university curricula. It seems an inevitable consequence that any linguistic theory about the nature of language, however communicative or dialogic it may be, will be totally irrelevant to the classroom teacher if it conflicts with the official teaching aims. At present, in the upper classes of German schools, official teaching aims unfortunately are dominated by what is called 'Wissenschaftspropädeutik' and therefore remain fixated on the mainly written analysis of literary English texts. The situation at university level is even worse, and the effects on the communicative abilities of German students are all too obvious.

The question for us is whether teaching as intentional activity represents an action game like the other ordinary games, for instance, representative or directive ones. Usually action is based on the concept of *intention* (Anscombe 1957). But does this suffice? If we intend to move an object from one place to another but do not succeed because the object turns out to be too heavy, did we carry out the action of moving? It seems that having the intention does not yet make up action, there must be some *effect* caused by the intention. Otherwise the intention is restricted to the attempt to act.

Let us now compare more precisely ordinary speech acts with speech acts of teaching. A representative speech act, for instance, expresses a claim to truth related to a specific proposition. By producing, e.g., the utterance *communication is always dialogic,* the speaker expresses his/her claim to the truth of the proposition. Speaking in this sense is acting:

speaking	=	acting
utterance		representative speech act
Communication is always dialogic.		CLAIM TO TRUTH

[always(dialogic(communication))]

Figure 6.1 Speaking as acting.

In contrast to orthodox speech act theory, I do not consider the single act as an autonomous communicative unit. Communication proceeds in sequences of initiative and reactive acts. By the very functional structure of the initiative act a certain expectation for the reactive act is set up: in our case, the representative speech act aims at a reactive speech act of acceptance. In general, the action principle thus entails the dialogic principle proper in the sense that the speaker expects the interlocutor to take up the very claim of the initiative act in accepting or rejecting it:

REPRESENTATIVE	↔	ACCEPTANCE
DIRECTIVE	↔	consent
EXPLORATIVE	↔	response
DECLARATIVE	[↔	CONFIRMATION]

Figure 6.2 Basic dialogic speech act types.

But where does teaching fit in? In contrast to ordinary speech acts, speaking is not yet teaching, nor can the goal of teaching, namely learning, be rationally or conventionally derived from teaching:

speaking =|= teaching
teaching ←|→ learning

Figure 6.3. Speaking, teaching and learning.

Even if we can presuppose that teachers have the intention of enabling their students to improve certain abilities, i.e. to learn, there is nevertheless no guarantee that learning will be achieved. There is no speech act nor sequence of speech acts of the kind that speaking counts as teaching. The intention of the teacher therefore can only be considered as an *attempt to teach* by the use of ordinary speech acts such as asking, informing, and requesting:

attempting to teach → learning
by asking
    informing
    requesting

Figure 6.4. Teaching as tentative action.

In the process of teaching, the ordinary action games of asking, informing and requesting are modified as we, above all, know from the so-called *teacher's question*. Teachers are not in need of knowledge but ask questions the answers of which they already know. They pose these questions in order to guide the process of learning.

In the same way as speaking does not yet count as teaching, the intentional attempt to teach does not necessarily lead to learning. We here address the often cited gap between the efforts taken by the teacher and the results demonstrated by the learner. Even if we can assume that teachers expect their students to learn, this type of expectation remains the *hope* that learning is made easier. We are confronted with an old problem of speech act theory, namely, the problem of *perlocutionary* psychological effects. Learning as the result of teaching seems to be some sort of perlocutionary cognitive effect that in the end is not in the intentional reach of the teacher. It is not as simple as with normal speech acts: produce the utterance and the effect will be there. The effect is desired, intended, at best approached. Whether it really occurs needs to be tested. *Tests* therefore become an essential part in the process of teaching and learning.

There are obviously action games such as teaching which use ordinary speech act sequences in order to influence the cognitive abilities and attitudes of the interlocutors. Advertising also belongs to this type. *Advertising* uses ordinary speech acts of directives, representatives, or exploratives with the intention of changing behaviour. Whether this intent will really have an effect is, however, not in the actual reach of the advertising company. Advertising thus, like teaching, inevitably remains an attempt at influencing behaviour.

At this point *didactic questions* about how to support the learning process come in. The teacher is supposed to be an expert, i.e. to have a higher degree of competence than the students in the subject matter to be taught. He therefore has to make efforts to present and explain the subject matter in a way that it can be grasped by the learner. I call this essential didactic exigency *matching horizons*.

Teaching a foreign language is not simply a matter of rules nor a matter of knowledge as, for instance, Gass and Selinker (2001) make us believe, since language use *goes beyond knowledge of rules* and to a large extent is simply *use*. Language acquisition happens in language use. Teaching a foreign language needs to make *conscious* what native speakers have learned in language acquisition in large part *unconsciously*. It is ordinary language use not artificially constructed models which will give us guidelines for our understanding of the nature of language.

THE PHENOMENON OF LANGUAGE

The object of teaching in our case is a foreign language. In order to understand a foreign language we need to compare it with our mother language. Having explicated my concept of language as an integrational phenomenon in detail elsewhere, for instance, in my papers given at the Integrational Linguistic conferences in London and New Orleans (Weigand 2002b, 2006a), I can now be very brief: I consider language to be the human ability to speak, an ability which cannot be separated but is always integratively used with other human abilities in dialogic interaction, among them the abilities to think and to perceive. Human beings are able to orientate themselves as social individuals in ever-changing surroundings in an adaptive and constructive manner. They are not the victims of the complex; on the contrary, they are able to master it by means of their *dialogic competence-in-performance*. Such a concept of language resembles Toolan's 'notion of creativity, as productive and interpretive proficiency in new or developing circumstances' (Toolan 1996: 271) and inevitably goes beyond the narrow scope of traditional linguistics as the science of language structure and necessitates a genuinely interdisciplinary approach (Weigand 2002b).

The history of linguistics is full of differing concepts of language. They are mostly set up rather arbitrarily. In contrast, the concept of language as an integrated part of dialogic competence-in-performance is justified by the survival needs of the species. To consider the human species simply as the symbolic species falls much too short. It is communication, not the creation of signs, which guarantees the survival of the dialogic species.

Foreign languages are not simply different languages, separate from our mother language. We can understand our mother language fully only if we know a foreign language, i.e. language comparison becomes a constitutive feature of analysis of every individual language. For instance, in order to know the meaning of *high* in English you need to know how it is used in English and how this meaning is expressed in a foreign language, for instance, in German. The English phrase *with high seriousness* is to be translated into German by using the so-called antonym *tief: mit tiefem Ernst*. Language comparison thus draws our attention to essential descriptive consequences which would otherwise remain hidden.

In any case, we have to refrain from contriving definitions and codes. Methodology has to be derived from the object not vice versa. In order to address an integrational complex object we need a key with which to open up the whole, and we need to know the minimal communicatively autonomous unit. The minimal unit in which interaction can take place is the cultural unit of the action game with human beings at the centre who act and react by means of their communicative abilities. There can be no separation of text and context, of language and interaction, or of language and culture. The *key* to opening up the integrational whole has to be a crucial feature of human beings' behaviour. In my view, it is basic needs, interests and purposes which are fundamental to human actions and, in the end, are verified by survival needs.

In the action game human beings negotiate meaning and understanding by means of principles of probability. They use rules and regularities as far as they go in order to structure the complex, but even the use of rules is dependent on probabilities which are the basic condition of performance. There are different types of probability principles: constitutive, regulative and executive ones. Constitutive principles—the action principle, the dialogic principle proper, and the coherence principle—constitute human dialogic interaction. They operate at the level of speech act categories such as representatives, directives, exploratives and declaratives and focus on basic premises of the concepts of action, dialogue and coherence. The Action Principle is based on what makes up action, namely, the correlation between purposes and means. Practical actions have a practical purpose that is pursued by practical means; communicative actions have a communicative purpose pursued by communicative means. The Dialogic Principle proper bears on the fact that every communicative action is dialogically oriented and is not autonomous. It is the very functional structure of the initiative act that indicates what reactive act can be expected. The communicative action is dialogically oriented and is not autonomous. It is the very functional structure of the initiative act that indicates what reactive act can be expected. The Coherence Principle is based on the integration of different communicative means, verbal, cognitive, and perceptual. It is human beings who therefore establish coherence in their minds in trying to understand the interplay of different types of communicative means.

Regulative principles mediate between different human abilities according to cultural parameters, for instance, between reason and emotion or between the interest of the individual and respect towards the other human being. It is precisely this principle of regulation between self-interest and respect or politeness towards the other human being on which Principles of Rhetoric are based. Both components of this Regulative Principle, trying to defend effectively one's own interest and respecting the interests of our fellow beings, are necessarily connected as a result of the double nature of human beings as social individuals:

EFFECTIVENESS ↔ RESPECT/POLITENESS
self-interest   interest of the other

Figure 6.5. Principles of Rhetoric.

Finally, there are executive principles which result from specific interests of individuals or institutions and are not usually explicitly expressed but can be detected as cognitive strategies underlying the dialogue (Weigand 2006b). They open up the vast field of complex action games, which needs to be investigated theoretically in a more profound way and with reference to authentic action games. Insofar as interlocutors can use them as deliberate strategies to achieve their interests and purposes, executive principles represent a subpart of Rhetorical Principles in general. In any case, they are principles of sequential structure, either dependent on speech act categories such as explorative sequences of clarifying or independent of specific speech act categories such as strategies of evading or insisting.

THE FOREIGN-LANGUAGE SYLLABUS

With the theory of dialogic action games we have a basically integrational theory which combines theory and practice insofar as it is a theory applicable to practice. We can, for instance, describe what jurists do in the area of legal argumentation, what businessmen do in the area of business communication or how the media are used in the area of media dialogues. Teaching a foreign language, however, means designing a *foreign language syllabus* which I consider to be a technique by which the natural object of language-in-use is transformed into the subject matter of the classroom.

As I see it, there are in principle two alternative methods: focusing on language use versus focusing on language system. Focusing on use does not necessarily mean not focusing on rules. In its extreme form, however, focusing on use simply means communicating or trying to communicate by renouncing analysis. Many foreigners *learn* a foreign language in this way by living and working abroad and seemingly imitating what they hear and perceive. However, whether these learners really learn by 'imitation' is doubtful since it is not clear what they might be imitating. It is of interest whether any language-acquisition processes may still be operating in these learners and what strategies they may apply. A study of pidgins may have something to offer here. This way of learning in untutored and unstructured situations, however, has little to do with teaching. In any case, however, using the foreign language as far as possible as the language of the classroom certainly is a valuable means for memorizing and practising language-specific routines.

The other extreme, focusing on the rule-governed language system, necessarily presupposes a type of linguistic analysis that cuts the integrational object of language into pieces and changes it to a compositional one. Such a type of linguistics seems to be preferred by some applied linguists because it allows them their own area of 'mediation' or 'of making linguistics useful', as Widdowson (2003: 8) calls it. One might wonder about the fact that even in this way learning happens to some degree. The reason is that human beings equipped with the ability to learn will anyhow manage to learn even if the teaching conditions are not the optimal ones.

In my view, we cannot ignore the fact that teaching a foreign language has to take account of the *nature of the phenomenon language* as part of a complex integrated whole. In this sense, I am now going to sketch a *foreign-language syllabus* which—as teaching and learning proceeds in time—necessarily has to deal with the complex whole to some degree step by step. The steps, however, are basically steps of increasing complexity by starting at the very beginning from the whole and always keeping track of it when focusing on components as they are related to the whole.

The Starting Point: Interaction Means Action and Reaction

The core and *starting point* of the syllabus has to be the view that by using language we interact. Interaction has to be made transparent at the universal level of meaning as action and reaction. The 'things we do with words' are negotiated at the level of interaction by making claims and fulfilling these very claims, i.e. by initiating and reactive actions. These interactive claims represent the key concepts for human dialogic interaction. We make claims about what we consider to be true and we make claims about what we want our interlocutors to do in convincing or persuading them or in influencing their action and behaviour, in any case expecting a reaction that corresponds to our claims. From here the syllabus should start with very simple examples, related to the communicative needs and purposes of the pupils, for instance, a request of the following type:

(1) REQUEST (GIVE (x,y,z))   ↔   CONSENT

   Could you lend me your book?   *You may have it. I don't need it these days.*

   I am sorry, I need it myself.

Even small children very quickly understand that they have such basic claims and that they can express them with specific utterances in specific situations. The underlying formula of the speech act F(p) and details of theoretical precision can be made transparent years later. Other examples of basic communicative purposes could include the following:

(2) question and answer   *When does our autumn excursion take place?*

(3) problem solving   *We should discuss what we are going to do.*
Where shall we go?
What shall we do?

(4) making proposals   *We could go to the zoo.*
Couldn't we go to the zoo?

(5) evaluating proposals   *It would be very useful for our next test to visit the zoo.*
I would prefer to make the trip by bike.

(6) warning   *You'd better not be late, we have to take the first bus. We have to start very early; otherwise the zoo will be overcrowded.*

Filling up the Set of Utterances

Whereas the first step focused on universal meaning concepts of action, the second step introduces the perspective of language comparison. It is the universal level of meaning where different languages meet, 'vergleichbar und unvergleichlich', as Mario Wandruszka (1969) called it. The perspective of language comparison focuses on comparing utterances of different languages and on the fact that there is always more than one utterance at our disposal to express our claims:

communicative purpose (state of affairs)   ↔   <set of utterances>

Figure 6.6.   The speech act as an open set of utterances.

Even small children easily understand that they have different utterances at their disposal, and they use them effectively in different situations and in different moves of the sequence. In learning a foreign language, students will become aware of the fact that there are, on the one hand, specific types of utterances which, as types, seem to be universal: the *direct, indirect and idiomatic utterance* (Weigand 2003²). On the other hand, they have to learn language-specific features, i.e. differences between their mother language and the foreign language. I cannot go into details of morphological form or inflection but would like to emphasize a few lexical and grammatical particularities in comparing English as a foreign language with German. Let us consider the following sets of utterances in English and German:

(7) REQUEST (FETCH (x,y)) ↔

I am asking you to fetch Doris.	*Ich bitte dich*, Doris abzuholen.	direct
Please fetch Doris.	Bitte hole Doris ab.	
Could you please fetch Doris?	Könntest du Doris abholen?	indirect
Didn't you want to fetch Doris?	Wolltest du nicht Doris abholen?	
Would you please fetch Doris?	Würdest du bitte Doris abholen?	idiomatic
Today *you are going to fetch* Doris.	Heute *holst du aber* Doris ab.	
etc.	etc.	

A German native speaker, for instance, has to learn that in English the progressive form is to be used, e.g. in *I am asking you* . . . or that the English verb *ask* corresponds to two different German verbs *fragen* and *bitten*. It will be important to emphasize the *integrational point*, namely, that verbal means, such as sentence types, particles or modals, represent only a part of the communicative means used for carrying out speech acts. Thinking and perceiving are always included. Consequently there cannot be a code between verbal means and purposes. It is in principle the whole utterance as a complex of communicative means which carries the speech act. Often the utterance form has to be learned as a whole and cannot be constructed from components. In this way, step by step a *comparative utterance grammar* will emerge.

Particles are a difficult subject matter in this respect. For instance, the German utterance

(8) Ist doch egal!

expressed with a certain intonation clearly means the opposite:

(9) Es ist überhaupt nicht egal.

But how to express this in English? The only possibility would be to express it by *it doesn't matter* with a specific intonation pattern.

Filling up the set of utterances available in the foreign language will be an objective of the syllabus which is continually to be pursued in the process of the advance towards proficiency. The decision whether an utterance fits the set has to be made on the basis of the criterion of communicative equivalence. When introduced at the beginning of the syllabus, it suffices to have a rather rough notion of communicative equivalence which distinguishes utterances according to basic action functions. In this rough sense, all utterances of (7) would be communicatively equivalent. On a closer look, however, which would attempt to differentiate subtypes of requests and specific situations, the utterances listed in (7) are not really functional equivalents, not real paraphrases. These subtle differences have to be taken into account in the course of the syllabus at a time when the students are more proficient in their use of the foreign language.

Principles of Politeness

In differentiating the utterances, especially direct and indirect ones, principles of politeness have to be addressed. The sociological concept of face addresses only one aspect of a multifaceted phenomenon which basically influences the choice of utterances. The theory of dialogic action games accounts for politeness as part of a regulative principle that mediates between pushing one's own goal and respecting the other human being. This regulative principle is highly dependent on culturally different systems of values and conventions (Weigand 2001: 96f.). Whereas, for instance, in German in a baker's shop we may simply use the direct utterance:

(10) Geben Sie mir ein Vollkornbrot.

without any explicit device of politeness; in English we have to stick to polite utterance forms of the indirect or idiomatic type such as

(11) Could I have a wholemeal loaf, please?

Especially with a negative reply, politeness in English can be expressed in a very subtle way which may seem amazing for German speakers as, for instance, in the following authentic example:

(12) A We'll have dinner together?

B It seems that probably I will not be able to be in time. So please go ahead without me.

If the syllabus claims to deal with such perfect ways of native-language use, authentic examples are needed. They can, however, not be formally retrieved from a corpus but need evaluation either by an insider of the action game or by the linguist as observer.

Predicating

In any syllabus, vocabulary will play a crucial role. In an action theoretic approach vocabulary contains the means for *predicating*. These means are not single words to be inserted into abstract syntactic structures nor do they have defined meanings. On the contrary, these means are phrases or multiword units which are used by speakers in order to predicate how they perceive the world (Weigand 1998).

Such a view of the lexicon naturally has important consequences for the description of lexical structures and for teaching a foreign language. Many problems overemphasized in orthodox theories vanish, e.g. polysemy; others have to be reconsidered, e.g. synonymy. Polysemy becomes evident as a problem of theory not of use. In learning a foreign language it is words-in-use which have to be learned because the use of words is neither totally based on free choice nor on rules as can be clearly seen by a few examples such as the following taken from a comparative analysis of *to fall* and German *fallen* (Weigand 2006a):

(13) big drops of rain fell   dicke Tropfen fielen
his hair *falls to* his shoulders   sein Haar *fällt auf* seine Schultern
to *fall on* a specific day   *auf* einen bestimmten Tag *fallen*
to *fall back on* easier solutions   auf einfachere Lösungen *zurückgreifen*
my work *falls into* three parts   meine Arbeit *gliedert sich* in drei Teile
to *fall into* a trap   in die Falle *gehen*
etc.   etc.

Words have meaning in phrases. The phrase is the unit which, in most cases, is unequivocal. Moreover, it is the phrase which determines synonymy as can be demonstrated by another example which starts from a comparative analysis of *thick* versus *dick* and leads to the inclusion of other 'synonymous adjectives' (see Weigand 1998: 35):

(14) *thick* wall   *dick*e Wand
thick forest   *dichter* Wald
thick crowd   dichte Menge
heavy drops   dicke Tropfen
heavy traffic   dicker/dichter Verkehr
swollen ankle   dicker Knöchel
swollen cheek   dicke Backe
etc.   etc.

For a theory of natural language and a corresponding syllabus which aims at competence-in-performance, it does not make sense to generate syntactic structures of the type NP → Det Adj N and insert lexical signs the connection of which is determined by rules, nor does a theory of mediation solve the problem. The lexical unit is not the single adjective but the collocation of adjective + noun or in syntactic terms the NP. Learning is facilitated if it is based on structures and networks, in the case of vocabulary on networks of phrases.

Sometimes differences between languages are not so clear-cut as in our examples (13) and (14) but refer to multifaceted language-specific details which are highly arbitrary and therefore pose problems for memorizing, for instance, in the case of speech act verbal phrases (Weigand 2002c):

(15)   to *make* an assertion   eine Behauptung *aufstellen*
       to *ask* a question   eine Frage *stellen*
       to *give* information   eine Mitteilung *machen*
       to *make* a recommendation   eine Empfehlung *geben*
       etc.

Knowing how words are used in phrases makes up a crucial part of learning a foreign language. Unfortunately, a comparative lexicography which indicates corresponding phrases or collocations is still in its infancy.

Referring

Whereas predicating is expressed by means of lexical phrases, referring has to do with grammatical means such as articles, pronouns and the like. It is, however, too rash to equate types of reference with expression types as happens in traditional linguistic accounts and philosophical argumentation. Reference is not at all a rule-governed matter but a very complicated affair. Like predicating, it is done with phrases which are sometimes dependent on the whole utterance and the speech situation and, in the end, on what the speaker believes to be definite or indefinite. Again, as was the case with predicating, the differences between languages are varied and arbitrary, as can be seen by a few examples:

(16)   Let's *go jogging.*—Machen wir *einen* Lauf.—Facciamo *la* corsa.
       Le rouge et *le* noir (Stendhal)—Rot und schwarz—*The* Red and *the* Black.
       Communism is losing significance.—*Der* Kommunismus verliert an Bedeutung.—*Il* comunismo perde di significato.

The learner will have to know that referring is not a case of changing articles but again a case of phrases and utterances which are to some degree conventional but to some degree dependent on the speaker.

It is, for instance, not a reasonable procedure to analyse the sequence of pronouns and proper names in face-to-face communication in order to find out rules for their use (cf. Weigand 1996). The use of these referential means has to be integrated with other cognitive means, namely, assumptions of the individual speakers about what can be presupposed as still being in the memory of their interlocutors.

Further Components of the Syllabus

A difficult topic in the syllabus will be the topic of *utterance syntax* or pragmatic syntax. If syntax is to be dealt with at all, it can no longer be treated as autonomous sentence syntax but has to be considered as a communicative means for expressing pragmatic meaning. Utterance syntax has to do with various types of grammatical expression, among them sentence types, particles, modals, intonation, etc. To a certain degree, these means can be considered to be speech act indicating devices. It is striking that for every basic speech act type there is a sentence type: for explorative speech acts the interrogative sentence, for representatives the declarative sentence, for directives the imperative sentence and for declarative speech acts the grammatical structure of the explicit performative utterance. For teaching communicative purposes, these correlations can be introduced as a preferred or economic correlation. They can serve as a starting point which, however, has to be continually differentiated for advanced students. It should be clear from the very outset that there is no code of correlation between sentence types and functions.

Furthermore there is the topic of dialogue structures to be addressed in the classroom. Again there are no independent patterns of how to structure dialogic sequences but rather principles and strategies pursued by the speakers in negotiating meaning and understanding such as, for instance, principles of insisting or clarifying. There is already some good teaching material based on short dialogues (e.g. Lorenzen and Taborn 1983). In this respect, the issue has to be raised whether teaching has to be exclusively based on authentic material. In any case, authentic material is a highly valuable source for understanding language and, if checked in a corpus, for verifying presumed conventions. Language use, however, goes beyond the possibilities of a corpus (Weigand 2004a), as, for instance, Widdowson (2003: 102ff.) also points out. As long as we remain observers, i.e. outsiders of the action game, we will only in part understand what is going on. Authenticity therefore must not be a fetish, neither in linguistics nor in language teaching.

LEARNING GUIDELINES

According to Elman and his group (1996: 22), learning is to be conceived of as a process of changes that arise as a result of interactions between the organism and aspects of the external environment. How this process can be intentionally influenced is an open question. I assume the following guidelines which are still to some degree programmatic in nature and need to be verified by further empirical research:

- Learning is improved if teaching is based on structures and networks.

The importance of structures and networks, for instance, becomes very clear with vocabulary. Words should be learned in phrasal structures or, as Sinclair (1998: 86) calls it, 'in larger bits'.

- Learning is improved if the teacher uses the foreign language in large measure as the language of the classroom.
- Learning is improved if the teacher starts from the cognitive level of the learners.

Teaching should proceed from simple cases to more complex ones, from few examples to many variants in a process that distinguishes different stages, starting from competence for survival via basic English and English for intermediate or advanced students to near native competence-in-performance. Matching horizons includes motivation: we learn more easily if we want to learn, and it includes testing in order to inform the teacher about the success of his/her efforts.

- Learning is improved if different teaching strategies account for different parts of the object to be learned.

In my view, it is important to distinguish between active and receptive competence-in-performance. Competence in understanding or receptive competence must be oriented towards understanding native language use. For active competence however it is sufficient if the learners have a suitable, even if restricted, set of expression variants at their disposal from which they can select verbal means for every move in the action game even if it is far more restricted than the set of expressions native speakers have at their disposal.

- Learning is improved by guidelines that can be derived from first-language acquisition.

In my view, we can learn a lot from the process by means of which children learn their mother language. Basically, it is a process of dialogic interaction between mother and child which demonstrates a few striking points. For instance, children *repeat* words they have just learned, and they repeat them in use. They are always confronted with the language they are going to learn. Mothers demonstrate the use and meaning of words by *paraphrases* and *reformulations*. They use *positive reinforcements* insofar as they are happy about the learning progress made by their children. The children themselves *play an active part*: they are motivated to learn; they intervene and pose questions. They proceed by trial and error but also by trying to understand and build up their world rationally, for instance, by first using the word *egg* for a ball. They have an extraordinary feeling for how specific utterances fit the situation and use whole utterances appropriately without knowing what the individual words mean. Even if first-language acquisition cannot be equated with learning a foreign language, the teacher can learn a lot from how nature has provided for it. Similarities in first- and second-language learning have, for instance, been empirically confirmed by Ervin-Tripp (1974) (cf. Fletcher and MacWhinney 1995, especially the contributions by Snow, and Ochs and Schieffelin, on different positions on child language acquisition).

CONCLUDING REMARKS

To conclude: Instead of establishing discipline boundaries between linguistics, applied linguistics, and the area of professional practice we should reflect on what we want to achieve by theories and in practice. There might be a real difference between theory and practice in physics, the difference between fundamentals and technical knowledge. To some extent, we can find this type of difference in linguistics, too, namely, the difference between natural language use and language use under specific technical conditions, for instance, of the new electronic media. Teaching a foreign language, however, is another issue. We do not need theories of mediation for it which presuppose linguistic theories based on the language myth. From the very beginning, we need integrational theories of language-in-interaction that are applicable to practice in various areas. In this endeavour we must be ready to cross traditional academic boundaries and to focus on the same complex object from different but joint perspectives. It will be the task of applied linguistics to develop syllabuses based on a theory of competence-in-performance and on the new insights of neuroscience.

Much has still to be done to make teaching and learning easier. For linguistics I would just like to mention the desiderata of good multilingual dictionaries of words-in-use which are based on corpora and of extensive comparative utterance grammars. For applied linguistics the desideratum remains to develop good teaching materials which cope with the claims of an integrational approach. Nevertheless, in the end, it will be the learner's challenge to bridge the gap between the protected space of the classroom and real life outside.

ACKNOWLEDGEMENT

I would like to thank David Beal (Ruhr-University Bochum, Germany) for valuable comments on an earlier draft of this paper from the perspective of an expert in foreign-language teaching at university level.
An earlier version of the paper has been published in 'Studies in Communication Sciences' 2006.6/1, 93–116. It is reprinted with the permission of the original publishers.

REFERENCES

Anscombe, G. E. M. (1957): *Intention*. Oxford: Blackwell.
Coulthard, Malcolm (1977): *An Introduction to Discourse Analysis*. London (Applied Linguistics and Language Study); new ed. 1985.
Ellis, Rod (2001): Investigating Form-Focused Instruction. In: *Language Learning*, 51, Suppl. 1. 1–46.
Elman, Jeffrey L. et al. (1996): *Rethinking Innateness. A Connectionist Perspective on Development*. Cambridge, MA, London: The MIT Press (A Bradford Book).
Ervin-Tripp, Susan M. (1974): Is Second Language Learning Like the First? In: *TESOL Quarterly*, 8/2. 111–128.
Fletcher, Paul and MacWhinney, Brain (eds.) (1995): *The Handbook of Child Language*. Oxford, Cambridge, MA: Blackwell.
Gass, Susan M. and Selinker, Larry (2001): *Second Language Acquisition. An Introductory Course*. Mahwah, NJ, London: Lawrence Erlbaum Associates, 2nd ed.
Gross, Paul R. et al. (eds.) (1996): *The Flight from Science and Reason*. Proceedings of a conference held in New York on May 31–June 2, 1995. In: *Annals of the New York Academy of Sciences*, 775. 1–593.
Gumperz, John J. (1996): On Teaching Language in Its Sociocultural Context. In: Slobin, Dan Isaac et al.: *Social Interaction, Social Context, and Language. Essays in Honor of Susan Ervin-Tripp*, 469–480. Mahwah, NJ: Lawrence Erlbaum Associates.
Harris, Roy (1981): *The Language Myth*. London: Duckworth.
Harris, Roy (ed.) (2002): *The Language Myth in Western Thinking*. Richmond, Surrey, UK: Curzon Press.
Leech, Geoffrey and Svartvik, Jan (1975): *A Communicative Grammar of English*. London: Longman.
Lewis, Michael (1993): *The Lexical Approach. The State of ELT and a Way Forward*. Hove, UK: Language Teaching Publications (LTP).
Lorenzen, Käte and Taborn, Stretton (1983): *Kommunikative Kurzdialoge im Englischunterricht der Klassen 5–10*. Bad Heilbrunn/Obb.: Julius Klinkhardt.
Murphy, Raymond (1994): *English Grammar in Use*. Cambridge: Cambridge University Press, 2nd ed.
Ochs, Elinor and Schieffelin, Bambi (1995): The Impact of Language Socialization on Grammatical Development. In: Fletcher and MacWhinney, 73–94.
Sinclair, John M. (1998): Large Corpus Research and Foreign Language Teaching. In: de Beaugrande, Robert, Grosman, Meta and Seidlhofer, Barbara (eds.): *Language Policy and Language Education in Emerging Nations*, 79–86. Stamford, CT: Ablex.
Sinclair, John McH. (ed.) (2004): *How to Use Corpora in Language Teaching*. Amsterdam/Philadelphia: Benjamins.

Snow, Catherine E. (1995): Issues in the Study of Input: Finetuning, Universality, Individual and Developmental Differences, and Necessary Causes. In: Fletcher and MacWhinney, 180–193.
Toolan, Michael (1996): *Total Speech. An Integrational Linguistic Approach to Language*. Durham, NC, London: Duke University Press.
Wandruszka, Mario (1969): Sprachen, vergleichbar und unvergleichlich. München, Germany: Piper.
Weigand, Edda (1989): Grundzüge des Handlungsspiels unterweisen. In: Weigand, Edda and Hundsnurscher, Franz (eds.): *Dialoganalyse II*, vol. 1, 257–271. Tübingen, Germany: Niemeyer.
Weigand, Edda (1996): Review of: Fox, Barbara (1987): *Discourse Structure and Anaphora. Written and Conversational English*. Cambridge: Cambridge University Press. In: *Studies in Language*, 1996, 236–243.
Weigand, Edda (1998): Contrastive Lexical Semantics. In: Weigand, Edda (ed.): *Contrastive Lexical Semantics*, 25–44. Amsterdam, Philadelphia: Benjamins.
Weigand, Edda (2001): Competenza interazionale plurilingue. In: Cigada, Sara et. al. (eds.): *Comunicare in ambiente professionale plurilingue*, 87–106. USL Lugano 2001 (VALS/ASLA Associatione Svizzera di Linguistica Applicata, Facoltà di Scienze della comunicazione dell'Università della Svizzera italiana).
Weigand, Edda (2002a): Constitutive Features of Human Dialogic Interaction: Mirror Neurons and What They Tell Us about Human Abilities. In: Stamenov, Maxim and Gallese, Vittorio (eds.): *Mirror Neurons and the Evolution of Brain and Language*, 229–248. Amsterdam/Philadelphia: Benjamins.
Weigand, Edda (2002b): The Language Myth and Linguistics Humanised. In: Harris, Roy (ed.): *The Language Myth in Western Culture*, 55–83. Richmond, Surrey, UK: Curzon Press.
Weigand, Edda (2002c): Lexical Units and Syntactic Structures: Words, Phrases and Utterances Considered from a Comparative Viewpoint. In: Gruaz, Claude (ed.): *Quand le mot fait signe. Pour une sémiotique de l'écrit*, 129–148. Publications de l'Université de Rouen 325 (Collection Dyalang).
Weigand, Edda (2003): Sprache als Dialog. Sprechakttaxonomie und kommunikative Grammatik, 2nd rev.ed., Tübingen, Germany: Niemeyer.
Weigand, Edda (2004a): Possibilities and Limitations of Corpus Linguistics. In: Aijmer, Karin (ed.): *Dialogue Analysis VIII. Understanding and Misunderstanding in Dialogue*, 303–317. Tübingen, Germany: Niemeyer.
Weigand, Edda (2004b): Empirical Data and Theoretical Models. Review article of: Eerdmans, Susan L., Prevignano, Carlo L. and Thibault, Paul J. (eds.) (2003): *Language and Interaction. Discussions with John J. Gumperz*. Amsterdam/Philadelphia: Benjamins. In: *Pragmatics and Cognition*, 12/2. 375–388.
Weigand, Edda (2006a): Indeterminacy of Meaning and Semantic Change. In: Love, Nigel (ed.): *Language and History. Integrationist Perspectives*, 79–98. London, New York: Routledge.
Weigand, Edda (2006b): Argumentation—The Mixed Game. In: *Argumentation*, 20, 59–87.
Widdowson, H. G. (2003): *Defining Issues in English Language Teaching*. Oxford: Oxford University Press.
Wilkins, David A. (1977): *Notional Syllabuses: A Taxonomy and Its Relevance to Foreign Language Curriculum Development*. Oxford: Oxford University Press.

7 Assessing Students' Writing
Just More Grubby Verbal Hygiene?

Michael Toolan

"*That which can be measured can be managed.*" (McKinsey slogan)

ON *VERBAL HYGIENE* AND CHANGING YOUR LANGUAGE

This chapter is a reflection on certain activities of assessment of language learning and language teaching, dwelling on what is controversial and socially embedded about them. The assessments are particular instances, but are also indicative and representative of widespread tendencies. Assessment has become so embedded in our ways of thinking about formal language learning and teaching that the latter are barely conceivable without some version of the former. And what is wrong with assessment, it might be complained? How else can one be assured that something has been learned, a competence acquired, a standard met or maintained? Everyone agrees, in principle, that levels of achievement in language proficiency need to be measured, and good practice recognized, low standards censured (even if friction arises from time to time as to whether censure/criticism is just "cultural insensitivity").

But in our practices of assessment can we escape the values-driven, moralistic judging that is apparent in the "minding your language", which seems a mild obsession in any literate society which places a premium on formal education? Such "minding your language" Cameron (1995) has dubbed "verbal hygiene" rather than prescriptivism, recognizing that it takes many different forms and inflections from the most progressive to the most conservative. According to Cameron, making value judgements on language is an integral part of using it; and people's folk beliefs about various language shibboleths and kinds of correctness are "a measure of their commitment to a discourse of value: a discourse with a moral dimension that goes far beyond its overt subject to touch on deep desires and fears" (Cameron 1995: xiii). Dictionary makers and language planners and anyone who has corrected errors of spelling and grammar in a student essay are norm enforcers, and verbal hygiene is this widespread normative activity of meddling with others' language, a normative activity of which descriptivism and prescriptivism are just different aspects. Nor is the having of norms and values something we can reasonably avoid.

> I have never met anyone who did not subscribe, in one way or another, to the belief that language can be "right" or "wrong", "good" or "bad", more or less "elegant" or "effective" or "appropriate". (Cameron 1995: 9)

It is as well, Cameron argues, if in whatever lay or specialist roles we use language (e.g., to our neighbours or in our formal writing) we recognize the gravitational pull of correctness, normativity, and received opinion about good, or appropriate, or standard writing.

With those thoughts as starting point, let me allude, also, to the widely accepted idea that our social categories and identities are not essential and inescapable givens, imposed upon us early and for all time. Following Judith Butler and many others (as Cameron does, also), we might consider critical theory's view that our status and identity are a matter of performance. In *Gender Trouble* (1990), for instance, Butler argues that a social identity label like "gender" is not a preexistent natural endowment, *reflected* in one's behaviour. Rather gender identity comes into existence when it is performed:

> Gender is the repeated stylisation of the body, a set of repeated acts within a highly rigid regulatory frame that congeal over time to produce the appearance of substance, of a natural sort of being. (Butler 1990: 33)

The kinds of repeated stylisations Butler has in mind would most directly include those to do with appearance, dress, demeanour, gesture and gait; but they could also refer to repeated distinctive ways of using language, perhaps especially speech. Part of the logic of Butler's thesis, and of constructivism generally, is that whatever is achieved and maintained by repeated regulated performance can be changed or abandoned by refusal to repeat, or by opting for a different repertoire of performance, repeated or otherwise. If you stop walking and talking (and dressing and ... etc.) like a heterosexual woman or a working-class male, then society will be increasingly hesitant to assign you to these normative categorizations; people will say you have changed, and you will have. Difference and change may, from this perspective, share a common foundation, whether one is contemplating gender behaviour or language behaviour.

If this model is plausible in relation to social categories such as gender and class, might it also be relevant to language activity and attainment, even though a depth of proficiency and awareness is entailed that is arguably of a different order from that involved in "knowing how to conduct oneself as, e.g., a heterosexual woman"? Can we really claim, without being accused of infuriating glibness, that being judged fluent and proficient in standard English is nothing more, essentially, than a matter of using English, performing in English, in the desired and valued way? Does it follow also that

English proficiency, being a kind of performance, is no more intrinsically admirable than any other form of behaviour (anymore than we could argue for an evaluative ranking of gender, class or ethnicity categorisations on inherent grounds)? This speculative chapter considers whether this might be so. Might we not argue that the development of first-language literacy at schools in the UK, guided by such instruments as the National Curriculum, is a training in the reliable production of repeated acts within a regulatory frame, so that the schoolchild comes to "perform" the identity known as "performing at key stage 2"?

Change and processes of change are crucial in all this, and formal education is centrally aimed at changing the pupil's performance and attainment (regardless of idealist notions that it is a drawing forth, an *e-ducere*, of a potential that is already within the child). Language usage and our reflections on it occupy a fertile middle ground, between the relatively "given" categories and identifications such as class and gender and the relatively changeable ones such as dress and diet preferences.

Our language behaviour is often conceptualised, in the culture, as a good deal less "fixed" or "given" than those attributes we seem to have limited control over such as our race, ethnicity, and sex, but not as freely changeable as perhaps our food or clothes are. Of course food and clothing choices and behaviour are not unconstrained domains of choice; but within Western societies there tends to be quite a lot of scope for choice, certainly by comparison with our ancestors. I can't imagine that my forebears three or four hundred years ago had the range of choices in food and clothing that I have, and by the same token I don't believe that, in the overwhelmingly nonliterate culture of those times, verbal hygiene played a major role. But today, in literate cultures, the average person is liable for and judged on their language to a greater degree than ever before; it is part and parcel of being embedded in a postindustrial society powered by information exchange and textual productivity—the production and circulation of texts in industrial quantities, you might say. As I wrote in my review of Cameron's *Verbal Hygiene* (Toolan 1998: 5):

> By and large our society conceptualizes language, particularly ways of written language, as open to choice: if you split your infinitives you have personally chosen to do so, and you are responsible. By contrast, the markers we each display which reflect our gender and class classification are not ones which society typically regards us as personally responsible for. At the same time, more so than in relation to food, and more importantly so than in relation to clothes, society "takes a view" of your grammar and usage choices: they are noted, and may be given in evidence against you. For (Cameron argues) society has certain normative expectations about language, and all lay thinking about language is permeated by this background assumption of normativity. It is not that the norms can be easily or explicitly stated on any particular occasion,

but more a matter of the general acceptance of the conviction that "there is a right way of putting things, of using the language; and some kinds of English *are* better than others." "Better in what respect?" you might wonder. The frank answer, from the true-believing normativist, is "morally better", pure and simple. . . . It is not that standards and evaluative judgement can have no role in language teaching . . . [but] where extant norms and standards are irrational or superficial they need to be exposed as such, and replaced by more worthwhile criteria of proficiency, effectiveness, and excellence.

Without subscribing uncritically to the claim that normative attitudes on language link up with morality, one can acknowledge that there is some association, even if indirect or considerably refracted, between normativity and morality. The enlightened normativist may recognize that all sorts of language practices are conventional rather than natural, but they also want to claim that the conventions involved are not stupid ones, but sensible and useful ones. The extra bits of rule following and self-discipline they involve, it is believed, are a small cost for the benefits of consistency and convergence that they reap.

CAUGHT IN THE WEB OF ASSESSMENT

My own learning from experience emerged from my being appointed, just a few years ago, to be external examiner for English language modules in the BA English Studies degree at a large and reputable university. As part of my duties, I was sent the coursework submitted by students taking what in the UK we now call a Level 2 module (in the former dialect, a second-year undergraduate course) entitled "Children's Language and Literature". The carefully polysemous module title permitted study of writing both for children and by children. The students' task in the particular coursework sent to me for review was to write a 2,500-word essay on the topic of *assessing children's writing*. More specifically, they were given samples of writing by two children (a boy and a girl, both aged ten), who have evidently been asked in class to write a short description of how to play a game that they were fond of. The boy has written an account of the game of football; the girl writes a description of the game Cluedo. Each composition is about 250 words long, and these came to me, as they did to the students, on a single sheet of paper with the boy's composition numbered as "1" and the girl's as "2":

> 1. *Ten-year-old boy giving an account of the game of football:*
> My favorite game is football. It is well none all over the world. It is not just a kids Game it is a Grown up game to. there are lots and lots of teams in Britain. There is Liverpool and Exeter City and

York City and West Ham United and Many more team these team meat up and play against each over it. Ends like 3 v 1 and things like that. this is how is how you play. You have a field and up each end of the pitch you have a goal. And the field has lines. thing you got to do is score in the goals. I mean you have to kick a ball in the Net and Goal keeper got to you from doing this. You elevan Players on each side if you are playing Proffesinill. And Ill Tell you the Rules. If the ball goes off the pitch it is a throwing. And if you kick some man you have a three kick. But you kick some in the Penalty. And if you handell it you do the same. I'll tell you the Bisians theres a Goal keeper and Theres Defenders, midfielders, Strikers. Wingers, Right Back, Left Back, and there's more too and that how you play fottball. and if you pracktise you may play for a profeinel, one day.

2. *Ten-year-old girl giving an account of Cluedo (board game):*
You have a board with rooms on it and in the rooms you put objects the objects are wrappon. you have three piles of cards a pile with the pictures of people on them you shuffle the people and take one out but don't look at it. you put it in the murder envelops. The second pile has got picture of the objects that you put in the rooms. you do the same as you did with the other pile you put another card in the envelope. The third pile of cards has got pictures of the rooms you put a room in the envelope. In the murder envelope you have how's the murder were it was done and what it was done by. around the board is people. you throw the dice and you move your counter which is ment to be a person which is on card. You have to find out who is the murder. You go to rooms and aksed things to come in. The three piles of cards is shared out to the people play. You have to ask if anybody has a card with a picture of anything in the room. They show you and you mark it off in your piece off paper. if you have got three things not marked off they are the thing you say I know. If you are right about two is the murder and it were it was done and with what you win. But if you are wrong to loss and the rest win.

This is how the boy's and girl's writing was presented to the students (it seems likely that these are typed transcriptions of the pupils' original handwriting, but this point was not clarified); the passages were prefaced by the question and four supplementary directions set out below:

Analyse the two examples of children's writing and assess them in terms of linguistic and communicative competence. You should also do the following:

i) State the criteria you use to evaluate the writing.

ii) Refer to relevant pedagogical material such as the National Curriculum guidelines (for relevant key stage) and language testing reports.

iii) Compare and contrast the children's written skills on the basis of your criteria.

iv) Discuss any problems/difficulties in assessing such writing.

In short, some teacher somewhere has set a writing performance task for their pupils; this work has been taken and treated as a representative sample by language lecturers at the university, and incorporated into an assessment question; in writing about the pupils' work and its linguistic and communicative competence (according to National Curriculum criteria especially) the students must show their own skills of mastery in the assessing of children's writing; the students' work is then graded and commented upon by the lecturers; and I am required to approve or ratify the lecturers' comments and marks. A complex layering of levels of reflexivity operates, a monitoring of language performances which is not entirely unidirectional (e.g., while the lecturers give marks to students' work and not the other way about, still students are entitled to expect certain standards of fairness, consistency, clarity, relevance, etc., in the marks and comments that their lecturers convey to them—and as external examiner I'm part of the machinery monitoring that bidirectional evaluation process).

When I got down to work on the sample of coursework sent me, one of the first questions I had was "Where did the pupils' writing come from, and what were the precise terms of the task the teacher had set the pupils?" I thought that richer contextualization might help me in my assessing of the students' assessings. But in practice I have yet to find out the answers to these questions; there was some change of duties at the university in question, or my e-mail enquiries got lost in the pressure of work (such pressure of work is part of the context too, I would emphasize; as is the fact that an external examiner is paid for this work at a rate that, if you were to charge say £20/hr for your work, would warrant you spending about twenty minutes assessing all the work sent to you in relation to this particular degree course). One way or another, the information got lost in transmission.

I looked at the essays of about a dozen students. The marks awarded to these essays by the two internal examiners ranged from 70 down to the failing mark of 38; my task, as external examiner, was to review the examiners' comments and the numerical marks they had awarded, and confirm that these were fair, reasonable, and in line with standards of marking and feedback at other UK universities. In other words, in the first instance an external examiner is assessing the internal assessing of the students' work, not directly the work itself. But in practice you can't do the former except by way of the latter; that is, the external examiner looks at the students' work, looks at the assignment that was set, looks at the course's syllabus and objectives and the schedule of seminar topics, factors in the students' level of preparation (are they first-year or third-year undergraduates, for example, and is the subject a core one in an honours programme or an ancillary one?) and so on. The examiner then looks again at individual pieces of student work and asks themselves how *they* would have commented upon and graded such submissions. And then they compare their hypothetical assessment with the real, internal one. When externals make notes about particular pieces of work sent to them, the notes are a hybrid, in that they seem chiefly addressed to the internal examiners (or their academic "manager", who is often the head of department) while some of the content amounts to a brief commentary on the work itself, and thus implicitly addressed to the student. For example, my note on the lowest-scoring essay, which earned an internal mark of 38, reads as follows:

Agreed fail; poorly written, frequently irrelevant to the set task . . .

When I write "agreed fail" I am implicitly addressing the internal examiners, but when I note that the answer is "frequently irrelevant to the set task" I am only echoing what the examiners already know, and saying what I would say to the candidate. Of the highest internally marked essay, partly I think reflecting my slightly grudging agreement that this merited a first-class mark, my notes read:

OK; not entirely methodical or sufficiently detailed, and with not a few gr/usage errors of its own; a bare first-class mark

Thus, while my complaint here purports to be directed at the student and the work, it is also implicitly addressed to the internal examiners, but off record, and could be interpreted as asking whether it was reasonable of them to give a 70 to work with these weaknesses. And of another piece, internally marked at 68 but one that I thought was just as good as the previous, I wrote:

Very good opening page on criteria of assessment; pretty good overall—I'd push up to 70; balanced, thoughtful, well-written

Nearly all the terms in these thumbnail evaluations could do with further discussion; for example, a verbal hygienic unpacking of what exactly someone means when he or she says an essay is "balanced". But what I particularly noticed afterwards was the way that my comments frequently focus on the students' *writing* quality (poorly written, well written, gr(ammar)/usage errors, etc.), as if, regardless of what they wrote *about*, or the quality of their insights or arguments, the quality of their own writing was almost always an important criterion.

As is often the case, some of the students' essays contain the sorts of gems and howlers that keep the examiner reading carefully. Thus I've noted that one student "introduces the strange notion that the writing is correct but not grammatical". And there are the usual own goals, as when one student types, without appropriate full stop:

> A ten year old boy writes the first extract on the subject of football Punctuation is a very important part of written work.

Somewhat similarly, another student writes:

> It is evident from the examination of both passages, that commas prove problematic.

But just looking at the *pupils'* writing efforts, a first question for me to ask myself, as an examiner of the *students'* work, is "What in these short compositions merits being commented upon, and in what terms?" Presumably the kind of commentary a primary-school teacher might share with the pupil, on what was good in the work and on what could be improved, need not be quite the same as the kind of commentary a student analysing the composition as part of a BA module might ideally supply, even if the two need to be related in some way. What weight should I put on the fact that Cluedo and football are very different kinds of game, the latter seemingly inescapable in modern Britain, and that explaining the former is arguably a far more taxing cognitive task. How much of the board game Cluedo can I remember, the better to evaluate the girl's account? (I remember Colonel Mustard and Miss Scarlett, but what are the other characters' names? By contrast, how removed from the world would you have to be in order *not* to know the name given in football to the player who is allowed to prevent the ball entering the goal by using the hands?). And as for the distinction in the rubric of the undergraduate module question between linguistic and communicative competence, how willing am I with my integrational linguistic inclinations to go along with this controversial separation? As a poorly paid external examiner I think that what is meant is the distinction between the mechanics, paragraphing, sentence initial capitals, correct spelling, consistency of tenses, etc., on the one hand, and things like clarity, orderliness, accuracy of description, enthusiasm or liveliness, on the other hand. But the distinction we know cannot be leaned on too hard (in some situations, at least, it is arguable that things like paragraphing, standard spelling, standard subject-verb agreement, etc. are forms of "clarity, orderliness, etc." at the micro level, enabling but not guaranteeing—not even necessary—for clarity and liveliness at the macro level).

Besides, as I know from my own long years of assessing essays, the micro material is so much easier to spot, count, measure, and manage (to bring in the crude McKinsey perspective). It is much easier to determine "how many spelling errors are there?" rather than "how engaging is it?"—particularly when you want to treat thirty compositions equally and reliably in a limited span of time. Liveliness of expression is so much more a matter of taste, and context-dependent, where a teacher's assessment might be coloured by their dislike of football, or Cluedo, or both; whereas there's only one correct way to spell *necessary*. Sometimes a covert and appalling *non sequitur* then comes into play in the assessment of pupils'—and students'—writing: "I don't have the time, energy, or Solomonic powers reliably to rate the liveliness and clarity of these thirty compositions, but anyone who is as accurate in spelling as pupil A is here is likely to be comparably proficient with regard to liveliness etc., while pupil B whose work is full of spelling errors is likely to be equally deficient in matters of 'communicative competence'." Note also that in counting the misspellings (assessors might notice the correct spelling of a few difficult words, but they rarely proceed positively, counting all words with the correct spelling) and attempting any link of this count to liveliness, fluency, or similar, a negative feature is incongruously used to illuminate a positive quantity. If kind and extent of spelling errors were taken as indicative of dullness or flatness, at least like would be being matched with like.

How, I ask the reader, would *you* rate or assess these compositions? How might one read aloud some of these sentences, for example these lines from the boy's text:

> if you kick some man you have a three kick . . . I'll tell you the Bisians

It is quite possible that the boy himself has a dialect which uses /f/ where standard English has /θ/ in word-initial clusters; under pressure from teachers and others who may have told him, roughly, don't say /f/ say /θ/ at word beginnings, he appears to have overgeneralized this *in his writing* to other words he would speak with an initial /f/ such as "free". This works well enough for *throwing* earlier in the same line (for standard *throw-in* or *throw in*: the boy probably says /frəʊwɪn/ or /frəʊwɪŋ/), but it can lead to error. Still, one doubts whether the boy would spell the word "free" with an initial *th* if the word were a more independent lexical choice (as opposed to the fixed expression it occurs in here), any more than he spells common words like "from" with an initial *th*.

There are similarly interesting things going on in the girl's writing, for example in her evident uncertainties about quite how to write, and reduce to space-demarcated word forms, phrases like "who is the murderer". In line 7 this is written out as *how's the murder*, which for the initial pronoun has the right letters but in the wrong order. More creative yet is the formulation in the penultimate line: *If you are right about two is the murder*, which I assume is equivalent to standard "If you are right about who is the murderer". The mistaken assimilation of a /t/ sound from the preceding *about* seems to prompt selection of a valid and loosely similar word form, *two*. Again, in a sympathetic spoken performance, with suitable pausing, misunderstandings and the sense of error can be minimized. Those are the things I find worthy of comment in the compositions and, I submit, these comments are far removed from verbal hygienic preoccupations.

The upshot of these remarks is that there seems much one could discuss with the pupils about their compositions, but it would be hard to have it fit into the procrustean assessment grid of the National Curriculum or standard measures of "linguistic and communicative competence". What the schoolteachers and the students and the lecturers and the external examiner (me) tend instead to be enmeshed in—all the assessing of the application of the criteria to the writing, and the marking of the assessing, and my checking of the marking—are layers and networks of verbal hygienic activity, all interacting in a complex economy.

And, like the Cluedo and football descriptions, we too often participate in this without really knowing all the rules of the game(s).

When I was examining the students' essays, I went to some of the National Curriculum Web sites to see if I could find the "National Curriculum guidelines (for relevant key stage)" referred to in the coursework question. In a short search, the best I could come up with was information of the following kind, for the designated "Levels" of attainment for writing (there are nine levels in all, numbered 1 to 8 with a ninth for "exceptional performance"):

Attainment target 3: Writing

Level 3

Pupils' writing is often organised, imaginative and clear. The main features of different forms of writing are used appropriately, beginning to be adapted to different readers. Sequences of sentences extend ideas logically and words are chosen for variety and interest. The basic grammatical structure of sentences is usually correct. Spelling is usually accurate, including that of common, polysyllabic words. Punctuation to mark sentences—full stops, capital letters and question marks—is used accurately. Handwriting is joined and legible.

Level 4

Pupils' writing in a range of forms is lively and thoughtful. Ideas are often sustained and developed in interesting ways and organised appropriately for the purpose of the reader. Vocabulary choices are often adventurous and words are used for effect. Pupils are beginning to use grammatically complex sentences, extending meaning. Spelling, including that of polysyllabic words that conform to regular patterns, is generally accurate. Full stops, capital letters and question marks are used correctly, and pupils are beginning to use punctuation within the sentence. Handwriting style is fluent, joined and legible.

Level 5

Pupils' writing is varied and interesting, conveying meaning clearly in a range of forms for different readers, using a more formal style where appropriate. Vocabulary choices are imaginative and words are used precisely. Simple and complex sentences are organised into paragraphs. Words with complex regular patterns are usually spelt correctly. A range of punctuation, including commas, apostrophes and inverted commas, is usually used accurately. Handwriting is joined, clear and fluent and, where appropriate, is adapted to a range of tasks.

Now everyone knows that such notional definitions of the kind relied upon in these descriptions have the potential to generate a huge variety of assumptions as to what kind of writing is fairly described as "imaginative and clear" or "persuasive," or shows "a variety of grammatical constructions" or "a range of imaginative effects." The difficulties only multiply when the distinctions between one level and the next are quite thinly described (concerning nonfiction writing, the level 7 and 8 descriptions advance from "in non-fiction, ideas are organised and coherent" to "non-fiction writing is coherent and gives clear points of view").

When I wrote a review of Cameron's *Verbal Hygiene* about a decade ago, one of the things I speculated about was whether verbal hygiene might go the way of "auto hygiene": the obsessive/compulsive cleaning and polishing of one's car, usually done by British males and usually on Sunday mornings, once religiously performed by most respectable burghers, but now rarely practised, except by way of the automatic car wash. Might verbal hygiene, in some of its forms, drop away as a thing to do, like the polishing of cars and shoes? Are there at least aspects of our negotiation of language difference where hygienic meddling might conceivably fall away? The one area where this might possibly emerge, I think, would be in responses to accent. Are we beginning to move away from the George Bernard Shaw world of discriminatory attitudes that we still sometimes seem to inhabit, where one British person cannot begin to speak English without there being some potential for fellow nationals (overtly or discreetly) to prejudge them? Might there come a time, and soon, when Glaswegian can speak to Brummie, and Brummie speak to Devonian, without routine activation of the differentiating and hypercritical attitudes so familiar to us?

A CHALLENGE TO THE "BETTER VS. WORSE" MODEL: ACCENT

Accent-based variation is the kind of linguistic performance diversity that British schoolteachers and university lecturers generally (there are no doubt ultraprescriptivist exceptionalists) would not regard as evidence of linguistic and communicative competence. In fact most aspects of speaking and hearing escape systematic attention in mother-tongue teaching and assessment, but accent in particular is especially insulated from attention; writing—stable, standardized, inspectable—is overwhelmingly the preferred mode. This is for the good and simple reason that (again by and large, and notwithstanding forms of prejudice against particular low-prestige accents), no-one can think of a respectable basis on which to devise a qualitative hierarchy among the kinds of speech production variation (corralled into named accents or contemplated in all its variability) encountered every day. *Bahth* vs. *bath* (/baθ/ vs. /bæθ/), which is "better"? A ludicrous question. And then if you say *bahth* must you also say *pahth*, *fahther*? Why, exactly; why is "consistency" better; or what precisely is the objection to 'speaking like a northerner' and then 'speaking like a southerner', even in the same sentence? What would be wrong in sometimes saying *bahth*, sometimes *bath* (just as many British speakers alternate unpredictably between pronunciation of *often* with or without a /t/ (/ɒfən/ vs/oftən), or *Tuesday* with initial stop plus glide, or full palatal affricate (Tyuesday/Chuseday)? Why is variation or variable production "wrong" or "less good"; what is wrong with variability, and why is monotonous and invariant spelling so much approved, when it is so much disapproved in other larger domains (talking, singing, writing, dancing, cooking)? Seeing where these rhetorical questions are leading, some in the teaching and assessing professions (to say nothing of parents, of course) will already be putting out red flags: there will be some teachers, in Britain and everywhere else where English is taught as a first or second language, who will already be objecting that the palatal pronunciation /ču:zdeI/ is "incorrect" or sloppy; but nothing makes it "incorrect" or sloppy other than an awareness that it is a departure from the conservative R.P. pronunciation, and that, in broad terms, its use is or is perceived to be more frequent among those who are lower class or less educated (or both) and rarer or only emerging among other classes or the more educated (or both). For some benighted folk, of course, attainment-by-association of this sort is good enough: get a person to *speak* the way educated people tend to do, and you've as good as produced an educated person.

Those who raise a red flag at the mention of /ču:zdeI/ do so because they foresee my next rhetorical question is that if offen/often variation is acceptable in speech production (rarely noticed in fact), why is it not also acceptable for there to be variation in spelling—between *offen*, *ofen*, and *often*, say—in a person's writing? Such inconsistency is deemed "uneducated", but why exactly? The answer seems to be because we take consistency and uniformity (of spelling, accent, grammar) as "good" and desirable for one or both of two main reasons:

1. because it is taken as reflective of a kind of self-disciplined consistency in other parts of a person's behaviour, the advantages of which are rarely spelled out but seem to stem from the idea that "you know

152 *Michael Toolan*

where you are" with a person whose behaviour is consistent and orthodox. As a result, spelling variation or inconsistency is dispreferred and may be penalized not for any intrinsic reasons but since it is effortfully avoided in and by the dominant cultures.
2. because consistency in spelling, especially consistent conformity to standard language spelling, is believed to make the discourse so written more reliably intelligible to a range of potential readers, including L2 readers, who may be particularly confused if you write that something is "well none all over the world" when you mean it is well known.

Proponents of language uniformity subscribe to much the same views that underpin enthusiasm for uniformity in school clothing—uniform clothing is easy, simple, removes competitive parading of variant styles, and all are freed from any stigma or prejudice that might exist against particular natural forms—but much more problematically, accent and voice being so much less easily donned or removed than a particular skirt or sweater. But who decides what the uniform shall be, and why should it be their decision? The advocate of uniformity and standardization recognizes the heterogeneity and even stratification (prestige *vs.* stigma) within the population, but has adopted a forced and harmful remedy: neither a respecting of the heterogeneity nor a dismantling of the stratification, but a concealing and denying of them by an outward uniform. Uniformity might conceivably emerge democratically, by a process of collective deliberation and agreement; more often it is evidently a question of the powerful or authoritative deciding, where those with authority in one area (e.g. teaching) are able to exploit that authority to make decisions in independent areas (such as what pupils must wear). In the arena of language, where palpably different pronunciations between different speakers are acceptable (northern bæθ vs. southern baθ) or from the same speaker at different times (offen/often), it seems that it is the sheer 'frozen' inspectability, in writing, of the misspelling in *Do you come here offen?* which helps render it an error to be expunged.

A corollary motivation, linking consistency to intelligibility as in the second formulated reason listed previously, arises the more forcefully because of an implicit but usually unstated principle of homologies: one word should normally or ideally have one form and one meaning. The past participle of *know* should have the one form *known* and not also, in free variation, like some Middle English glossary nightmarishly projected into the 21st century, *none*, *knowen*, and *knowon*; and one of those 'variants', *none*, is especially to be shunned as it 'already has its place': it is already an English word (with its own single form and notionally stable single meaning). Tolerance of variant spellings would lead to tolerance of such bamboozling sentences as *Dad was none two like a bit of meet*; whereas the Education Act of 1870 and a steady series of institutionalizing initiatives since (including the university education of teachers and the National Curriculum) might be regarded as centrally concerned with 'raising' everyone above such levels of quaint illiteracy—varieties of writing which, at our kindest, we would have to say do not travel well. We all wish to banish bamboozlement, so the correction of *none* to *known* is itself clearly, in all the given circumstances, appropriate and desirable.

And yet, as we equally well know, accent- and dialect-based variation in pronunciation and lexis are not production errors, so that even if they sometimes cause misunderstanding they cannot logically be 'corrected'; rather, in the process of coping, it is the recipient who here must adjust or work harder, not the producer. And we also know that the 'one word one form one meaning' is as much honoured in the breach as in the observance, routinely and pervasively. Finally, we know that sanctioned words, forms and meanings are at best semi-permanent, rather than 'good for all time': for example, the ordained standard spelling of quite everyday words like *to-night*, *gray*, and *encyclopaedia*, has changed in a relatively few decades, to say nothing of the constant emergence of new meanings for words. So our own commitments, as teachers, to consistency, and uniformity and norms of usage, grammar, and punctuation, are always shadowed by our awareness that these desiderata and their presuppositions are much less than the whole picture.

Not all our language-assessment practices of rating and measuring escape the criticism that they are managing merely for the sake of managing. And matters are made worse if one begins to suspect that principles of uniformity and standardization, of one set of rules applying to all, are only selectively applied, with norm observance waived for elite groups.

The kinds of material most routinely attended to by teachers' red pens and grading mind-sets are relatively shallow items, metaphorically and sometimes literally diacritical: split infinitives (which one might more positively characterize as 'adverb-adjoining infinitives'), misuse of apostrophes of possession and contraction, run-on or comma-splice sentences, and so on. The last-mentioned of these errors invites further reflection, it is certainly one that lowers the perpetrator's reputation in my estimation (unless done with conscious irony). As I attempt to 'teach' my final-year English undergraduates how not to comma-splice, it becomes newly apparent to me that I appear to be quibbling over the use of a comma where a semicolon or full stop should appear: a tiny dot above or in place of the comma is all that is at stake, it seems. And for such minor infractions, especially where repeated, the student-writer is taxed, in terms of marks lost; and one also begins to wonder whether the 'tax' or marking down is not merely heavy, but regressive. Is it vaguely but disturbingly analogous to the way the tax system captures the vast mass of income earners, while the superrich pay disproportionately little tax—as if they were not bound by the same kinds of rules at all?

The reasoning is as follows. Standard written English—with its stipulations about grammatical concord, correct spelling, appropriate use of possessive and contraction apostrophes, tense-matching, and so on—is a mildly onerous collective commitment to a set of norms, in the (common) interest of enhanced clarity and intelligibility. Standard written grammar, in short, is a communication tax. Standard grammar therefore invites some comparison with taxation. Direct taxation, in particular, might be viewed as a parallel imposition, by the collectivity on all of its members, to the ultimate greater benefit of the individual as well as the whole community. Some community members (usually the less affluent and less well-educated) will be found failing to observe the standard grammatical norms, in circumstances where they are customarily expected or required; they will pay costs, directly or indirectly, accordingly. Similarly, community members found to have dishonestly evaded their tax obligations are penalized. But what are the implications, for individual and collective commitment to community obligations generally (including those concerning especially the written language), when it becomes widely known that, for a whole class of elite members of the community, it is as if the tax code were null and void (Murphy 2008; Peston 2008)? When the principle of collective conformity is undermined in such an important area as income and wealth creation, the tremors are felt also in other areas of personal constraint, under penalty of incurring costs, in the collective interest. In the interests of the larger community, we discipline both the language we produce (paying our dues to the standard grammar god) and the wealth we produce (paying our dues to the Inland Revenue). But if some powerful group are found not to be paying their wealth dues, without the slightest sanction, people might begin to wonder whether the whole communitarian paying-of-dues model was brainwashing by the powerful.

I began this paper by wondering to what extent the English National Curriculum teaching goals of getting the schoolchild at some determinate age to 'perform at key stage 2 level' was chiefly self-fulfilling, chiefly a matter of performance, without anything robust in the way of a natural or logical foundation upon which it could be shown that performing key stage 2 tasks was a *necessary* condition for certain kinds of basic literacy, clarity, orderliness, relevance, appropriateness and effectiveness in language use. By the same token must German users of English be taught to say *for five years* and not *since five years* for clarity and effectiveness? Must British people write *behind* rather than *in back of*, avoid adverb-adjunction of infinitives (a.k.a. "split infinitives"), maintain the apostrophe in *its very disappointing*, and so on? Is *'See you later'* really the only correct spelling of this valediction, for educated people, given the advent of SMS-messaging? My general conclusion is that some at least of the phenomena taken as the necessary core of educated writing (writing that is correct, fluent, and appropriate) may in particular circumstances be rather more supplementary or diacritical considerations; they may be subtleties of signalling the observance and importance of which must (by integrationist logic) be more open to local determination and evaluation, in ever new and changing contexts of use, than is usually allowed. This is a plea, then (echoing those of Davis and

Hutton in this volume), for all teachers and guardians of the language (any language) to maintain a self-critical stance with regard to every prescription or proscription, every 'key stage attainment', they promote or invoke. None of this is in any way a denial of the importance of correctness and the identification of errors; but it is a reminder that linguistic proficiency entails a great deal more than 'absence of errors', and is therefore harder to measure and even harder to manage.

REFERENCES

Butler, Judith (1990). *Gender Trouble: Feminism and the Subversion of Identity.* London: Routledge.
Cameron, Deborah (1995). *Verbal Hygiene.* London: Routledge.
Murphy, Richard (2008). *The Missing Billions: The UK Tax Gap.* London: TUC. http://www.tuc.org.uk/touchstone/Missingbillions/1missingbillions.pdf.
Peston, Robert (2008). *Who Runs Britain?: How the Super-Rich are Changing Our Lives.* London: Hodder & Stoughton.
Toolan, Michael (1998). Don't Leave Your Language Alone. Review article on D. Cameron's *Verbal Hygiene* (1995), in *Language and Communication*, 18: 87–99.

8 Integrational Linguistics and Language Teaching

Charles Owen

Measles gives you spots; pregnancy, a baby. Other conditions, e.g. high blood pressure, are symptomless and you only discover the truth about your health by chance. How does one know if one has integrationism? Since reading the foregoing chapters, I have been anxiously anticipating developments, but so far I seem to be much the same as I was before I started it. Does that mean I wasn't paying attention? I hope to persuade you that I was, and to leave it to you to decide if I have been infected. Here, in no significant order, are some things I still believe in, just as I did before reading the essays in this book:

   a. languages such as English, French, Russian, Welsh, Chinese, Malay, Tamil
   b. geographical areas such as England, Germany, Wales, China, India, Tamil Nadu
   c. linguistic categories such as verbs, nouns and prepositions
   d. native speakers of languages
   e. nonnative speakers of languages
   f. people of whom it is impossible to say that they are native or nonnative speakers of any language
   g. bilingualism
   h. grammar
   i. accents (e.g. 'she speaks fluent English but with a noticeable French accent' or 'Roy Harris's French accent is almost native-like')

Here are a few things whose ontological status I find perplexing or debatable, but whose existence I am hesitant to deny since they help me write about language, which is what I have been asked to do here:

   a. human language as a discrete mode of communication, distinct both from paralanguage and from nonhuman communication
   b. words
   c. Standard English
   d. language teaching, indeed any kind of teaching

e. any useful relationship between description (analysis-based codification) and language learning (or acquisition, whichever term you prefer)
f. integrationism

Let us begin with Harris, since he is the inventor of integrationism and hops watchfully from one contributor's shoulder to the next. I am old enough to have been exposed to almost the same Latin and French teaching methods as Harris, but perhaps my English lessons were already tainted by the early stirrings of postwar liberalism. I remember a teacher who insisted on lining us up with our backs to a wall. He would bark words, in no sort of context, and we would have to spell them and say what part of speech they were. If you answered correctly, you stayed where you were. If you answered wrongly, you swapped places with the boy on your left. Several wrong answers would maroon you at the left-hand tail, and one more would see you relegated to your desk as a grammatical failure. The winner was the last man standing, and he would receive a stale chocolate gold moidore. Thus I learned, at the sunset of empire, that coolies, stevedores and moidores were nouns, no less than *mensa*, *puer*, *cheval* or *Français* with a capital F. Simultaneously I certainly learned many other things—Harris is by no means the first to have observed that there are two (usually more than two) levels of activity in any teaching enterprise. When you answer that *stevedore* is a noun, you show you know what stevedores are. Actually, the first time you play you don't know this, but you whisper to the chap on your right: 'What's a stevedore?' and with any luck he tells you, before adding the really important point that a stevedore is a noun. In addition, you submit to the ideology of the teacher, which includes the belief that parts of speech are real categories and, somewhat more contentiously, that knowing them is essential. Yes, the process is highly reductive, but it is surely an error to regard it in isolation. At the age of ten, you may not see the point of it, any more than you see the point of algebra or the feudal system, but that does not mean there is no point. The fact that you can already speak English, and put together a reasonably coherent (for a ten-year-old) written composition, does not of itself prove the uselessness of learning that *stevedore* is a noun.

So why might it be useful and why do I want to defend the existence of nouns? Linguistics has always been an exercise in mapping and modelling. Therefore, the integrationist attack on classification is an extreme form of doubt about the integrity of classes, taken to such lengths that its proponents deny the possibility of classification. Most of us who have taught linguistics have enjoyed telling students that word classes in ancient Greece were quite different from those we recognise today. Lyons (1968:10–11) says that Plato allowed only nouns and verbs, lumping words we would call adjectives in with verbs. Aristotle added conjunctions, which covered everything else—a sort of dustbin class, rather like adverbs, first added by Harris's friend Thrax. I speculate that a dustbin which has lasted for over 2,000 years must be of reasonable quality, even if it is just a dustbin. Sinclair (1991: 81ff.) devotes a great deal of energy to proving that *of* is not a preposition but a one-member class all by itself. Although his argument is attractive, it is one which could in fact apply to any word. The view that we cannot disentangle grammar from lexis has come to be known as 'lexicogrammar' and the central claim is that words are not independently selected, but always co-selections, with the 'co-' here applying not simply to other words but also to preferred patterns, or structures, if I may be so bold as to use such a term. In this respect, lexicogrammar is quite close to integrationism because it resists atomisation, albeit not quite so religiously.

It might be thought that arguing whether *of* is a preposition or not confers legitimacy on the term *preposition*—reifying it if you like. And of course it does—to a degree, just as one reifies when one argues about whether a wolverine is a weasel or a wolf, or whether an okapi is an antelope or a giraffe, or whether Pluto is a planet or not. One suggests that categories such as *weasel* are robust, and that what we are trying to do is to assess the membership credentials of a specific candidate. This gets very tricky with things like race and culture, to such an extent that the discourse of debate in these areas is intractably and notoriously bedevilled by reification. Does this mean we cannot debate? Does it mean that all attempts to classify phenomena are doomed to failure? Obviously not. Rather, it means that the process of classification, to which humans are evidently very attracted, is a natural way of making sense of our environment. We can coherently argue that prepositions are a class arising from a consideration of European languages, and do not seem to fit Chinese quite so well, since in that language a preposition-cum-verb class may be more useful, but I do not see that this deconstruction makes the practice of classification worthless. Integrationists like to argue that humans make sense of their environment in the here-and-now instant of communication. Why, one may ask, should they not also attempt to do so by means of classification, and why should one form of making sense be elevated to the status of unchallengeable writ while another is condemned as mythology?

In principle, this should be a question of usefulness. A map or model which is so crude or so misapplied to data that it is unrevealing is clearly useless, and needs replacing with a better one. I would like to be able to say that this is the integrationist position on Aristotelian and Saussurean models of language, but in fact that is not possible. To say so would be to suggest that integrationism has an alternative map or model in mind—a different way of analysing the phenomenon we know as language. Unfortunately, it quite specifically rejects any model which engages in analysis or assumes there are any 'independent' facts to be described at all. Any claim to describe a linguistic fact must be treated with suspicion since, by definition, the claim will tell us more about the describer than the supposed fact being described.

You visit your local bookshop to inspect maps of Germany. There are several on offer, some larger scale than others, some opening up to a large sheet of paper, others in book form. Some show physical features such as mountains, but few centres of population, while others give lots of detail about towns and villages but do little to represent terrain. Being an integrationist, you decide that none of these maps tells you anything at all about Germany. Moreover, no conceivable map could have told you anything. After all, Germany has changed since the maps were drawn; indeed, it has changed since you entered the shop. Germany is only meaningful at all in real time, when two or more participants experience it together and agree that it is indeed Germany they are experiencing. You complain to the bookseller: 'Deutschland ist bloss ein Augenblick. All other talk of Germany is fiction—pure mythology. Look, this map has a dotted line showing the border between the former Bundesrepublik Deutschland and the former Deutsche Demokratische Republik! How quaint is that?' Warming to you, the bookseller replies: 'Not half as quaint as one I have at home which has dotted lines showing Lower Silesia and West Pomerania as part of Germany; that's all the territory of the former German empire to the east of the Oder-Neisse line. It's shown as being "under Polish administration", and the map was published about twenty-five years after World War 2.' You have found a soul mate, and continue: 'Just goes to show you learn nothing at all about Germany from these maps, only about the political leanings of the people who drew them. Cartography is mere social construction.' 'Exactly my sentiments,' the bookseller replies. Toolan tells us straight: 'Despite the elaborate machinery of scientific linguistic categories and analyses, there are no politics-free linguistic facts.'

It is important not to dismiss social constructionist attacks on reification merely on the inadequate grounds that they defy common sense. I mentioned race earlier. In the interests of economy I must summarise, but it is at least fair to characterise attitudes to the concept of race as very variable both synchronically and diachronically. Doubtless there are people on the streets today, even if you are not among them, who think that there is a 'black race' or a 'white race' of humans. Deploring such taxonomic crudeness, nineteenth-century anthropologists, assorted imperialists and political mischief-makers expended much energy in nailing down the finer points of discrimination between the many different races they held existed. Late-twentieth-century social theorists pointed to the lack of solid biological foundation for this kind of essentialising, and argued that all racial classification was socially constructive. Most recently, though, advances in genetics, especially in the field of medicine, appear to be identifying shared genetic characteristics of certain groups of humans, not necessarily coinciding with the coarse racial labelling of the past, but worth paying attention to. So is race fact or socially constructed myth? Probably it is both, and probably the same can be said of language and languages, and probably integrationists are not alone in identifying this as an epistemological conundrum.

The first book on dialectology I pull down from the shelf (Petyt 1980) makes clear that the political basis of 'languagehood' (or lack of it) far outweighs issues of comprehensibility. The linguistics lecturer who problematises Thrax will also enjoy making the point that there are villages near national frontiers where it is a bit hard to say what the locals are speaking. The existence of a continuum of mutual intelligibility stretching from the English channel to the Mediterranean has been known about for a long time. Likewise, awareness of political facts which cause the villagers on one side of the border to say they are speaking French while their friends on the other side claim equally fervently to be speaking Italian (or some version thereof) is hardly recent. All linguistics students know that in China there are mutually incomprehensible 'languages' which the Chinese themselves prefer to call dialects of Chinese. In 1979 the government of Singapore launched one of its many social engineering campaigns with the slogan: 'Speak more Mandarin and less dialects.' Keeping my eye strictly on prescription, I complained in a letter to the *Straits Times* (published on p. 19 of the 26 October 1979 issue) that the slogan should say either *fewer dialects* or *less dialect*, and it was altered, sensibly, to *less dialect*—possibly the only recorded instance of a linguist having influenced Singapore government policy. Thirty years later we know that the campaign was a success—you hear a lot less Hokkien on the boulevards of Singapore these days. By contrast, no Singaporean, and certainly not Nair either in her fascinating chapter on Indian scripts, would ever claim that the mutually incomprehensible languages of India ('the most conservative estimate gives us about 325', she says) are in fact 'dialects'. Notice that you can, if you desire, come up with all sorts of philologico-historical explanations for this, sagely declaring that the languages of northern India are Indo-European whereas Malayalam and Tamil are Dravidian, a situation which contrasts markedly with the shared Sino-Tibetan characteristics of both Hokkien and Mandarin. But if you do go down that road, you are abandoning integrationism just as firmly as if you argue that Hokkien and Mandarin are separate languages. In truth, the sociopolitical dimension to our identification of separate languages is neither a new insight nor peculiar to integrationism. Harris is of course aware of the wider consensus on the fragility of the sociolinguistic foundations for separate languages, so he hastens to distinguish mere awareness (e.g. Chomsky's stance described on p. 30) from his own position. Chomsky, he says, merely complains about inconsistency, whereas he denies any possibility of defining separate languages. I remain unconvinced. The conclusion that languages exist only as ideology, not as linguistic substance, seems quite unproven. It is true that it is also very hard to disprove because there are no questions or tests one can set to help with proof. That treacherous ally 'common sense' might suggest asking things like: 'Can a Sicilian peasant have a conversation with a burgher of Calais?' or 'why do we need interpreters and translators?' but I think integrationism would rule out such questions a priori as missing the point: 'Cast a Sicilian peasant and a burgher from Calais away on a desert island, and you'll find they can converse very effectively. Interpreters and translators are not needed for communication; their intervention changes the interaction into something else.'

Let us, though, also consider the psychological side of the argument. Harris may be right to suggest that most children in monolingual societies first discover there are other languages through pedagogy. I would say this is a contingent and not very interesting consequence of the way we live. More interesting is his contention that children growing up in bilingual families do not know they are bilingual until a teacher tells them. That I find implausible, and Harris cannot really believe it either, for he says (38): '... the differentiation of words and constructions as belonging to two separate systems is a gradual process.' Quite so—words/constructions/two separate systems—and not a flash of lightning administered by a teacher but a gradual realisation. When did Nabokov first have the experience of speaking to someone in Russian and, on receiving no reply, trying French instead? My supposition is that he would have been about three. Before then he may well have mixed them up 'indiscriminately' in a 'primitive state', and even after his third birthday he probably used French words when speaking Russian and vice versa. But by three, I suggest, he would have been able to choose what I am disposed to call a language—either Russian or French. The fact that Nabokov himself did not know he was speaking Russian or French is irrelevant. A three-year-old is quite capable of telling the difference between an interlocutor who fails to respond because a. she has heard but is busy, b. she hasn't heard because she is upstairs, c. she is deaf or d. she doesn't appear to understand. The response to a. and b. is to shout louder; to c. to resort to nonverbal communication and to d. to try French, even though you don't know that's what it is called.

Harris is persistent though; he imagines a strange world in which a hypothetical Nabokov grows up speaking what I would call two languages but never has the opportunity to discover this. Nobody ever fails to understand him because all speakers are in the same isolated boat. There is no reason for anyone to think they are speaking x rather than y. The choice of words (*chien*, собака) is, in effect, random. There is no code-switching because there are no codes. In such a world, the distinction between languages x and y collapses, he argues, citing work by Asher on the Total Physical Response method in support. I find this all very odd, especially the notion that Asher is a closet integrationist, a point I shall return to. Here I want to focus on the terms of the argument, the conditions if you like, i.e. the strange Nabokovian world outlined earlier. As far as I know, there are no societies which regard the sun and the moon as being the same entity, but we can imagine one which does. In that society, by definition, the sun and the moon are the same—no doubt about it. In other words, if this entirely imaginary Nabokovian speech existed, then, tautologically, the case would be made; but it doesn't, never has and never will.

Young children, who are ignorant of politics, geography or sociology, do know whether they are trying to communicate in one form of speech or another even if they lack the metalinguistic awareness to call it Russian or French. The completely indiscriminate stage, the existence of which is disputed in the literature, is transient, and there are good logical reasons for that. I have already alluded to lexicogrammar. Both lexicogrammarians and integrationists would surely agree that young children produce unanalysed stretches of communication which typically reflect statistical imperatives of the heard environment language. To argue that a young child exposed to both English and French in equal measure (and that in itself is unlikely) might indiscriminately produce utterances such as:

> Un canard yellow
> A jaune duck
> I want du lait
> Où est my pyjamas?

is odd. Of course, many such utterances are reported in the research literature, but Harris is not suggesting mere possibility. Rather, indiscriminateness implies that such utterances would have just as much potential for occurrence as their one-language equivalents, and evidence for that is lacking. Notice that I haven't even begun to consider what it might mean for the phonological substance of two languages to be 'indiscriminately mixed', but such research evidence as there is suggests that this does not happen. Genesee (2000: 332) summarises the situation rather well: 'In the absence of sound and complete data on language use in different language contexts, an explanation of bilingual mixing in terms of undifferentiated language systems is open to serious question.' Nailing the matter down more specifically in relation to syntax, Meisel (2000: 367) asserts on the basis of French-German bilingual child data: 'I believe I have shown that bilingual children consistently use different word order in both languages no later than with the appearance of two—or more—word utterances.' In other words, the conventionally described differences between French and German in terms of subject, verb and object placement in a sentence appear in the speech of bilingual children as young as two.

Harris's thesis that the separation of languages is only a socially conditioned political construct, with neither sociolinguistic nor psychological substance, is not proved by observable data but is a conjecture. I realise that my use of the expression 'psychological substance' begs many questions, and will arouse integrationist ire. Is not 'psychological substance' conjectural? I agree that the precise details of it are, but if we are looking at the available evidence, it points to differentiated language systems—a term actually used by Harris himself. You may be asking why I have laboured over this issue so inordinately when the book contains so many other interesting points. It is because I want to establish, as firmly as I can, that there is something for the language teacher to teach, and that this something can be named, and that to do so is a rational and justifiable course of action, and does not amount to a post hoc rationalisation of politically driven behaviour. I will return presently to the complicated issue of the form teaching might take, but I want first to take a brief look at the discourse of integrationism.

Something which troubles me considerably about the desire to deconstruct the 'myth' of separate languages is that the postdeconstruction terminological vacuum we would naturally expect does not in fact materialise. The authors in the earlier chapters still talk happily about French and Russian, Hindi and Welsh, Arabic and Chinese, not forgetting English. Presumably, their explanation for this is that we all live in the world as we find it. None of us can escape the ideological conspiracies we were born into, and we must be practical. By analogy, and thinking back to our discussion of race, too much censorship of approximative terminology would hinder debate unacceptably, they might argue. If we were to be more precise, every time we use a term like 'Welsh', we should really say: 'the form of language used by people in a part of the world known as Wales, and associated by them with the history and culture of Wales . . . and indeed conventionally called 'Welsh' even though there is really no such thing.' Since this circumlocution would be extremely tedious, we shall adopt a convenient shorthand way of referring to this more complex concept, namely, the word *Welsh*. We shall do this notwithstanding the great degree of variation which the conventionally named form of language exhibits. Besides, people will know what we mean when we refer to 'Welsh', even if we are somewhat contributing to the reification of a nonexistent entity. To borrow from Frege, *Welsh* only means 'Welsh' if there is such a thing as 'Welsh'; since there isn't, it doesn't.

I hope the foregoing will not be seen as a trivialisation. If it sounds a little abrasive, it is because integrationists appear to be constantly sawing at the branch on which they are perched. Or, put another way, any integrationist discussion of the phenomena ordinary folk call separate languages is doomed to terminological self-destruction. The integrationist insistence on the lack of existence of separate languages, while it has some interest from a philosophical point of view, is of questionable value for the language teacher. Early in his chapter, Harris admits that teachers are puzzled by it: 'If a language does not exist, how can one teach it?' He promises an answer, but although he says many other interesting things, I doubt whether the typically puzzled teacher will be satisfied on this point. Fulminating that teachers are teaching a myth conjured up by the institutionalised practices of pedagogy is probably not going to win many converts to integrationism.

So what is language teaching? Harris says that if someone teaches you to swim, then you can swim, whereas if they teach you French, you cannot necessarily speak French. This is true, but a red herring. If you say:

'John taught me swimming', does that mean you can swim? Not necessarily, although, as I shall show presently, it probably does mean you can. Similarly, if someone teaches you *to speak French*, then presumably this is no different in terms of outcomes from someone teaching you *to swim*, except for the contingent point that speaking French is more gradable than swimming, as Harris notes. In summary:

no necessary implication of success	implication of at least some success
taught me swimming	taught me to swim
taught me French	taught me to speak French
taught me physics	taught me to do physics

Harris leaves the significance of his swimming/French example unexplained, but I take it to mean that 'having been taught French is no guarantee of having any practical command of French at all' implies there is no such thing as French. We might just as well say that 'having been taught swimming is no guarantee of having any practical command of swimming' implies there is no such thing as swimming. It is instructive in this connection to find out what people do in fact mean when they say 'x taught me y'. This is where corpus linguistics comes into its own. If you enter 'taught+me+NOUN' as a search term in the Bank of English, you get quite a few lines where NOUN is a language. Here (with the exception of the Shakespeare example) are the ones clearly relating to a foreign language:

1. And when she invited me to a French restaurant, her light blouse sported an inscription in Chinese. Never in my life had I been so interested in Chinese ideograms. And late that evening, she **taught me Chinese** on her wide bed which, at night, looked as though it was suspended over Hout Bay.
2. That's where I met Vessna. I was nine. She was eight. We spent most of our time at the beach or under the fig tree in the back of my great-aunt's house. She **taught me Croatian**, and I **taught her English**. We laughed all the time. We'd spend hours alone on the beach imagining the Romans sailing their great ships on those waters.
3. 'Sorry, Toby, I remember now. The friend you had from—where was it-Sarawak? Wasn't he at Balliol or . . .' His smile was kindly on my embarrassment. 'Indonesia. Java, to be precise. **Taught me Dutch, Malayan and Tamil.** That's it. You introduced me once. Just after I'd come up. He was over from Oxford for the day. Christ, I was impressed. You were collecting languages like a schoolboy does postage stamps.'

4. Vera says she is 86. She is shabby and wears a grubby skirt. Her lined features hang off her face. In her cracked hand, she holds a bunch of dying carnations. She also speaks impeccable English, with an upper-class accent. 'I was rich once,' she says. 'I was married to a German. He **taught me English**. But he died 15 years ago.'
5. My wife, Melissa, comes from Gabon, the Paris of Africa—it's one of the most beautiful countries in the continent. She **taught me French**, because when I met her she couldn't speak much English, and our children are growing up bilingual.
6. If Caliban's emotions mirror those of the Indian people, then his words also do. In telling Prospero, 'You **taught me language**; and my profit on't is I know how to curse', he foretold one consequence of the introduction of the English language into India.
7. In Klein there was a visible poet and a dedicated one. He **taught me Latin** and the text was Virgil, Book Two. I remember Klein's thunderous vocables, and I'll never forget the marvellous music and his delight in poetic sound.

The teacher in 1 is probably teaching other stuff alongside Chinese—let's hope so anyway—and we do not know how good the writer became at Chinese. The writer in 2 is both learner and teacher, reciprocally. The teacher in 3 is multilingual in three languages from completely different language families (remember that I believe in such things) and looks to have been equally successful in others unnamed. In 4, the teacher is German but teaching English to an Arabic speaker. In 5, while we have no evidence, it seems likely that the teacher has French as a second/colonial language. I include 6 just because it is so thought-provoking and in 7 the language is dead but the writer clearly thinks he learned something. None of these speakers implies that the teaching was a failure. Furthermore, if you widen your search to include the many other things people say others taught them, e.g. Braille, cleanliness, discipline, happiness, history, maths, oenology, patience, physics, piano, salmon, sin and tolerance, you quickly get a sense that people talk about teaching in the past not as an activity which took place in a confined space and time, the outcome of which is of no interest, but one which had consequences, normally beneficial although sometimes double-edged, as Shakespeare so shrewdly observes. There is no good reason to think that these examples are peculiar. A proper study of context shows that Harris's claim that 'John taught me French' does not imply success bears no relation to the way people actually talk about language teaching.

The examples do show, however, that these writers have been in a close personal relationship with their teachers. None of the learners 1–5 suggests that their teacher used a grammar book, or gave them vocabulary tests or substitution drills. Writer 7 learnt Latin by reading Virgil and I concede that his ability to converse in the forum may not have been fully developed. The data, therefore, lend support both to a widely held theory and to something many of us have experienced in practice, namely, that you learn a language best when you are obliged to communicate with fellow human beings in everyday ways. Is this a great revelation for applied linguistics? Hardly. In the epilogue to his magisterial *History of English Language Teaching*, Howatt (1984) muses wistfully on rational and natural approaches to language teaching. 'Nature in language teaching, it would seem, is intractable. Reason typically intervenes in the shape of linguistically organized syllabuses, sociologically responsible curricula, or psychologically well-argued methods.' Meanwhile, Harris furiously attacks the confusion between 'proficiency in' and 'knowledge about'. I rather feel there are many who have made the same point previously. Insofar as a syllabus itemises the unitemisable, it is guilty as charged. Insofar as teachers try to teach so many words a day, or the present before the past or the subjunctive only after GCSE, they too are guilty. Insofar as learners want to learn something called 'Standard English' rather than something called, say, Birmingham English, they are guilty of adopting a political position. Insofar as Asher believes that ordering his learners to stand up, sit down and hide in the cupboard is the key to rapid language learning, he is no different from Harold Palmer, Maximilian Berlitz or Michel de Montaigne's father, who, notoriously, allowed his son to hear and utter nothing but Latin until he was seven.

I suppose what I am saying here is that there is little new under the sun, but many new ways of expressing it. Howatt (ibid: 296) observes: 'Natural language acquisition through orate interaction occurs in pre-literate infancy. The experience of becoming literate at school brings with it an awareness of language which is quite alien to the pre-school child, a consciousness of linguistic form and a measure of deliberate control over the use of language in different spoken and written contexts.' He goes on to comment on the difficulty of ever reproducing the preliterate stage of language development, once it has passed. This all sounds like something integrationists would agree with; Pryor's interesting experiences of learning Arabic clearly speak to the truth of Howatt's comments. I would be interested to know, however, what more battle-hardened integrationists make of Pryor's account of her attention to repeated data. She says she noticed strings of speech—*attini, mralfa*—occurring in different contexts, and started to pay attention to them. She comes to the same conclusion that Wilhelm von Humboldt reached in his earliest writings on language (*Über Denken und Sprechen*, 1795–97):

> ... dass ... die Wörter verschiedener Sprachen nicht vollkommene Synonyma sind, und daß wer 'equus' und Pferd ausspricht, nicht durchaus und vollkommen dasselbe sagt.

> [... that ... the words of different languages are not perfect synonyms, and whoever utters 'equus' and 'horse' does not utter entirely and perfectly the same.]

Since she wants to avoid giving the impression that the repeated data she has noticed are in fact discrete items of data at all, she asks: 'How might an integrationist explain what I was learning?' This is a useful question, and a point where I felt, briefly, that we might be approaching some kind of definitive answer to the many problems thrown up by integrationism. She tells us she wasn't learning the meaning of *attini* and *mralfa*, since they have no meaning outside the instance of use. Nor was she learning how to ask for spoons, since there is no way of asking for spoons which can be learnt. For there to be a way, you would need to think of asking for a spoon before you open your mouth, and that never happens; to claim that it does makes you guilty of falling for the notion of telementation. You may ask for a spoon many times in your life, but on every occasion, you will be doing something different from the last time. There are no resources for you to draw on. So what *was* she learning? 'I was learning to make contextualised connections between activities (speaking, listening, fetching, and so on). I was narrowing down a range of possibilities by excluding irrelevant ones. I was learning local patterns of behaviour, that is, relationships' (132). But why is Pryor so confident that this is what she was learning, and what does the word *learning* mean here?

For a large part of the twentieth century, disputes raged over behaviourism. When we say that a rat has learnt a maze, how can we be certain that it has 'learnt' anything at all? It may respond in certain repeated ways, but unless we can find some tangible bit of grey matter in which the learning resides, our attribution of 'learning' to the rat is really mere speculation based on observation of repeated behaviour. A rat which cannot regularly find the cheese will be said not to have learnt, but for all we know, every time the rat successfully reaches the cheese, it is creating this pattern of behaviour 'anew'. Well, enough of this. We do say that the rat has learnt the maze, because *learning* is a word which conveniently captures what we observe. Chomsky famously derided the notion that humans learn language in the same way; who has not reeled at his mighty put-down of B. F. Skinner in his review of *Verbal Behaviour*? It might be worth revisiting a very small part of his attack:

> In the typical Skinnerian experiment, the problem of identifying the unit of behaviour is not too crucial. It is defined, by fiat, as a recorded peck or bar-press, and systematic variations in the rate of this operant and its resistance to extinction are studied as functions of deprivation and scheduling of reinforcement (pellets). This is perfectly reasonable, and has led to many interesting results. It is, however, completely meaningless to speak of extrapolating this concept of operant to ordinary verbal behaviour. Such 'extrapolation' leaves us with no way of justifying one or another decision about the units in the 'verbal repertoire'. (Chomsky, 1959: 34)

Almost half a century has passed since these words were written, and during that time much ink has been spent on justifying decisions about the units in the verbal repertoire and, even more pertinently in the current context, the meaning of *learning*. If one rereads the Chomsky review carefully, one finds that his critique is very largely directed at vagueness of terminology—a failure to say how terms such as *stimulus, response, operant* and *reinforcement* can have any clear meaning when deployed in a discussion of language. What would constitute a stimulus? How do we know what the boundaries of an operant are? Above all, he argues (convincingly in the opinion of many), the terms are reciprocally dependent and therefore empty. He scarcely touches on his own ideas about the relevant units, which were in any case still at a formative stage.

Pryor very reasonably cites Harris's comments about the integrated nature of vocalization, gaze, gesture, posture and so on, but what I find hard to grasp is the leap from recognition of the multifaceted nature of communication to the denial of any kind of analytical characterisation of the verbal repertoire, or even of a verbal repertoire at all. If you do not believe in any kind of analytical structure of language, or if you believe that all such analysis is a misguided attempt to systematise the unsystematisable, that languages have no categories or rules, you may feel a lot of sympathy for poor old Skinner. Boiling his ideas down to the essentials will surely leave 'local patterns of behaviour' as a likely irreducible core.

I have expressed considerable scepticism about integrationist thinking on the nature of language and languages, but it does not follow that integrationist opinion on second-language learning is necessarily wrongheaded. Much of what is said about the doubtful utility of making learners learn paradigms and rules, conjugations and declensions, the passive voice, how to use the subjunctive and so forth, does tend to support the experience of many teachers and learners—up to a point. I am bound to observe, though, that this is by no means a new position. By linking radical views on the nature of language and languages to rather well-trodden paths of applied linguistic theory and practice one can make everything seem new even if it is not. Consider the work of Stephen Krashen (e.g. Krashen 1981). It really does not matter whether you agree with this or that detail of his theory. What you cannot deny is that he has argued consistently for two kinds of 'knowledge', which he has called 'acquired' and 'learned', and that he has also argued that there is no transfer of the latter to the former. If you learn in class that you should use *for* with durations and *since* with fixed points of time after the present perfect—'I have been learning English *for* ten years and *since* 1998'—there is no possibility of this learning transferring to your acquired system. If you do produce *for* and *since* in line with the preceding rule, the likelihood is you have 'acquired' this bit of grammar, but not because you 'learnt' it. Krashen's position has been intensely debated, and many researchers, teachers and learners refuse to accept it. I don't know whether he is right or not, but what is abundantly clear is that he has been saying the same thing for a long time. Superficially, his position seems close to Harris's, yet I doubt Harris would agree with it because it suggests that there is something to be acquired, namely, the grammar of the past perfect combined with different prepositions. In other words, linguists who hold that grammar exists and can be described, and can be acquired by exposure to quality input and natural interaction (preferably with native speakers) but not by classroom learning of grammar—such linguists would, for integrationists, be making the fundamental error of attempting to itemise. They might be preferable to linguists who still believe you can teach grammatical rules in class, but not much.

Let us now consider in more detail the practical consequences of applying theory to pedagogy. In principle, Krashenite teachers and syllabus designers should not try very hard to make learners use *for* and *since* 'correctly', let alone waste valuable time on cognitive explanations with squiggly lines on the blackboard showing fixed times and durations. If they can contrive situations in which their learners find themselves having to use the present perfect, this at least sets the conditions favourably, but this probably defines the limits of their ambition. There have been countless ideas about how best to achieve this, i.e. set favourable conditions in class, particularly in the absence of a plentiful supply of itinerant native speakers willing to wander through the classrooms of the world. These all attempt to simulate 'real communication' and range from sociological (functional) syllabuses, e.g. Corder 1973, Wilkins 1976, Munby 1978, to more corpus-based (lexical) approaches such as that suggested by Sinclair and Renouf (1988) and Willis (1990). This list represents but a tiny fragment of the total effort which has been devoted to this issue. The degree of success is obviously very difficult to measure and extreme variability of circumstance prevents us from recording any results which we could, with scientific certainty, identify as progress. This is the point Toolan makes in his introduction, and it is well made. Perhaps the sad truth is that all such attempts, no matter how valiantly the teacher may try to achieve immersion and communicative authenticity, are merely 'constructed cultural institutions' (Davis 77).

So is language teaching in classrooms pointless? Reading this collection, one does feel that the authors, whether employed as language teachers or not, are inclined to that view, or at least to the view that all such teaching is marginal to the desired outcome of learning. Weigand, whose proposals for an interaction-based syllabus would be understood by teachers who have never encountered integrationism, is the main exception to this mood. By the same token she is the least integrationist writer in the collection (apart from me), since she believes in things like separate languages, structures, words and so forth, i.e. categories which should really be anathema. Take this statement: 'Words have meaning in phrases. The phrase is the unit which, in most cases, is unequivocal. . . . The lexical unit is not the single adjective but the collocation of adjective + noun or in syntactic terms the NP' (158). Most nonintegrationist linguists could easily agree with this— there is nothing very contentious about it. But how can this be argued by an integrationist, for whom there should be no such thing as an NP? The very act of identifying an NP surely abstracts syntax from the overall communicative event, which is not permissible. I am not persuaded that Weigand is a true integrationist.

Let us accept, if only for a moment, the integrationist view that all known approaches to language teaching are based on a myth; can we not still point out that, even if the situation is not ideal, teachers are paid a wage to encourage, to motivate? This might mean that teachers can achieve some success, even if not by the route they imagine. There are many who say that religion is based on myth, yet send their children to church schools because they seem to get the results they are seeking, both morally and academically. Looking at this in more detail, if learners get their *for* and their *since* muddled, perhaps the teacher can intervene at that point with some comprehensible input? These are difficult questions to answer because I am writing in the abstract. Unless we know something about the learners, the teacher, the reasons for learning, the amount of time available and the state of the paintwork on the classroom ceiling, how can we assess the value of a teacher's intervention? To that extent we can all agree with the integrationist insistence on the importance of circumstance. The fact remains that Krashen's theory depends on 'comprehensible input'—a concept it shares with many other theories, including especially Asher's TPR. As Toolan notes, a class of Germans may well confuse their *for* and their *since* quite happily without impeding mutual comprehension, so the only input which would, conceivably, serve to counteract the confusion would have to come from the teacher. The intervention might be worthless in direct cognitive terms, but it might be indirectly beneficial. For example, learners might say to themselves: 'Dammit, got it wrong again. I really don't understand this *for* versus *since* business. I am determined to get it right. I will listen very carefully to all future instances. I know I can do it.' I suspect that most Krashenite teachers relax their principles and consent to intervene, and even offer rule-based explanations. This is contrary of them, because they know it doesn't work—Krashen has said so (Harris, too, of course)—but they do it anyway. What about integrationists? Surely they at least should resist the temptation to try to explain the difference between *for* and *since*?

Integrationist disapproval of prescriptive explanation goes well beyond the argument that it does not work. It also runs the risk of becoming an unwarranted intrusion on the learner's linguistic rights, of imposing a false consciousness of language on learners, and indeed teachers. A lot is said about false consciousness in this book, so I must devote some attention to it. First of all, let us just agree that prescription is ideological; the integrationist denial of any essential or inherent merit or standardness in any form of language is uncontroversial in conventional linguistics. If an activity is ideological, is it ipso facto reprehensible, misguided, self-defeating, pointless? If that were true, it would make life very difficult. Hutton's chapter on Hong Kong and Toolan's on normativity in the UK education system both wrestle vigorously with the ideological nature of language teaching. Both worry that teachers, and the social system which trains, recruits and pays them, impose norms for no justifiable reason. Most of Hutton's essay is devoted to undermining the term 'native speaker', particularly in regard to the question of 'ownership' of language. One of the most interesting moments is when he asks:

> Ironically, in other language subjects in most contexts, the politically correct view is that the native speaker is the most qualified person to teach a language, since it is assumed that no one else is qualified to speak on behalf of the culture that is associated with the language. Can one imagine a teacher of Arabic or Chinese producing musings equivalent to these from a university teacher in Germany when contemplating the status of the structure "*I learn English since ten years*"?

The musings in question argue, roughly, that if such structures are common in the entity we loosely refer to as "World English", why should any teacher, especially a parochial citizen of the UK, claiming to know best on grounds of native-speaker competence, seek to teach otherwise?

I like to think of myself as a democrat and would be quite willing to consult my class of Germans. I would say: 'Regarding this *for/since* problem, you know it really won't make any difference to the message if you get them confused—confused, that is, from the perspective of people who claim to be native speakers. How would you like me to proceed? Do you want me to try to explain what I think the difference is, or would you like me to ignore any instances I perceive to be confused, or what? You tell me. English is a world language, and there are tons of people out there saying things like: *I am learning English since ten years*. If you like, I can even show that the grammar books are, as ever, a bit of a simplification. Just for a laugh, how about this example? "He asked the girl if there were any left alive of her household but she said there were none save only she for her mother **was dead years since**." You may think this is archaic, although actually it appeared in *Esquire* magazine for men in 1994, so probably came in a bit of creative writing; a short story, for example. Isn't it a bit odd that the writer implies that the direct speech version of the girl's utterance is: 'My mother is dead years since'? Here is another example, found on the Internet:

> Semiotics and rhetorics bear, among many qualities, spatiality and temporality. And this, as I see it, undergirds Dambrot's hirability at Akron. He has a great local reputation in northeastern Ohio where his rhetorical legacy in mid-Michigan has been—**in these ten years since**—overhauled by a surprisingly powerful ethos, made over by social/regional heroism, a winning record in well-liked programs (this season at Akron excluded), and access to elite recruiting channels.

I could then go on to discuss the implications of this, and I hope it would be interesting for my German learners. Would this liberal, consultative, context-based, although probably confusing, approach to the vexed issue of *for/since* make me, even briefly, an apprentice integrationist? If so, then I am glad to know it, but I think I know what the answer is going to be.

Toolan concludes his dissection of language education in the UK with: 'Not all our language assessment practices of rating and measuring escape the criticism that they are managing merely for the sake of managing' (182). Not all, perhaps, but the implication is that most are, i.e. that normativity is seldom based on objective or rational foundations but is more a function of arbitrary convention, policed by elites. As far as foreign- or second-language teaching is concerned, this theme is hardly new but rather a widespread post-Kachru development. Hutton marches in step to well-drilled antilanguage-imperialism drumbeats when he argues that normativity must find a new reference point, possibly on the Internet. Similar sentiments abound in journals and conferences; they are arguably well on the way to becoming a new orthodoxy. As far as the education of native speakers goes (I use the term unselfconsciously), this seems to be a restatement of the objection to the ideological, power-based foundation for verbal hygiene, although quite a trenchant one. Toolan usefully reminds us of Cameron's original coinage of 'verbal hygiene' (Cameron 1995). As I understand Cameron, we need to distinguish between hygiene and prescription, even though they overlap. Hygiene is the natural exercise of value judgements about language and part of what it means to be a human user of language—something none of us can escape. Prescription, by contrast, is hygiene based on false consciousness or deference to social power structures. Endemic in false consciousness are precisely those 'myths' which integrationism attacks, for example, the notion of standardness. Whether this distinction really holds water is something one could discuss at length, but I outline it here as background to a curious event.

Just recently, and rather unexpectedly, Professor Harris found himself in a dispute with Professor Jenkins of Southampton University, who attacked him in the pages of the *Times Higher Education Supplement* (Jenkins 2007). To any reader who has stayed the course of this book so far, this dispute will be rather baffling. For it was Harris who had complained about the nonstandardness of the written English of some overseas students at Oxford, and Jenkins who vilified him for claiming ownership of English, not the other way round. At one level, this is just one of those academic spats which flare up from time to time, generating more heat than light. However, it seems to me to shine a ray of light on a truth too often neglected, which is that we absolutely cannot step outside our roles as social language users. Cameron's point about hygiene is that it is a necessary, inalienable attribute of language. So if Harris complains about the level of written English by foreign students currently said to be tolerated in UK universities, is that hygiene or is it prescription? If Jenkins argues that Harris's normativity is out of touch with reality (viz. the inexorable march of World English), is that an argument against prescription or a denial of Harris's right to do a little hygiene? This is complicated territory, but it is clear to me that if Cameron is right about the inherent contestability of language, and I believe she is, then the logical conclusion is that the boundary between hygiene and prescription is also naturally contestable. Cameron seems to gloss over this in her own account, in which she scorns editorial gatekeeping ('characterized by authoritarianism, mystification, irrationality and lack of critical engagement', p. 77); condemns Orwell ('The theory of communication underlying Orwell's work is rarely subjected to critical scrutiny; but on closer examination it turns out to be based on simplistic and questionable assumptions,' p. 70); and defends feminist verbal hygiene in the following terms: 'The positive side of verbal hygiene—seldom realized, admittedly, but not to be ruled out in principle—is that by drawing attention to the way identity is created in everyday linguistic practice, it enables us to reflect on the identities we currently perform, and beyond that, to imagine alternatives' (p. 209). Absolutemily right, and why should this not apply to a child finding her way in the linguistic jungle, or to any learner of a second language, just as well as to a woman seeking to escape linguistic prejudice?

Let us return to Hutton's interesting observation that English, as preeminent world language, is unique in throwing up these intractable issues of ownership. In fact that is not strictly the case. Setting aside French cultural attitudes for a moment, I suggest that many of the issues surrounding the teaching of French in francophone former colonies must be the same as those which trouble Hong Kong. But when it comes to Arabic or Chinese, Hutton says, the politically correct view is that native is best on grounds of association between language and culture. I take it that his use of "politically correct" imputes a questionable value judgement to all participants: learners, teachers and policymakers. Is this fair? Is it necessarily "politically correct" to believe that a native-speaker teacher would serve you best? If you are an integrationist, you will not believe in native speakers anyway, but let us say you are an ordinary person who wants to learn Arabic. You will doubtless know perfectly well that if your teacher has the same mother tongue as you, but has become really competent in Arabic, he may have some advantages; he will have been through the mill, as it were. On the other hand, his pronunciation will almost certainly not be native-like. But which native model should you favour? Spoken Arabic comes in many forms. If you are not planning to go to one particular Arabic-speaking society, maybe you don't mind, but you do want a teacher who would at least be recognised as native. Your deliberations and your decision may be misguided but they are not politically correct, or even political, except in a way which is so vague that it has no force. I accept that many of the judgements made about language proficiency in places like Hong Kong are very questionable. Yet, if we take Cameron's argument seriously (and of course she did not discuss second-language prescription at all), we should hesitate before assuming that all the amusing examples Hutton shares with us are mere prescription. They may be rather understandable hygiene.

The same can be said for normativity in the UK. I am not really convinced by the analogy between verbal hygiene and school uniform. The arguments for making children wear uniforms usually invoke a need to eliminate conspicuous social differences (wealth, class, culture). Mothers often add that it avoids bickering with children about what they should wear. Whether those arguments are rational or not is beside the point; what is important is that the arguments for insisting on conformity to conventions in children's writing are quite different. They do not revolve around the wish to conceal differences in the social status of writers. Nor is it really a question of trying to avoid argument. It is not a coincidence that prescription is at its fiercest in discourse judged to be of organisational importance and at its weakest in informal and creative discourse; we do not moan about punctuation and spelling errors in a postcard, but we may well do so if we spot them in a legal statute. One can call that political if one wishes, but to what purpose? The social value of prescription in the education system is not to insist on well-punctuated postcards (the language equivalent of knee-length skirts if you like), but to enable all children to become statute writers, should they desire it, to 'imagine alternative identities they might perform', as social constructionists such as Butler or Cameron might put it. Nor, actually, is prescription just a matter of insisting on conformity. As Hutton notes, some of the more interesting language teaching involves creative writing, where learners have their attention focussed on choice for effect. There is absolutely no reason why this same phenomenon cannot apply to punctuation in any kind of writing, whether or not it is labelled as 'creative'. In short, whether you want to call it hygiene or prescription, the teaching activities under discussion are not just a question of insisting on uniformity, but of helping learners to make effective choices. I can hear the integrationist exclaiming: 'But what you mean by effectiveness is simply a retrospective attribution of value. There is no logical or objective reason why statutes should be punctuated differently from postcards. Your argument is circular.'

To which I would say that one of the things which puzzles me most about integrationism is the apparent inconsistency between the emphasis on the importance of circumstance, on the one hand, and the willingness to disregard it on the other. On the one hand, it is wrong to teach learners that language has rules, categories or typically representative locutions—there are no such things; the act of telling anyone to mind his or her language (second-language learner, primary-school child, teacher trainee, journalist) is a. theoretically unsound because it misrepresents language, b. pointless because it will not 'work' and c. offensive because it is ideologically biased. On the other hand, if someone objects that actually it is a matter of horses for courses, that yes, language teaching can be pointless, is inevitably ideologically biased, can induce false consciousness, but can also escape or at least mitigate these vices by taking circumstance into account, then the charge is likely to be one of retrospective or self-validating circularity. To be sure, integrationism is a very awkward customer.

I shall sum up. I have enjoyed reading this book because it contains stimulating reflections on language. I have huge difficulty in accepting some of the underlying theoretical positions, but many of the statements on language teaching are uncontroversial, familiar even, to the average applied linguist. Targets for critique are often deserving of such, but again, in many cases they are hardly new. I do not think the book offers very much by way of practical guidance to teachers, but this is not its aim. Rather, it tries to transform thinking, and since all teachers benefit from exposure to as wide a range of thinking as possible, I would recommend the book for that reason alone. Has it transformed my own thinking? In a way, yes, because it has forced me to rethink many issues, even if I find, in the end, that my immune system is too resistant to let me succumb to integrationism.

REFERENCES

Cameron, D. 1995. *Verbal Hygiene*. London: Routledge.
Chomsky, N. 1959. 'Review of B. F. Skinner's *Verbal Behaviour.*' *Language*, 35, 1.
Corder, S. P. 1973. *Introducing Applied Linguistics*. Harmondsworth, UK: Penguin.
Genesee, F. 2000. 'Early bilingual development: one language or two?' In: Li Wei 2000.
Howatt, A. P. R. 1984. *A History of English Language Teaching*. Oxford: OUP.
Jenkins, J. 2007. 'Lashed by the mother-tongue.' *Times Higher Education Supplement*, 7.09.07. London: Times Newspapers.
Krashen, S. D. 1981. *Second Language Acquisition and Second Language Learning*. New York: Pergamon. Also available online at: http://www.sdkrashen.com/.
Li Wei (ed.). 2000. *The Bilingualism Reader*. London: Routledge.
Lyons, J. 1968. *Introduction to Theoretical Linguistics*. Cambridge: CUP.
Meisel, J. M. 2000. 'Early differentiation of languages in bilingual children.' In: Li Wei 2000.
Munby, J. (1978). *Communicative Syllabus Design*. Cambridge: Cambridge University Press.
Petyt, M. 1980. *The Study of Dialect*. London: André Deutsch.
Sinclair, J. McH. and A. Renouf. 1988. 'A lexical syllabus for language learning.' In: Carter, R. and M. McCarthy (Eds.), *Vocabulary and Language Teaching*. London: Longman.
Wilkins, D. 1976. *Notional Syllabuses*. Oxford: OUP.
Willis, D. 1990.*The Lexical Syllabus* London: Collins Cobuild ELT.

Contributors

Daniel R. Davis is Associate Professor of Linguistics in the Department of Language, Culture, and Communication, University of Michigan–Dearborn. His research interests include Celtic languages, varieties of English, and language pedagogy. He has edited anthologies reprinting crucial early linguistic analyses in *Celtic Linguistics, 1700–1850*, *The Development of Celtic linguistics 1850–1900*, and *American English 1760–1925* (all with Routledge). He coedits the journal *World Englishes*.

Roy Harris is Emeritus Professor of General Linguistics in the University of Oxford and Honorary Fellow of St Edmund Hall, having previously held teaching or research posts at universities in Hong Kong, Boston, Paris, South Africa, Australia, and Delhi. His books on integrationism, theory of communication, semiology and the history of linguistic thought include *The Language Myth*, *Rethinking Writing*, *Saussure and his Interpreters*, *Introduction to Integrational Linguistics*, *The Necessity of Artspeak*, *The Semantics of Science*, and most recently, coauthored with Christopher Hutton, *Definition in Theory and Practice: Language, Lexicography and the Law* (Continuum: 2007). He is coeditor of the journal *Language and Communication*.

Christopher Hutton teaches in the School of English of the University of Hong Kong, where his research focusses on political issues in language and linguistics. At present he is investigating the links between linguistic theory and race theory, and the history of race theory, following on from his 1999 study of linguistics and ideology in Nazi Germany, *Linguistics and the Third Reich*. He has also researched the sociology of the language situation in Hong Kong and Southeast Asia, looking at topics related to colonialism, language identity and the politics of linguistic description. Recent publications include *Race and the Third Reich* (2005) and (with Roy Harris) *Definition in Theory and Practice* (2007).

Rukmini Bhaya Nair is Professor of Linguistics and English and Head of the School of Humanities at the Indian Institute of Technology, Delhi. Her research interests include narrative, pragmatics, language acquisition, postcolonialism, hypermedia, and epithymetics. Her recent books include *Translation, Theory and Text: The Paradigm of India* (2001), *Lying on the Postcolonial Couch: The Idea of Indifference* (2002), and *Narrative Gravity: Conversation, Cognition, Culture* (2003); she is currently completing a study of *Gossip, Gesture and Gender: Conversational Narratives and Cultural Norms*. She has also published several acclaimed collections of poetry: *The Hyoid Bone* (1992), *The Ayodhya Cantos* (1999), *Yellow Hibiscus: New and Selected Poems* (2004). She is editor of the literary journal *Biblio: A Review of Books* (http://www.biblio-india.org).

Charles Owen is Senior Lecturer in the Department of English, University of Birmingham, where he teaches courses in discourse analysis, grammar, stylistics and general and applied linguistics. His research interests include applied linguistics, forensic linguistics, and corpus-assisted discourse analysis. He is completing a book on hybridization in contemporary managerial and institutional discourses.

Sally Pryor is an internationally award-winning digital artist/programmer/animator who has been working with computers and art for nearly thirty years (http://www.sallypryor.com). Her most recent interactive artwork examines the connections between writing and the human-computer interface. Her current research integrates embodied human-computer interaction with specific learning activities. She lectures in digital media at the Faculty of Arts, Melbourne University.

Michael Toolan is Professor of English Language and head of the Department of English in the University of Birmingham, where he teaches and researches chiefly in literary linguistics and narrative and discourse analysis. His publications include *Total Speech* (1996) and *Narrative: A Critical Linguistic Introduction* (2nd edition: 2001); and he edits the *Journal of Literary Semantics*. His *Narrative Progression in the Short Story: A Corpus Stylistic Approach* will appear in January 2009 from Benjamins.

Edda Weigand is Professor of Linguistics at the University of Münster, Germany after having been Professor of German in Italy. She is also president of the International Association for Dialogue Analysis (IADA, Bologna). She works mainly in two fields: dialogue analysis and comparative lexical research. On the basis of a general dialogic notion of language (*Sprache als Dialog. Sprechakttaxonomie und kommunikative Grammatik*, revised ed. 2003), she has written many articles and authored or edited several books on pragmatics, speech act theory, dialogue theory, lexical semantics and other topics. She is editor of the series 'Dialogue Studies' published by John Benjamins.

Index

A
abstraction and externality 14–15
Akbar 70
Al Biruni 63–64
Anderson 17
Anscombe 123
anusaaraka transliteration 66–67
applied linguistics as mediation 13–14, 99, 129
Arabic 20–21, 101, 104–114, 173
Aristotle 70
Asher, J. 36, 40–41, 161, 166, 170
Asher, R. 40

B
Barthes 31
Batchelor 90
'benchmark' examination for English teachers in Hong Kong 92, 94–97
Berger 98
Berlitz 41, 166
Bhaya Nair 17–18, 160
Bishop 81
Bloom 47
Bolinger 74
Bolter 117
Bolton 74
Buddha 70
Butler 141

C
Cameron 84, 140–142, 150, 172–173
Canagarajah 76
categorisation 157–158
Chinese 101, 160
Chomsky 26–27, 48, 160, 167
class 22, 39
Cole 57

Collingwood 31
Confucius 70
Corder 169
correctness as ideological 40
cotemporality 13
Coulthard 121
Coupland 81
Crowley 97

D
Davidson 26–27
Davis, D. 9, 10, 20, 85, 154
Davis, H. 77, 83, 99
decontextualization 41
Derrida 48, 57, 58–9, 63
dialogic action games 20, 124–126, 127–128
Dionysius Thrax 29–32, 35, 39, 42, 43, 157
Disraeli 34

E
Ellis 121
Elman 121, 135
English in Germany 11, 94; in Hong Kong 9–10, 19, 88–102; in India 18, 59, 68
Erling 11, 94
Ervin-Tripp 137

F
Farrow 83
Fife 83
Fletcher 137
Freud 70

G
Garrett 81
Gass 121, 122, 126

Index

Gödel 70
Genesee 162
Goody 48, 61, 67
Graddol 8–9
grammar as control of literacy 84; historical contingency of 85; teaching of 157
grammatistes, the 29
Grimm 101
Gross 120
Gumperz 122

H

Harris 2–3, 10, 13, 15–16, 47, 48, 49, 66, 69, 70, 71, 73, 75, 77, 83, 84, 90, 97, 107, 108, 109, 111, 113, 117, 120, 122, 157, 160, 161, 162, 163, 165, 166, 168, 172
Havelock 42
Hindi 49, 57, 62
Howatt 166
Humboldt 166
Hutton 10, 11, 12, 18–20, 77, 155, 170, 172, 173, 174

I

immersion language class as temporary community 78
implicit instruction 16, 25
Indic scripts, diversity of 18–19, 53–56, 61, 62; and identity 50, 64, 68; vs. Roman script 57–58, 62, 69
integrational semiology 2, 14, 26, 107–109, 113–114
integrationism as infection 22, 156, 175
interlanguages 121

J

Jenkins 172
Johns 8
Jones 39
Jones 80

K

Kabir 70
Kachru 12, 74, 76, 172
King 80
Krashen 168, 170

L

language acquisition 166–168

language assessment 21, 43, 140–155; of writing and by writing 144–148; and reflexivity 146–148
language as fixed code 2–3, 47, 108
language vs languages 4, 26–27, 41, 76–77
languages, differentiation of as taught 33, 36
language immersion 10, 74–78
language learning failure 8
language myth, the 3–4, 11, 26, 47; literacy and 42–43; ethnocentrism and 45
Lanza 47
Leech 122
Levy Bruhl 57, 58
Lewis 121
linguistic vs. communicative competence 147–148
linguistic proficiency 32
linguistic reflexivity 5, 9, 48, 108
Lippi-Green 84
literacy and elitism 61, 84, 90
Lorenzen 122, 135
Love 77, 79
Luckmann 98
Lyons 157

M

Macaulay 91–92
MacWhinney 137
Manoharan 50
Manning 80
Marx 70
McKay 93
McLuhan 57, 59
Meadows 118
Meisel 162
metalinguistic awareness 31–33, 108
Microsoft Word grammar- and style-checker 96
Milroy 84
Montaigne 166
mother tongue 18, 19; in colonial and missionary education 91
Munby 169
Murphy 122
Murphy, R. 154

N

Nagami 61
National Curriculum 145, 149–150, 152, 154

native speaker, the 4. 8, 20, 27, 75,
    92–95, 171–172; Romantic concept of 19, 98, 100–101
Nabokov 29, 33–34, 35–36, 161
Nehru 62
NET (Native-speaking English Teachers) scheme 92–98
Neumark 112
nomenclaturism 37
Nowakowski 24–25, 41

O

Ochs 137
Olson 57, 59
Ong 57, 59
Orwell 173
Outer Circle vs. Expanding Circle, English of 12, 93
Owen 22

P

Palmer 40, 166
Panini 49
Parry-Williams 82
Pattanayak 64
Pennycook 99–100
Peston 154
Petyt 160
Phillipson 99
Piaget 121
Plato 42, 157
Porter 5
Pratt 45
postcards 21, 118
precepts vs. rules of English 97–98
prepositions 10, 158; Welsh 82–85
prescription 172–173, 174
projective vs. reductive modes of language teaching 34–5
Pryor 20–21, 104, 166, 167, 168

Q

Quirk 93

R

race 159–160
regionalism in usage norms 11
Renouf 7, 169
Rhys Jones 80
Richards 74, 75, 78
Rodgers 74, 75, 78
rollover human-computer interaction 104, 112–113, 115
Rushdie 69

S

Saussure 3, 7, 9, 37, 41, 114
Schieffelin 137
science, linguistics as a 6–7; methods and assumptions of 6
scientific progress 5–6
Scribner 57
scripts and identities 51
scriptism 48
script conversion, electronic 51, 63, 66–67
Selinker 121, 122, 126
Shaw 150
signs as new 1–2; indeterminacy of, 1–2, 15, 43
Sinclair 7, 122, 136, 157, 169
Singh 50
Skinner 167–168
Snow 137
Standard English 38–9, 88, 97, 98, 101, 153–155; performance of proficiency in 141
standard languages and nationalism 4, 11, 17, 18, 26, 30, 38, 45
Strathern 67
Svartvik 122
Sweet 81–82
synoptic view, as pedagogy 31, 35

T

Taborn 122, 135
Tagore 24–25, 30, 34, 40, 43, 45
Taylor 75, 77, 83, 84
telementation 2–4, 20, 47
Thomas 80,
Thorne 80
Tognini-Bonelli 7–8
Tomasello 47
Toolan 73, 77, 84, 107, 109, 114–115, 126, 159, 169, 170, 172
Total Physical Response 36
transliteration 66
Trudgill 98

V

variation, sociolinguistic 80; vs. 'unified' standard language 98, 150–154; vs consistency or uniformity 152–153, 174
verbal hygiene 140

W

Wandruszka 130
Watt 61

182 Index

Watts 98
Webcorp 12
Weigand 20, 120, 122, 123, 126, 128, 131, 133, 134, 135, 169–170
Welsh 79–85
Widdowson 13–14, 73, 93, 99–100, 121, 122, 129, 135
Wilkins 123, 169
Williams 80
Willis, D. 7, 169
Willis, J. 7

Wittgenstein 37
Wolf 107
World Wide Web, language on the 102
writing as precondition of synoptic language teaching 42, 47; and Arabic 110–112; and linguistic scientism 49; and cognition 57

Y

yessence vs. nonsense 24, 45